A THANKFUL HEART
and a Discerning Mind

Published by Lonely Scribe
www.lonelyscribe.co.uk

Copyright © The Contributors as listed 2010

Cover design and typesetting
copyright © Armadillo Design Ltd 2010

The right of the Contributors to be identified as the authors of this work has been asserted by them in accordance with the Copyright, Designs and Patent Act 1988

ISBN: 978-1-905179-05-3

All rights reserved. No part of this publication may be reproduced, distributed or transmitted in any form or by any means, electronic or mechanical, without the express written permission of the publisher.

This book is sold subject to the condition that it shall not, by way of trade or otherwise, be lent, resold, hired out, or otherwise circulated without the publisher's prior consent in any form of binding or cover other than that in which it is published, and without a similar condition being imposed on the subsequent purchaser.

At the request of John Newton and the contributors, all royalties from the sale of this work are donated to **Christian Aid.**

A THANKFUL HEART
and a Discerning Mind

— Essays in honour of John Newton —

Edited by Dr Mervyn Davies

Give to me, Lord, a thankful heart
And a discerning mind;
Give, as I play the Christian's part,
The strength to finish what I start
And act on what I find.

Caryl Micklem (1925–2003)

Cover images: (front) John Newton preaching at St Paul's Cathedral at the centenary service for Cardinal Newman, 23 November 1990; (back, top to bottom) Principal of Wesley College, 1973; John Wesley in a 19th-century engraving, pub. L. Tallis; meeting Pope John Paul II as President of the Methodist Conference, 1982; Metropolitan Cathedral of Christ the King, Liverpool; receiving an Honorary Degree from John Moores University, 1993; at Liverpool's Anglican Cathedral in June 1995 with Bishop David Sheppard and Archbishop Derek Worlock.

Contents

Introduction..7

John Newton: A life...15
Henry Rack

PART ONE: HISTORICAL

Proto-Methodists of Anglican Piety in Post-Revolution England............27
Tim Macquiban

John Wesley and Eighteenth-Century Dissent.............................40
Henry Rack

The Rise of Methodism in Southern England..............................57
John Vickers

Two Preachers at St Mary's: Wesley and Newman..........................72
Mervyn Davies

PART TWO: ECUMENICAL THEOLOGY

Now and Then: Ecumenism over time......................................91
Frances Young

Conference Episcope: History and theology.............................110
Brian E. Beck

A Methodist Re-Reading of St Paul.....................................127
Neil G. Richardson

Calvinism and Arminianism – Again!: A contribution to
Anglican-Methodist relations..144
John Munsey Turner

Newman's model of the Church: A helpful paradigm for
ecumenical ecclesiology?..165
Wendy Allen

Convergence in Catholicity and Communion..............................186
David Carter

Mary – Mother of all God's children 206
Norman Wallwork

Rescue, Release and Redemption: Mary and Exodus traditions in
the Gospel of Matthew and their relevance for today 222
Sandy Williams

Whither the wider ecumenism?: A Methodist perspective 238
Martin Forward

PART THREE: CHRISTIANITY AND THE FUTURE

Two Women Facing Death: Julian of Norwich and Etty Hillesum 254
Melvyn Matthews

Schools of Formation: What kind of theological education is needed
for a learning and missionary Church? 271
Graham Dodds

Are the 'New Atheists' the 'New Fundamentalists'? 291
John A. Harrod

Notes on the contributors 310

Introduction

Give to me, Lord, a thankful heart
And a discerning mind;
Give, as I play the Christian's part,
The strength to finish what I start
And act on what I find.

Caryl Micklem (1925–2003)

This hymn by one of the most notable Nonconformist hymn writers of the twentieth century is one of John Newton's favourites and many of its words and phrases could be said to be exemplified in his life, as can be seen in Henry Rack's biography. His joy in his vocation and the wisdom and commitment he brought to all his endeavours have given inspiration to many people, not least to the friends and fellow scholars who have in gratitude contributed essays to this volume. While most of these are Methodists, four of the essays are by Anglicans and Roman Catholics. Although the volume attempts to include material that is representative of John Newton's varied interests and work, no claim is being made here to have exhausted this. Many other collections of essays would be needed to do justice to someone who has done so much for the Church in this country and for the many individuals whose lives he touched during fifty years of ministry.

Tim Macquiban's essay assesses the contribution of two figures with Salisbury connections to illustrate some aspects of post-Restoration and post-Revolution Anglican Spirituality. They are both women, and women are under-represented more generally in the study of Anglican spirituality. One is Susanna Wesley, whose work John Newton has highlighted in aspects of his writing. The other is Elizabeth Burnet, wife of Gilbert, Lord Bishop of Salisbury, whose

Method of Devotion, published posthumously, was widely read in the early eighteenth century. It casts further light on the religious and cultural milieu which shaped Methodist spirituality, with its particular emphasis on the method which gave the movement its name as well as shaping its ethos.

This is followed by Henry Rack's exploration of Wesley's dealings with contemporary Dissenters. The significance of Wesley's Dissenter ancestry has been variously estimated, he argues, but the chief influences on his development at Oxford and in Georgia were from high church and non-juror sources. His rigid high-churchmanship was modified by encounters with Moravians and evangelistic needs. Five conflicts with Dissent are discussed. The softening of Wesley's early prejudices against Dissent were subject to considerable limitations. Though coloured by Anglican prejudices and doctrinal differences, Rack argues that his position was chiefly conditioned by the fear that Methodists might be drawn away from the Church of England and become localised sectarians, their evangelism and attractiveness crippled by the legal and social limitations of Dissent.

John Vickers's essay focuses on central southern England, an area in which Methodism was particularly slow to become established and to spread during Wesley's lifetime. He explores the reasons for this, including the predominantly rural nature of the area, the strength of the parish system and the existence of strategically located dissenting causes. All these factors contributed to Wesley's comparative neglect of the area. Until a year before his death, the Salisbury Circuit still embraced most of Hampshire and Dorset, where the only towns of any size were Portsmouth and Southampton. He suggests that Southern Methodism's relative weakness, which continued after 1791, can be examined at strategic points, for example in 1825 (through the Marriott collection of circuit plans) and 1851 (through the returns in the Religious Census of 1851). The pattern of public worship and of ministerial deployment in the period after Wesley's death are examined in some detail at grass-roots level in the preaching plans.

In the first of two contributions on Newman and Wesley, Mervyn Davies compares and contrasts these two famous preachers in St Mary's, Oxford, although from different centuries. As well as being

Oxford men, they had much in common in terms of upbringing, education and Evangelicalism. They were committed to the idea of Christianity as revealed and sought to reinvigorate the Church in England by preaching. A study of their sermons shows they shared a passionate commitment to a God who has revealed his purposes for humankind, the need to live a holy life, a condemnation of worldliness, the emphasis on the lack of deep religious zeal in the nation, and also on the healing grace of God. Newman's sermons, like those of Wesley, were practical but dogmatic. Both had read patristic writings, especially Augustine and the Eastern Fathers, as well as the Anglican Divines and *The Book of Homilies*, and were steeped in Scripture. Each of them rejected Calvinism as well as the excesses of Pietism, emphasising the importance of Word and Sacrament, Justification by Grace, Sanctification, the work of the Holy Spirit, the reasonableness of Faith in the face of increasing scepticism and the importance of Holiness in Fellowship rather than mere individual piety.

Frances Young's essay opens the section on Ecumenical Theology and argues for the importance of tradition as being part of something bigger than ourselves, for an ecumenicity over time as well as over current denominational and cultural boundaries, and advocates a different approach to what tradition is, and why it is important – in other words, for a common shift in perspective on the subject of tradition, both as far as Methodists are concerned, and on the part of our ecumenical partners to whom tradition matters. The approach she explores is one that takes seriously the necessarily hermeneutical process involved in engaging with the past. There can be no simple appeal to precedent, she claims, because actions and words carry different meanings in changed cultural contexts. Responsible historical awareness of the 'otherness' of the past is necessary, so that the kind of listening, respectful dialogue learned in ecumenical encounter becomes the stance adopted towards tradition.

Brian Beck follows this by suggesting that the point is often made in ecumenical conversations that although British Methodism lacks the office of bishop it has *episcope*, exercised by the annual Methodist Conference, and, through delegation, by various categories of individual officers and groups. In this *episcope* lay and ordained share. The use of the term *episcope* is relatively recent, but the reality it expresses goes back to the eighteenth century. Since then, however, neither the constitution of the Conference nor the understanding of the nature of its authority have remained constant. His essay outlines the history of Conference oversight and explores the theological, as distinct from the legal, basis for it in its present form.

Neil Richardson argues that every Christian reading of Romans is shaped by, though not ideally determined by, the Christian tradition in which the interpreter stands. How different will be, or should be, a Methodist reading of Romans more than two and a half centuries since John Wesley's famous conversion experience? This essay contends that two influences have profoundly affected our reading of Paul: major debates in Pauline scholarship and the modern and post-modern Christian experience. The essay looks, in turn, at Paul and Wesley's conversions and the implications for understanding Christian conversion today. He concludes that a Methodist re-reading of Romans in the twenty-first century still stands, in several important respects, within the authentic Methodist tradition, while differing significantly from earlier Methodist interpretations, including those of Wesley himself.

John Munsey Turner revisits the eighteenth-century divisions between 'The Calvinists of the heart' and 'The Arminians of the heart' in the Evangelical Revival, which raised fundamental questions about the Nature of God and the doctrine of grace and salvation. 'Faith working by love' was John Wesley's emphasis. He urges Methodists to be more positive about John Calvin, who stressed the Trinity and the sovereignty of God and Christian vocation. Wesley was not always consistent in his definitions of both sin and perfection, and disputed with 'Arminians of the head' like John Taylor. Was perfection or 'perfect love' a matter of slow growth, or could it come instantly, like conversion? Albert Outler saw in Methodism the Anglican trio of Bible, Tradition and Reason, added to by the vital role of Experience, which he saw as Wesley's legacy. Geoffrey Wainwright adds the role of a 'generous orthodoxy', social concern and the Lord's Supper. In several doctrinal statements there is a stress on the witness of the Spirit, the pressing on to 'perfect love' and the vital place of Christian groups in that, coupled with the importance of fresh expressions of mission, linking people's need for a religion of the *heart* as well as of the *mind*.

In the second of the two contributions featuring Cardinal Newman, Wendy Allen suggests that Newman's ideas about the papacy, infallibility and conscience might help to bridge the gaps between Methodist and Roman Catholic understanding of the place of authority in the Church. Newman valued each stage of his Christian journey, and his experience in two communities means that he is well placed to bridge any difficulties in terminology. Newman's model of the Church focuses on the dynamic interaction between the diverse roles of Prophet, Priest and King and offers, she believes, a constructive and challenging 'organically ordered' model of the Church. This model might help to challenge the self-understanding and reflection of different ecclesial communities, including Roman Catholicism. In this essay she outlines the diverse roots of his model, describes and interprets it, and finally suggests how the model can make a helpful difference to ecumenical understanding by holding diverse ecclesiologies together.

David Carter follows Wendy Allen's essay by surveying aspects of the developing Roman Catholic–Methodist relationship, beginning with the assertion, in 1937, of the classical Wesleyan theologian, Henry Bett, that the two churches with their respective emphases on authority and experience were poles apart. He goes on to contrast this with the receptive attitude taken by the representatives of the two communions in their most recent ecumenical dialogue report, *The Grace Given You in Christ* (2006). It looks at the growing awareness among people in both churches of common emphases, for example on the primacy of the universal call to holiness, the interdependent nature of the Church at every level and the common search for greater catholicity, which have helped the two churches look at each other with new eyes. It takes as a particular example the reassessment of a previously hotly-contested issue, devotion to and learning from the example of the discipleship of the mother of Jesus both through formal dialogue and the informal work of the Ecumenical Society of the Blessed Virgin Mary, to both of which John Newton has contributed. He then looks at aspects of the ecumenical dialogue achievement which might now be deepened and lead towards further rapprochement.

Two essays then follow, one by Norman Wallwork and the other by Sandy Williams, which explore Mariological perspectives. Wallwork argues that the titles and the vocation of Mary are derived from and are wholly dependent upon the titles and vocation of her Son, and that it is quite impossible to maintain that while there was a dynamic movement within the New Testament concerning the evolution of Christology, there was no fairly early movement in the church's understanding of and devotion to Mary.

Sandy Williams suggests in her essay that studies about the significance of Mary have tended to focus on the Lukan birth narratives and less has been written about the way Mary is portrayed in the first gospel. This paper argues that the Matthaean account can have particular relevance for people in today's world, especially for those fleeing from the horror of genocide, and that Matthew's Mary continues to be a representative figure. Her discussion is based on the premise that the Exodus story of 'rescue, release and redemption' provides the biblical world-view – the meta-narrative – for God's people then and now. The methodology includes an exegetical study that uses typology to examine both how the Exodus traditions in Matthew 1-2 elucidate the significance of Joseph, Mary and Herod, and also how the story of the Exodus resonates with the experience of displaced people today. Consideration is given to how the text invites reader response and challenges God's people to enter into the Exodus story and allow it to shape their Christian journey.

Martin Forward concludes this section by inquiring whether inter-faith relations remain controversial for many Methodists and other Christians (some of whom still hope that dialogue will 'wither away'). He makes the point that Methodists have been in the vanguard of contemporary inter-faith relations, and uses recent Methodist scholars and practitioners to illustrate why and how this is so. Geoffrey Parrinder drew upon Methodism's Arminian roots to protest Calvinist exclusivism, and proposed a view of the cosmic Christ to understand and appreciate other religions. Will that do nowadays, or is it too paternalistic? Kenneth Cracknell has drawn our attention to John

Wesley's cautious affirmation of people of other faiths, in noticing that pure and undefiled religion can be found in Islam and elsewhere. Where do we go from here? Is it possible to discern a Christian (even a Methodist Christian) spirituality that would contribute to where the wider ecumenism will find itself in 2050?

Melvyn Matthews, in his essay, brings into parallel consideration the writings of two women of entirely different times and faith perspectives, and shows how their understanding of God and the language used to convey this understanding has striking similarities as well as differences. He suggests that these similarities were engendered by the terrible circumstances in which the two women lived, namely the famines, persecutions (Lollards), ecclesiastical wars and the plague of the fourteenth century which all affected Julian, and the Holocaust which brought about the death of Etty Hillesum and her family in Auschwitz. In the face of these tragedies the two women develop similar understandings of the relationship of God to the human soul and similar understandings of the manner in which God deals with personal suffering, guilt and evil. He examines the way in which the language of these two writers subverts conventional theological language and offers alternative means of theological expression, which ecclesiastical writers have been and are slow to adopt.

This volume would not have been complete without contributions on theological education, an area which occupied a substantial part of John Newton's ministry, and an examination of the virulent attack on religious faith that has been such a feature of the new millennium. Graham Dodds explores the context of theological education today. For a contemporary evaluation of theological education to be described, and for the exploration of its direction to be discerned, a theology of education is necessary, he argues. Although this will differ in configuration, depending on ecclesiological considerations, some principles are delineated. 'What makes for a learning Church?' is discussed in a case study, which assesses the development and impact of an influential report, *Formation for Ministry within a Learning Church*, published in 2003. Drawing on the work of Newman, Congar, Hull, Banks, Craig, Farley and Slee, among others, he asks: 'What kind of theological education is necessary for clergy and laity in the light of declining numbers of leaders and members, and the ambition to pursue a missionary purpose?'

John Harrod argues that we need to engage both critically and creatively with the 'new atheism'. He acknowledges that religion is vulnerable to terrifying distortions and that religion is often an area of human life as flawed as any other – and sometimes more so. Religion can correlate with human life at its worst – but also at its best. The new atheism does a service in exposing religion's manifold failings. In this essay Harrod examines the main characteristics of the kind of attack mounted by writers such as Dawkins in *The God Delusion* and suggests that in many ways the arguments are not recent ones. What is new is the passion with which religion is attacked, the lack of measure in the attack and the particular combination of aspects of the contemporary critique. This represents a challenge to the Church and to theologians if atheism is not to have the last word.

This volume could not have been produced without the help and encouragement of many people, not least the contributors themselves. Tom Cairns and Susan Last of Lonely Scribe have been unfailing in their advice and assistance, especially in the early stages of planning. Warm thanks are due to Mike Brealey, Librarian of Wesley College, for his help in locating documents and references, to Janet Henderson, former Librarian of Wesley, for her encouragement, suggestions and support, and to Jayne Giltrow of Wesley College for her help in word-processing. Rachel Newton generously lent her photographs of John, from which a selection was made, and who in all sorts of ways assisted with the project from the very beginning. I am grateful also to Ward Jones, Chair of the Bristol District, and Jonathan Pye, Principal of Wesley College, for their support and encouragement, and particularly to Norman Wallwork for his help in finding a publisher. Thanks are also due to the Editor of *The Epworth Review* for permission to include the biography of John Newton by Henry Rack and to the Editor of the *Bulletin* of the Methodist Sacramental Fellowship for permission to reproduce the essay by Tim Macquiban.

John Newton: A life

Henry Rack

Lincolnshire is not, perhaps, one of the best-known or most picturesque of English counties. Yet it has had its share of notable sons and daughters, including those with Methodist connections. It was the home of the Wesleys of Epworth; that exotic rarity, the Methodist Squire Brackenbury of Raithby; and Sir Henry Lunn, the controversial missionary, pioneer ecumenist and travel agent. Most famous in recent times has been the daughter of a Wesleyan grocer from Grantham who became the first British woman prime minister. By a curious coincidence the subject of this profile was also born in Grantham and his family was connected with the same Wesleyan chapel as the grocer.

Although John was born in Grantham in 1930, the family moved early to Boston and it is with that historical town that he probably feels most affinity. St Botolph's famous tower ('Boston Stump') is a reminder of the town's mediaeval eminence, but for John's future interests it is also memorable for its Puritan associations. From here John Cotton and other Pilgrim fathers emigrated to America, and Boston was to be famously reborn in Massachusetts.

Here John grew up and he has given us an attractive account of his early experiences of family and church in the late Monica Furlong's collection of such accounts in *Our Childhood's Pattern*. It includes a photograph already attractively recognisable, though with an unfamiliar head of hair! John's memoir has the significant title 'No Holiness but *Social* Holiness' – John Wesley's famous dictum which, though primarily referring to the mutual spiritual help of Christians, soon included an instinctive concern for physical needs. This was a lesson which John received from his early experiences in family and church. He was largely brought up by his mother since his father was absent during the war and did not return later. Busy with a shop and small children to bring up, John's mother instilled in them a deep respect for the Christian faith and a great compassion for the poor. As

John recalls, he would later recognise in this a reflection of the free, unmerited, universal love of God.

A much more specific Methodist nurture came from his grandfather, a retired railwayman and able local preacher. A year of illness when John lived with his grandparents left a lasting impression on him. If grandmother was rather severe, grandfather became something of a surrogate father. Well-read, a man of principle (not least a teetotaller) he was also full of fun and whimsicality. The local Methodist chapel included other examples of outstanding laypeople who expressed both kinds of 'social' Christianity. To the common diet of preaching, hymns and extempore prayer was added, after being received into full membership at the age of fifteen, the experience of sacramental worship which would become a vital part of John's spirituality. As he says, this local Methodist community became for him a surrogate family. In retrospect one can perhaps say that he was fortunate in the time and place he experienced this. Provincial Methodism of this kind in the 1940s and 1950s produced some outstandingly dedicated, self-educated preachers who also had strong social consciences. This was also the heyday of Methodism's commitment to youth clubs. John's dedication of his life to Christ came in response to an appeal by Philip Race at a youth weekend, though this might only have happened after the experience of the chapel 'family'.

Meanwhile his more formal education was in progress. From 1942 to 1949 he attended Boston Grammar School, then entered University College, Hull, to read history (in those far-off days Hull, like a number of other provincial universities, still took London University degrees). After taking his BA in 1952 John began research on 'Puritanism in the Diocese of York 1603–40' under the leading Reformation scholar A.G. Dickens. Though absent in the USA soon after John began his work, Dickens was an exemplary supervisor who enabled John to become a Junior Research Fellow at the Institute of Historical Research in London (1953–55) where he benefited from meeting the celebrated R.H. Tawney and the doyen of Puritan studies, Geoffrey Nuttall. And so John obtained a well-earned PhD in 1956.

Unusually for that period there was no Methodist Society at Hull, though an active SCM and Christian Union. By the time he finished

Above: John as a Local Preacher in the Boston Circuit, Lincolnshire, 1948.

Right: Graduation from Hull University in 1953.

his PhD John had offered for the ministry and so fulfilled by proxy what his grandfather had wished to do but was prevented by family needs. John should have begun ministerial training in 1955, but at short notice was summoned by the Secretary of Conference, the formidable Eric Baker, to fill a temporary gap as acting chaplain of Kent College, Canterbury. This was the first of several unexpected calls which would mark his subsequent ministry. In this case it was a matter of being an untrained minister and untrained teacher of religious education, as well as taking on the multifarious duties of a boarding-school master.

It may have seemed a relief to move from this exacting year to the more straightforward life of a theological college. In those days, however, almost all Wesley House students took the theological tripos in two years. One wit described the House as 'Mr Flemington's stable for theological race-horses'! John would certainly have enjoyed a third year, when he would have specialised in church history, but instead was sent to Richmond College as assistant tutor (1958–61). Here he met Marcus Ward, a valued friend whose biography he was later to write.

From unpromising beginnings, with little encouragement, Marcus became a considerable scholar and outstanding teacher in Bangalore before coming to Richmond. He was influential in the creation of the Church of South India and wrote a history of its early years, as well as being a dedicated ecumenist.

Ordained in 1960, from 1961 to 1964 John had his first taste of circuit ministry in Louth, moving to Stockton-on-Tees in 1964–65. In Louth he was to lay the foundations of that combination of pastoral and scholarly activity which would particularly characterise his ministry. Here, too, he met Rachel, and their marriage in 1963 began a partnership which enlarged that sense of family which had marked his early development so profoundly.

John's circuit experience might well have continued for several more years and could still have led to the leading positions in Methodism he would later experience. But once again he responded to Connexional needs as tutor in church history at Wesley College, Bristol (1965–72). His first significant publication on *Methodism and the Puritans* had already appeared in 1964 as a lecture for Dr Williams's Library, the centre of study for the older Nonconformity. It was a subject John was peculiarly fitted to explore, combining his own experience and study of early Puritanism.

He now became part of a formidable team of Methodist scholars, and to the wide-ranging demands of teaching ministerial students he brought a freshness of experience, pastoral care and scholarship. In 1968 his *Susanna Wesley and the Puritan Tradition in Methodism* (second edition 2002) added an important dimension to Wesley studies.

But this was a time of great uncertainty in ministerial training, with college closures and amalgamations constantly under debate. As John recalls, by the early 1970s it was expected that Wesley College would close and the staff were prepared to move on. Then an unexpected vote in Conference led to Wesley being retained. But in the meantime, out of the blue, John had been invited to go to Africa to help to develop St Paul's United Theological College in Limuru, Kenya. This was in 1972 and John expected this overseas ecumenical experience to last for five years, but once again the unexpected intervened. In 1973 he was summoned back to the reprieved Wesley College, this

Principal of Wesley College, around 1974.

time as principal as well as tutor in church history. Five fruitful years followed and it was during this period that John produced his *Search for a Saint: Edward King* (1977). The apparent shift in scholarly interest was deceptive. John had been exploring spirituality for several years. His early Methodist experience had already broadened to include sacramental and ecumenical elements. This reflected the mixture of high church, puritan and catholic elements which Methodism had inherited from John Wesley. John's sacramental and pastoral concerns led to a sympathetic understanding of Edward King (1829–1910), Bishop of Lincoln. King had a place in church histories as the target of a prosecution for 'ritualism' in 1888–90, which may have helped to discredit this kind of persecution. For King was a man of deep piety and devoted to the pastoral care of clergy and other individuals. He especially attracted John for his Lincolnshire connections. He had indeed commanded respect and affection from local Methodists and John found memories and anecdotes still alive in Lincolnshire Methodism.

In 1978 John took up the very difficult appointment of superintendent of the West London Methodist Mission. Here he followed the long and celebrated ministry of Donald Soper, at the best of times a difficult and delicate prospect. Behind the famous open-air ministry and worshipping community at Kingsway Hall lay an extensive body of social work. It had been decided to transfer the centre of the work from the declining Kingsway congregation to Hinde Street. This predictably caused distress and opposition. It says a great deal for John's diplomatic and pastoral, as well as practical, skills that the transfer was made successfully. It was equally to Lord Soper's credit that he scrupulously avoided any kind of interference with his successor and gave short shrift to anyone who might have made matters difficult for him.

John cannot have had much time for scholarly work in this period, but he managed to produce a wide-ranging study of spirituality in *The Fruit of the Spirit in the Lives of Great Christians* (1979). Election as President of the Conference for 1981–82 was perhaps not a surprise to his friends, though it had not been expected for that year and was complicated by being the point at which the final move to Hinde Street was made. John recalls that his aim for his year in office was to encourage spiritual education for the whole Church. This was expressed in the three-fold offer and challenge: 'A Christ for All, A Church for All, A Theology for All'. Once again this brought together the whole range of his interests and concerns.

Yet this was perhaps even more the case when he moved from London in 1986 to become chairman of the Liverpool District for the next nine years until his retirement in 1995. Liverpool, as everyone knows, is famous not only for its football, the Beatles and fine buildings, but also for its painful transition from a once-prosperous port to the scene of struggles with local government and

Meeting Pope John Paul II as President of the Methodist Conference 1982.

urban decay. Once again John was plunged into a peculiarly fraught situation. This was the heyday of Derek Hatton and the Militant Tendency, the municipal workforce threatened with the sack and the city with bankruptcy. Yet one of the signs and sources of hope, it is fair to say, was in the churches. Liverpool had had an ugly sectarian history in which Catholic versus Protestant hostility had once infected local government in a way only parallelled in Northern Ireland. By the time of John's arrival this situation had strikingly improved. The partnership of shared ideals and the personal friendship between Archbishop Derek Worlock and Bishop David Sheppard inspired by example, and action well beyond superficial ecumenism led to a many-sided ministry of religious and social cooperation in the service of the city's communities and churches. John soon became the third member of this remarkable partnership, which extended to all levels of community life. It was expressed in joint worship, small group activities, social work and work for racial equality in this multicultural

As National Free Church Moderator with Cardinal Hulme and Archbishop Robert Runcie and Bishop Graham Leonard in 1990 at St Paul's Cathedral.

At Liverpool's Anglican Cathedral, June 1995, with Bishop David Sheppard and Archbishop Derek Worlock.

city. Characteristically, John still found time to publish, in 1994, *Heart Speaks to Heart: Ecumenical Studies in Spirituality*.

It was during this period, too, that John began to accumulate titles and honours – some decorative but most as onerous as they were honorific. He was joint president of the Merseyside and Region Churches' Ecumenical Assembly (1987–95); twice Moderator of the Free Church Federal Council and co-president of the Churches Together in England (1990–94). Within Methodism he was chair of the governors of Westminster College, a trustee of Wesley House, a governor of Rydal School and president of the Wesley Historical Association. In the wider world he was made an Honorary Fellow of John Moores University and – which must have given him particular pleasure – Honorary Canon of Lincoln and Hon. DLitt of Hull, his old University. The award of a Lambeth DD was a graceful acknowledgement of John's ecumenical work and scholarship. In 1997 he was awarded the CBE for his work in Liverpool. In retirement his ecumenical work was extended as a member of the Roman Catholic–Methodist International Commission (1997–2002). Finally, another almost accidental position came his way in 1991 when his interest in G.K. Chesterton was recognised by his election as president of the Chesterton Society. What GKC would have thought of a Methodist being so honoured can only be guessed! But one can see the shared concern for (in the best sense) 'popular' theology, spirituality, and social concern as well as literature.

It is no surprise to find that (official) retirement in 1995 led to changes in activity rather than anything like vegetating. Settling once again in Bristol, it was highly appropriate that John should have become Warden of the New Room for five years – a position which entirely suited his tastes. Invitations to teach and lecture came in seemingly unabated and until recently he lectured part-time at Wesley College. John and Rachel have settled in a delightful home with a view of the mediaeval clergy house of Westbury. In their pretty back garden John has built a neat study which houses part of his library, which also creeps beguilingly around the house, along with pictures of places and the family. He is working on what will surely be the definitive life of Bishop King. Along with this his old hobbies of walking, gardening and (of course) book-collecting continue.

Without Rachel's partnership many of these years of varied activity would have been impossible. Besides bringing up four lively boys, who have followed interestingly varied careers, Rachel has had what must surely be seen as a creative ministry of her own. Trained in drama and applying her talents to special needs teaching, she was for a time chaplain at Wesley College after she and John moved back to Bristol. But in Methodism at large she is probably best known for her portrayals of Susanna Wesley, mother of the Wesleys and gifted pastoral guide.

Reflecting on his own life what has most struck John is the way in which practically all the tasks he has undertaken seem to have been thrust upon him. Or at least they have not been from his own planned choice, but have resulted from the pressing requests of others, and often to meet awkward and difficult situations. He says that his writings seem to have been chosen for and not by him as well, though they have also fulfilled long-standing concerns and interest. We can only guess how much these varied and exacting tasks have cost him in anxiety and difficult personal adjustments. But it is also a signal compliment to John and a sign of sense as well as necessity in the Church that has employed him, that his special combination of gifts has been recognised, drawn out and used in this way. He has been qualified to shine in purely academic or pastoral or other specialised branches of the Church's work. Yet it seems that it has been in the expression of these abilities joined together that he has excelled. What is more, the maintenance of scholarly interests along with all his other ministerial activities throughout his career has allowed each concern to enhance the others – an example of ministry perhaps too seldom seen nowadays.

The watchwords from his presidential year – 'A Christ for All, A Church for All, A Theology for All' – embody his abiding concerns. In expressing them he has an enviable ability to adapt his message to every kind of audience. It can fairly be claimed that he has also expressed much of the original Wesley spirit and concerns: what Albert Outler termed 'plain truth for plain people', backed by serious study and wide-ranging curiosity, a spirituality which embraced elements in both Catholic and Protestant traditions with what Wesley called 'the catholic spirit' and applied in social as well as spiritual service. To these John has added a natural, unforced wit and – what Wesley perhaps lacked! – an engaging sense of humour and warmth in personal relationships along with a natural modesty. For he is still the unspoilt and unpretentious friend and recognisably the same kind of person that the writer of this profile encountered over 50 years ago, but with a wealth of experience added. Long may he continue to refresh, instruct and entertain us.

. . . .

Reprinted by permission from The Epworth Review

Bibliography

Books:

Susanna Wesley and the Puritan Tradition in Methodism, Epworth Press, 1964 (Revised edition 2003).
The Palestine Problem, Pergamon Press, 1971.
Search for a Saint: Edward King, Epworth Press, 1977.
The Fruit of the Spirit in the Lives of Great Christians, Epworth Press, 1979.
A Man for All Churches: Marcus Ward, 1906–1978, Epworth Press, 1984.
Heart Speaks to Heart: Studies in Ecumenical Spirituality, Darton, Longman and Todd, 1994.

Articles and Shorter Publications:

'The Yorkshire Puritan Movement 1603–1640', *Transactions, Congregational Historical Society*, Vol. XIX, No.1, August 1960.
'Methodism and the Puritans', Friends of Dr. Williams's Library, 18th Lecture, London: Dr Williams's Trust, 1964.
'Susanna Wesley' (1669–1742): A bibliographical survey'. *Proceedings of the Wesley Historical Society*, Vol. XXXVII, 1969-70.
'Perfection and Spirituality in the Methodist Tradition', *The Church Quarterly*, Vol.3, No.2, 1970-71.
'The Ecumenical Wesley', *Ecumenical Review*, Vol. XXIV, 1972.
'Faith and the Creed', in *About Faith*, ed. John Stacey, *Local Preachers Department of the Methodist Church*, 1972.
'Edward King', in *A Dictionary of Christian Spirituality*, ed. Gordon S. Wakefield, SCM Press, 1983.
'The Theology of the Wesleys', The Methodist Heritage – The Principal's Lectures, Southlands College.

'Samuel Annesley (1620–1696)', *Proceedings of the Wesley Historical Society*, Vol. XLV, 1985–86.

'Analysis of Programmatic Texts of Exodus Movements', in *Exodus – A Lasting Paradigm, Concilium*, T. & T. Clark, 1987.

'What I owe to the Wesleys', Methodist Sacramental Fellowship, 1998.

'John Wesley and Methodism', *Priests and People*, Vol.2, No.5, June 1988.

'Wesley and Women', in *John Wesley: Contemporary Perspectives*, ed. John Stacey, Epworth Press, 1988.

'Spirituality and Sanctification', *One for Christ*, 1988/3.

'The Wesleys for Today', *Methodist Newspaper Company/World Methodist Historical Society Publications*, 1989.

'Amazing Grace: The Spirituality of John Newton', The John Newton Lecture 1990. *The John Newton Project 1990*.

'Christians Together in a Hurt City' (Liverpool), The George Jackson Lecture 1990, *Edinburgh Methodist Mission*, 1990.

'No Holiness but *Social* Holiness', in *Our Childhood's Pattern: Memories of Growing Up Christian*, ed. Monica Furlong, Mowbray, 1995.

'The Eucharist in Methodism', *Methodist Sacramental Fellowship Bulletin*, No.125, 1996.

'Charles Wesley, Ecumenical Hymnographer: Names and Sects and Parties Fall', *Proceedings of the Charles Wesley Society*, CVol.4, 1997, Madison, New Jersey.

'The Trial of Bishop King' (Read v. Bishop of Lincoln), *Ecclesiastical Law Journal*, Vol.5, No.25, July 1999.

'The Rev. Neville Ward of Bath: a Methodist Mariologist', *The Ecumenical Society of the Blessed Virgin Mary*, 2003.

'Protestant Nonconformists and Ecumenism', in *Protestant Nonconformity in the Twentieth Century*, ed. Alan P.F. Sell and Anthony Cross, Paternoster Press, 2003.

'Methodism and the Articulation of Faith: No Holiness but Social', *Methodist History*, Vol.XLII, No.1, October 2003.

PART ONE
Historical

Proto-Methodists of Anglican Piety in Post-Revolution England

Tim Macquiban

Introduction

Over forty years ago John Newton published his *Susanna Wesley and the Puritan Tradition in Methodism*,[1] providing not only the most scholarly full-scale biography to date of this remarkable woman, but also a stimulus to further studies to locate the development of later Methodist spirituality within the wider sweep of Christian history. John and his wife Rachel have subsequently, in their local ministry and contribution to Methodist theological education, and more particularly latterly in the enhancement of education and spiritual formation in places of Methodist heritage such as Epworth Old Rectory and the New Room Bristol, made sure that Susanna has been given equal place of honour amongst the founders of the Methodist movement.

I want here to take two significant figures, both connected with Salisbury, where this paper was originally given to a conference of the Methodist Sacramental Fellowship presided over by John Newton, to illustrate some aspects of post-Restoration and post-Revolution Anglican Spirituality, drawing on the twin strands of Caroline and Puritan influence within the Church of England. They are both women, and women are under-represented more generally in the study of Anglican spirituality, in line with the overall neglect for women and gender in spirituality studies until recently. As Ursula King has commented: 'gender perspectives remain often hidden and unacknowledged in writings on spirituality'.[2] Indeed, I searched in vain for references to the two subjects of this study in major works on spirituality. This absence merely underlines for me the insufficient regard for their contemporary impact or for the legacy that they have bequeathed to us. They are **Elizabeth**, third wife of Gilbert Burnet, Lord Bishop of Salisbury, who died in 1709, and **Susanna**, wife of Samuel Wesley, Rector of Epworth, Lincolnshire and mother of John and Charles Wesley, Anglican clergymen but also co-founders of the Methodist Movement; she died in 1742. Too often have they been sidelined thus, as useful and godly appendages to their clerical husbands. In this they share the experience of other women who 'throughout history… have struggled, often against great odds, to pursue a spiritual path contrary to the wishes of their families, friends and religious authorities'.[3] Both were in their own right fascinating figures who contributed to the spiritual life not just of their families and social circle, but also their wider church communities, influenced by their writings and example. It is with the hope of recovering the voices of women's spirituality and what they have to say to us that I offer these two vignettes, in the added hope that interest will be kindled and further research done. I will share a little of their social and familial contexts before looking at the similarities and differences in their method as well as aspects of their spiritual experience and writing.

Biographical background

Susanna Annesley was born in 1669, at Spital Yard, Bishopsgate, London, the youngest daughter of a prominent Presbyterian pastor, Samuel Annesley, whose ministry in Spitalfields after his ejection from the nearby parish of St Giles' Cripplegate in 1662 extended to his death in 1696. Susanna's formation in Puritan piety and pastoral care remained an abiding influence, despite her marriage in 1688 to the young curate Samuel Wesley (also of Nonconformist antecedents). They were both converts from Nonconformity to high church Caroline Anglicanism.[4] Samuel's parochial ministry took him from London into Surrey, then on to Lincolnshire, where he was Rector of Epworth from 1697 until his death in 1735. Here Susanna raised a large family, saved Samuel from ignominy on a number of occasions when he fell foul of parishioners and church authorities, provided a stable home and education for her children, led groups of local people in instruction when Samuel was away and found the time to write from her wide reading. Of course today she is remembered primarily as the mother of John and Charles, the wife of Samuel, the minor poet and bible commentator, and the daughter of the prominent dissenting minister, also Samuel. But she was, for many later Methodists at least, a saint, an archetype of evangelical womanhood whose intellectual and spiritual contribution is only now being fully evaluated since the complete edition of her writings has been made available.[5] More recently acknowledged has been her influence on Charles Wesley's formation through the inculcation of her catechetical writings (such as those on the Apostles' Creed and Ten Commandments written in 1710–11) and spirited daily conversations with each of her children.[6] In widowhood, partly spent in Salisbury with her daughter, she wrote some important works in defence of reformed Anglicanism. She was buried in 1742 in Bunhill Fields, London, with Bunyan and other Nonconformist worthies, not far from the Foundery Chapel where a society was established by her son John as a centre for the Methodist work in London.

The formative events of family life which shaped her spirituality were first her dispute with Samuel over the saying of the Amen at the end of the prayer for King William in 1701, demonstrating her defence of the liberty of conscience as a High Church Anglican and supporter of the Stuarts, born of her fierce dissenting spirit. John was the first fruit of the reconciliation between man and wife, born in 1703. It is perhaps not surprising that the last son was christened Charles as an indication of this adherence to the Stuarts. Secondly, John's miraculous preservation in the fire (along with the other children) which destroyed Epworth Rectory (including all Susanna's writings) in 1709 gave her a special sense of God's providence and grace, which had marked her and Jacky out as divine instruments. And thirdly, her holding of 'irregular' services in the Epworth Rectory kitchen while Samuel was away at Convocation in 1711–12 demonstrated that her methodical approach to her own personal life spilled out into an imperative to educate others, family and parishioners. She justified it in terms of a holy stewardship entrusted to her:

> *I cannot but look upon every soul you leave under my care as a talent committed to me under trust by the great Lord.*[7]

Holy living, in the context of a catholic spirit which defended liberty of conscience and reasonable enthusiasm, was the hallmark of an Anglican spirituality informed by its Puritan legacy (though now politically suspect), which gave birth to the Methodist Movement and aspects of the Evangelical Revival.

Elizabeth Blake was born in 1661 near Southampton, the daughter of Sir Richard Blake. From the age of eleven she read religious books. At seventeen she was married to Robert Berkely, whose estate in Worcestershire provided a comfortable gentry existence. Edward Stillingfleet, Lord Bishop of Worcester and a leading Latitudinarian, was a close friend. He said of her that 'he knew not a more considerable woman in England', noting her devotion and generosity in instructing the poor. During the reign of the Catholic King James II, she and her husband joined other Protestant refugees in the Netherlands until they returned in the Glorious Revolution of 1688. When her husband died in 1693, she was left a considerable fortune and more time for leisure. She gave much away and spent more time in reading, starting to compile books of rules and directions for holy living.[8]

In 1699 she married Gilbert Burnet, Lord Bishop of Salisbury, noted historian and supporter of William III, whose previous two wives had died. Elizabeth took responsibility for the upbringing of his children, as well as continuing to spend much time 'in writing upon Divine and Moral Subjects'.[9] In the last year of her life, in declining health, she had published her *Method of Devotion*, which her biographer said was 'all entirely her own composing without any Assistance or Addition by any Person whatsoever.' Despite a visit to the 'spaw' (Bath?) in 1708 to try to reverse her ill health, she was taken ill with pleurisy on her return home to Salisbury and died in February 1709. In her will she desired to die 'as she lived, in a full Communion with the Established Church of this realm, and in a Communion of Charity with the whole Body of Christians throughout the world.' Lest we think that she exhibited that most catholic spirit others desired, we have to remember that she excluded from her ecumenical outlook all Roman Catholics whose 'Idolatry, Superstition and Cruelty' she commended to the Almighty's displeasure and action in her prayers of intercession.[10] She bequeathed to the world her living example of Protestant saintliness, admired by those in Salisbury and beyond. Her *Method of Devotion*, which went into several editions (including a life added posthumously) beyond 1709, in which the strict rules of piety in private and public devotion were laid out, was held up as the basis for a holy life 'in conformity to the holy will of God'.[11] It was modelled perhaps on that greatest of the seventeenth-century Anglican spiritual writings, Jeremy Taylor's *Holy Living* (1650), itself a guide to prayer, with examples, and a book of meditations with general directions for living the good life.

Method and Rules

What then were the aspects of their spirituality which were common? First, I will look at the method and then the content. In terms of **method**, they were both daughters of the Puritans with their emphasis on an ordered timetable for the spiritual life with regular exercises in Christian obedience as they strove towards perfection. Newton claims that 'the framework of Susanna's piety was that of Puritan Method' formed in the 'serious godliness of the Annesley household.[12] They shared with most earlier Puritan divines a sense that journaling was important. Such a devotional diary is considered by many to be the Puritan substitute for the confessional, though rather more often entered, in what Martin Thornton calls 'a disciplined response to the leading of the Spirit'.[13] Such submission to God as part of Christian discipleship was common to men and women. But for women it may have had the added dimension of being one of the few means of expression of revolt against a patriarchal society where women, as Susanna noted in a marginal note (for her eyes only?) were allowed to 'think much and speak little'. This may explain the reticence to publish at all the writings of their innermost feelings. Elizabeth Burnet spent every evening in recollecting her 'actions and discourses', while Susanna Wesley urged all to 'make an examination of your conscience at least three times a day and omit no opportunity of retirement from the world'.[14]

One way of holding to this method of devotion was through **rules** and a disciplined life. Jeremy Taylor's *Holy Living* had devoted its first section to the 'care of time' and the second on 'purity of intention'. Susanna's insistence on regular self-examination was the most difficult thing in the world: 'to preserve a devout and serious temper of mind in the midst of much worldly business',[15] especially when one had, as she did, 'a numerous family and a narrow fortune'. A carefully ordered timetable in which even household tasks became religious acts was an essential for a disciplined life, particularly for women in the family context. Elizabeth's *Method of Devotion* was a highly structured timetabled approach to the day and the week, with specific rules for a holy life. In the morning, she enjoined six rules to prepare one's being for the day, giving examples of patterns of prayer. Every moment had to be accounted for in a sacrificial service to God:

> *I offer my Soul and Body, my Will, my whole Self as a sacrifice, a whole Burnt-Offering to Thee.*
>
> *O Thou, whose life is only a Perfect Pattern, and whose Doctrine is only a Perfect Rule, enable me, and all who profess Thy holy name, so to obey the one and to follow the other, that at the great Day of Account, we may know that comfortable sentence, 'Well done, good and faithful servants, enter into the Joy of the Lord.*[16]

Holy Time

Another aspect of this reverence for Holy Time was the centrality and importance of the Lord's Day. Susanna has several meditations on the 'most happy day', which served to remind people that 'these sacred moments may ever be employed in Thy service', a day for devotion rather than diversions, with all things 'devoutly performed' in praise and thanksgiving.[17] She reminded Samuel 'never to spend more time on any matter of mere recreation in one day than you spend on private religious duties.'[18] Elizabeth has a whole section of her *Method* setting out how to spend the day, including advice against putting on new clothes, entering church gravely and preparing for worship, and the timely warning: 'be not offended at and much less despise the Preacher tho' he is not greatly learned and wants the Ornaments of Wit and Eloquence.'[19]

Holy Living

Holy Living is to be experienced in relationships, with God, with family and community, and with all God's children. Within the Puritan tradition there was stress on the centrality of the concept of Church as the household of God, the gathered congregation, modelling its life on the pattern of Jesus Christ for its moral behaviour. Richard Baxter, in his *Reformed Pastor* put much store by catechising families in homes; the Christian life was to be built on family life: 'the life of religion and the welfare and glory of church and state dependeth much on family…'. Susanna modelled the Epworth household on these models adapted from à Kempis, Baxter, Lucas and others, and her own experience of the Annesley Puritan household.[20] She devoted specific time to each of her children each day of the week, taking two children on Sunday. She shared in family prayers, bible reading and taught them in a rigorous educational scheme. Elizabeth set out prayers for family devotions in her *Method*, noting that 'Where no Chaplain is kept, nor the Master of the Family is willing to perform this part of his Duty, doubtless the Mistress may supply that Neglect to her children';[21] and also to women in the house, though not to men, to whom recommended reading was to be provided. Female devotional methods were constrained within the limits of a patriarchal society.

Both Susanna and Elizabeth imbibed the broad **catholic spirit** of Baxter, Tillotson, and Stillingfleet, whose preaching and friendship they shared. Baxter's *The Saints' Everlasting Rest* was a particular favourite, which her son John included in his *Christian library*.[22] Elizabeth commended to God's protection 'all Churches and States professing and maintaining true Religion, according to Thy holy Word'.[23] This, however, did not prevent her from reminding Almighty God of the 'miserable yoke of Papal Usurpation' or the 'cruel Tyranny of Infidels' under which the 'once glorious Churches of the East' then laboured.

Holy Living was to be found in a quest for **Christian Perfection,** with a reasonable enthusiasm borne out in an active life based on contemplation. Both Susanna and Elizabeth stressed the person of Christ as the model and pattern for moral behaviour, an *imitatio Christi*, perhaps influenced by the work of Richard Lucas, whose maxim 'the world is an excellent school to a good Christian' guided the ethical dimension of holy living sought by them in their discipline.[24]

Susanna's bringing together of reason and conscience so that 'we make the light of Scripture and reason shine so bright' found an echo in the writings of Gilbert Burnet, which she quotes:

> *Experience without Reason may be thought of delusion of our fancy, so Reason without Experience had not so convincing an operation. These two meeting together, must need give a man all the satisfaction he can desire.*[25]

Such **Reasonable Enthusiasm,** together natural and revealed religion, 'by the direction and assistance of (God's) Holy Spirit', released the spiritual life from the dullness of Deism or the laxity of Latitudinarianism in a more affective response to the reading of Scripture (Newton, 149).[26] Susanna wrote that spiritual indisposition should not result in inactivity. Even if she could not pray, she would meditate. If she could not meditate, then read. If she could not read, then she got on with doing good. Such pragmatic common sense challenged the quietist approach of the Moravians and others, while preserving the priority of prayer and contemplation at the heart of the spiritual life. She took comfort in the words of Isaac Watts:

Where reason fails, with all her powers,
There faith prevails, and love adores.[27]

Means of Grace

The means of grace employed by God for building up holy living were, for both, prayer, self-examination, meditation upon and reading the scriptures and regular holy communion. Susanna's 'ways and means of religion' listed in her 1718 journal are very close to her son John's means of grace informing the life of the Holy Club in Oxford in the 1730s, as was her theology of the real presence in communion, set out in a letter to John in 1732.[28] Susanna regarded prayer as the chief weapon against temptation, while meditation was 'incomparably the best means to spiritualise our affections, confirm our judgement, and add strength to our pious resolutions'. Whenever there is any fervent prayer against any particular imminent, dangerous temptation, the remembrance of that prayer is a check upon the mind.[29] Of Elizabeth it was said that she prayed, read and wrote so much that 'you could think she spent all her time in the closet'.[30] Her *Method* is full of examples of her prayers for every time of the day and every occasion. One example may suffice to give a flavour of her intentions:

> *O Lord give me a pure Mind, holy Thoughts, a recollected Spirit, that I may this Day, and all my Days, walk in the awful Apprehensions of thy sacred Presence, that thy Glory may be the End of all that I do; that my Studies and my Labours, my Duty to my several relations, my Neighbours, and myself, may be rend(e)red acceptable to Thee through Jesus Christ, Amen.*[31]

She has notes on how to meditate and how to read the scriptures, all designed to the end 'of forming the Mind to a Christian Temper of Love, Humility and Truth and the Life to an exact Obedience to the Laws of the Gospel'.[32] All this is illustrated with practical advice, such as the reminder to 'lose not the morning by being too long in eating your breakfast and Dressing'.[33]

Self-Examination

This was, of course, crucial to the method of both, each day regularly, but particularly before taking holy communion in order 'to rely only on Jesus the mediator of the new covenant', confessing sins in order to underline one's reliance on the mercy of God.[34] Elizabeth sets out a list of questions, framed it seems by the concept of stewardship in the light of Matthew 25:[35]

- Help your neighbour – instruct the ignorant
- Comfort the afflicted
- Reprove the wanderers
- Assist all with good advice
- Bear patiently ingratitude when doing good
- Pray for others: 'tho' you can't relieve all, you can pray for all'
- Support strangers
- Rejoice in neighbours' good fortune
- Feed the hungry, give drink to the thirsty, clothe the naked
- Be kind to strangers
- Visit the sick
- Set honest prisoners at liberty

The introspection of dealing with personal sin is naturally woven in with the ethical response demanded by holy living.

For both women, the systematic regularity of preparing for and receiving communion was of greater priority than for many of their contemporaries. It flowed out of the emphasis on self-examination after meditation as a hallmark of serious piety.[36] For Susanna, the sacrament was a seal of the covenant of Christ with his Church, esteeming the Lord's Supper as a sovereign means of grace and requiring rigorous preparation. She wrote to her son Samuel while at Westminster School:

> *There is nothing more proper or effectual for the strengthening and refreshing the mind, than the frequent partaking of that blessed ordinance.*[37]

By 1732, she confirms her belief in the real presence of Christ in the sacrament, which so affected or mirrored the eucharistic spirituality of her sons.[38] Elizabeth too encouraged 'frequent and devout attendance', but stressed the more memorialist aspect of the sacrament and its place as a pledge of the 'promises of the New Covenant' in Christ's Blood, realising the benefits of his passion.[39] Nevertheless she concluded the rite with a prayer:

> *So live in me as to enable me to live and walk in the practice of these and other heavenly virtues.*[40]

Conclusion

Space does not permit many further examples of the god-fearing piety of these two remarkable women displaying what Susanna's father, Samuel, called 'serious godliness'. Susanna's piety was thoroughly Christo-centric and doxological, informed by her wide reading of scripture and contemporary works including Locke and Pascal, as well as Puritan and Caroline Divines like John Pearson and Jeremy Taylor. She displayed a warmth and enthusiasm which expressed itself in spontaneous ejaculations of praise to God and obedience to God's will. Elizabeth's piety was perhaps more measured (as befitted a Bishop's wife?) with excellent time management and zeal for the public good in making holy living something which all could practise (or at least those of her class and leisured existence!). Both shared the ideal of the redemption of time for God's holy service as the central feature of their methodistical approaches to the spiritual life. Ursula King has chronicled the 'rediscovery of countless women saints and mystics of the past' whose experiences and life stories, spiritual search, struggles and achievements, 'can greatly appeal to both women and men'.[41] She argues that most women's practices and devotions were 'usually of a more domestic, private, and folk nature rather than being part of official religion'.[42] Further research remains to be done on testing the hypotheses offered by others (e.g. Chilcote and Ruth) in the differences between male and female spiritual writers of this period and the influence of Susanna on the spirituality of the Wesley brothers and the wider Methodist movement. While the motives for the writings of Susanna Wesley and Elizabeth Burnet were undoubtedly focused on their own households, though very different, their influence, through the evangelical ministry of the Wesleys by Susanna, and the reputation of Gilbert Burnet as a forward-looking reformist pastoral bishop in his diocese of Salisbury, ensured that the method and spiritual exercises they put into practice for themselves and those around them had a far wider effect on the life and development of English religion and spirituality.

Notes

1 Newton, John (1968), *Susanna Wesley and the Puritan Tradition in Methodism*, London: Epworth Press.
2 King, Ursula (2009), *The Search for Spirituality: our global quest for meaning and fulfilment*, Canterbury: Canterbury Press, p122.
3 Op. cit. p132.
4 Wallace, Charles (2007), 'Charles and Susanna', in Newport, Kenneth C.G. and Campbell, Ted A. (eds), *Charles Wesley: Life, Literature and Legacy*, Peterborough: Epworth Press.
5 Wallace, Charles (1997), *Susanna Wesley: The complete writings*, Oxford: OUP, p3.
6 Wallace (2007), pp70-72.
7 Quoted in Wallace (1997), p13.
8 Goodwyn, T. (1709) 'Some account of her Life', added to Elizabeth Burnet's *Method of Devotion* (2nd Edn).
9 Goodwyn (1709), pp i-xviii for details of her life.
10 Op. cit. p42.
11 Op. cit. p21.
12 Newton (1968), pp132-36.
13 Wallace (1997) p197.
14 Op. cit. p197.
15 Op. cit. p208.
16 Goodwyn (1709), p284.
17 Wallace (1997) p303.
18 Newton (1968), p55.
19 Goodwyn (1709), pp197ff. Section on the Lord's Day.
20 See Newton (1968), Chapter 2 on Family.

21 Goodwyn (1709), op. cit. 197ff.
22 Newton (1968), p139.
23 Goodwyn (1709), p43.
24 Wallace (1997), p327.
25 Op. cit. p338.
26 Newton (1968), p139.
27 Quoted in Newton (1968), p152.
28 Wallace (1997), p79.
29 Op. cit. p201.
30 Goodwyn (1709), pxxi.
31 Op. cit. p88.
32 Op. cit. p79.
33 Op. cit. p99.
34 Wallace (1997), p224.
35 Goodwyn (1709), .p354.
36 Newton (1968), p139.
37 Op. cit. p147.
38 Op. cit. pp147-48.
39 Goodwyn (1709), p277.
40 Op. cit. pp291-92.
41 King, p128.
42 Op. cit. p123.

John Wesley and Eighteenth-Century Dissent

Henry Rack

Introduction

In 1779 Wesley published in his *Arminian Magazine* a letter written thirty years before by Charles Skelton, a former Methodist preacher now turned Dissenting minister. The letter told of spectacular conversions among criminals awaiting execution. But Wesley added a sharp postscript: 'Did God design that this light should be laid under a bushel, in a little, obscure Dissenting meeting house?'[1] While there may be a touch of Anglican snobbery here, along with a certain resentment Wesley was liable to show towards those who left Methodism, the remark nevertheless reflects serious differences of principle and practice between Methodism and Dissent. But was this slighting judgement typical of Wesley's attitude towards Dissent?

Although there has been a fair amount of comment on Wesley's debt to the Puritans, much less attention has been paid to his views of, and relationships with, contemporary Dissent.[2] The present paper will concentrate mainly on Wesley's relationships with his contemporaries rather than with Puritanism and earlier Dissent.

Wesley's Changing Views of Dissent

Despite his later irregularities, Wesley began his career as a stiff high churchman, much influenced by the even more extreme Nonjurors who left the Church of England in protest against the deposition of James II. He also denied the validity of non-Episcopal orders. Yet he was the grandson of distinguished Dissenting ministers, though his parents conformed to the Church of England when still young. He may well have been kept in ignorance of that ancestry until late in life.³ He only learnt of his grandfather John Wesley's Nonconformity in 1765, but in 1768 marvelled at three generations of his family 'preaching the gospel, nay the genuine gospel, in a line.'⁴

What is most striking about Wesley's reading and devotional disciplines at Oxford is the very small number of 'Puritan' works he records, alongside some of the continental Pietists.⁵ The most obvious characteristics of his piety in this period are his reverence for 'primitive antiquity' in doctrine, worship and discipline, enhanced by the influence of the Manchester Nonjuror Dr Deacon via Wesley's Oxford associate John Clayton.⁶ It was the Moravians, not English Dissenters, who challenged these influences and led to Wesley's conversion in 1738, though he played down his Moravian debt later. Indeed, despite his doctrinal shift to justification by faith, he continued to emphasise his long-standing pursuit of 'perfection' and his rejection of the predestinarianism of seventeenth-century Puritanism and Dissent, adopted also by many new evangelicals. These emphases are reflected in the doctrinal discussions of the early Methodist Conferences in 1744–47. But the Conferences also displayed a striking change from Wesley's high church views on church order. The Church of England is defined in minimal, pragmatic terms as 'the congregation of English believers in which the pure word of God is preached and the sacraments duly administered.' The early development of church order is seen in naturalistic terms as evolving from congregationalism through presbyterianism to episcopalianism, no system being of divine ordinance.⁷

What caused these striking changes? Could they have been influenced by earlier or contemporary Dissent? Wesley was certainly acquiring some knowledge of contemporaries by reading and personal contacts. He read Isaac Watts's *Psalms* in 1737 and met him in 1738. He corresponded with Philip Doddridge in 1739 and met him in 1740. Though nothing of these conversations is recorded, he addressed Doddridge's academy students in 1745.⁸ In January 1740, to the Scottish Presbyterian Seceder, Ralph Erskine, he made the remarkable concession for an English Episcopalian that 'every Christian congregation has an indisputable right to choose their own pastor.'⁹ In the proposed agenda for the first Conference in 1744 under 'Discipline' it was asked 'What may we adopt from C[ount] Z[inzendorf], the Kirk [Church of Scotland] and the Quakers?' though the Conference minutes do not record this being done.[10] Although Wesley liked to claim that Methodism was merely an auxiliary to the Church of England and denied he was founding a new sect, it is clear that Dissenters also became Methodists. In old age Wesley gloried that it was 'peculiar to the people called Methodists' that they can hold any opinions and remain Churchmen or Dissenters. The early 'Rules of the United Societies' (1743) only required a desire to 'flee from the wrath to come' and showing this in their conduct.[11] He also acknowledged in 1745 that the shift from his old exclusive churchmanship was the result of encountering 'those at the smallest distance from us [the Church of England] whether they be termed Presbyterians or Independents' 'in whom "the root of the matter" is undeniably found.' But he criticised these and other Dissenters, as he had already criticised Anglicans, for failing to live up to their own avowed principles.[12]

Yet it seems unlikely that Dissent was the origin of his revised views on doctrine and church polity. Minimising Moravian influences, he ascribed his altered views to Scripture and 'antiquity' as viewed through his reading of Lord King and Bishop Stillingfleet, though the needs of Methodist development may have been equally important.[13] In Part III of his *Farther Appeal* he inveighed against Dissenters in the past for disputing over 'opinions' and 'externals' in religion, though excepting people like Philip Henry, whom he claimed did not dispute and were forced out of the Church.[14] Although to 'John Smith' in 1746 he defended sixteenth-century Puritans like Thomas Cartwright as being 'the most learned and most pious' Englishmen of their time, on rereading Daniel Neal's *History of the Puritans* in 1747 he was amazed equally at 'the execrable spirit of persecution' which drove them out of the Church 'and at the weakness of those holy confessors' in disputing about surplices, hoods and kneeling at the Lord's Supper.[15]

In principle, at least, Wesley became increasingly tolerant of religious differences, reflecting the 'enlightened' view of his time that persecution purely for religion is not justified. Once, he admitted, he had thought all English people should belong to the Church of England. But on this principle the Reformation could never have taken place for it would undermine 'the right of private judgment on which the whole Reformation stands.' This claim comes from his sermon on 'The Catholic Spirit' in which he argued that Christians could unite on essentials while agreeing to differ in 'opinions' on lesser matters like modes of worship and church polity. In 1766 he claimed that liberty of conscience is a right by the law of God and nature as well as of England.[16] Though a keen sacramentalist he was prepared to allow not only that particular forms of baptism are matters of 'opinion', but that even baptism itself is not essential for salvation, otherwise (absurdly) Quakers would be damned.[17] As his views on the way of salvation became more flexible in later life, he was prepared to allow that so long as holiness was achieved 'by whatever means' he was 'content'.[18] Yet this toleration co-existed with the view that Roman Catholics, though open to salvation, could not be trusted with full civil rights.[19] His views on the restriction of full civil rights for Dissenters appear not to have been recorded but, as we shall now see, he was selective in the apparent softening of his earlier hostility to Dissent.

Cooperation and Conflict with Dissent

Wesley's distrust and hostility were aroused partly by the doctrines of certain types of Dissent. To Miss Bishop in 1778, when she had criticised Anglican clergy for not preaching the gospel, Wesley claimed that Independents and Baptists were worse, 'for Calvinism is not the gospel, nay it is further from it than most of the sermons I hear at Church' and more dangerous to Methodists.[20] At Ilchester in 1786 he thought the society would do well despite the opposition of Calvinists and 'Socinians' (probably Presbyterian anti-Trinitarians).[21] Suspicions of this kind were aggravated by threats to Methodists' beliefs and preachers lost by becoming Dissenting ministers, often as Calvinistic Independents. A recent analysis suggests that rather more ex-Methodists became Dissenting than Anglican ministers.[22]

Wesley's attempts at organised evangelical cooperation were mainly directed towards Anglican evangelical clergy, though he abandoned these attempts in the 1760s.[23] Cooperation with Dissenters was very limited and on an individual basis, chiefly (it has been argued) with Presbyterians. These, however, seem mainly to be in the established Church of Scotland, so not legally 'Dissenters'.[24] In 1755, under pressure from some preachers for ordination and separation from the Church, it is not surprising that Wesley thought it a 'prudential' rule for Methodists not to attend Dissenting meetings unless already Dissenters, these being encouraged to attend their own communion services.[25] In 1779 he thought it safest not to allow Dissenting 'teachers' [ministers] to occupy Methodist pulpits as they had suffered for allowing this.[26] In all of these cases his underlying anxieties included the desire not to separate or seem to separate from the Church. This also explains his reluctance to allow preachers and preaching houses to be registered for protection under the Toleration Act or, when they were, to admit that this made them Dissenters.[27]

Most of Wesley's public, private and extended controversies were with Church of England clergy. Apart from personal and passing encounters there are few literary controversies with Dissenters. In 1748 he wrote a letter to an unnamed Quaker, criticising Robert Barclay's *Apology* (1676) as (perhaps misleadingly) a standard of Quaker doctrine. Their main faults (he claimed) concerned dependence on the inner light instead of Scripture for authority, on justification, the sacraments and worship.[28]

Also in 1748 Wesley met Gilbert Boyce, a Baptist minister. The most significant issue to emerge in the correspondence which followed was Wesley's regular claim that differences on 'opinions' need not change the love he felt for Boyce. But for Boyce believers' baptism was not an 'opinion' but a biblical rule. Wesley's response was the remarkable claim, cited earlier, that even baptism itself was not essential for salvation, otherwise (impossibly) Quakers would be damned.[29]

In 1758 he wrote to Micaijah Towgood to refute his *Dissent from the Church of England fully justified*.[30] The Wesley brothers read the book in 1755, clearly with some of their preachers' current objections to the Church and pressure for ordination and separation in mind. Though John at first conceded that the book was able and 'contains the strength of the cause' (i.e. in favour of separation), he soon condemned Towgood as a 'bitter, sarcastic jester'.[31] What Charles Wesley described as his brother's 'excellent treatise' in response has disappeared, but parts of it were probably used in various writings including his address to the 1755 Conference on 'Ought we to separate?'[32] However, despite his arguments against separation, John acknowledged both in his 1755 address and to Rev. Samuel Walker of Truro later that year that he could not answer some of the preachers' criticisms of the church. Nor, he admitted, could he now subscribe to the Book of Common Prayer as wholly scriptural.[33]

In January 1758 he responded directly to Towgood, by now describing the book as 'the most saucy and virulent satire against the Church of England that ever my eye beheld.'[34] Why he had delayed is not clear, though debates over separation and pressure from the preachers to certify themselves under the Toleration Act evidently continued during 1756 and 1757.[35] Wesley's letter to Towgood focuses on what the latter claimed (and Wesley agreed) was the fundamental issue in dispute. For Towgood argued that Christ is the sole lawgiver in his church and therefore the Church of England has no authority to decree rites and ceremonies. Hence separation from it is justified. Wesley argued, like Hooker against the sixteenth-century Puritans, that the church does have the right to make rules on 'things indifferent, not defined by Scripture'. That Christ is the 'sole sovereign power' does not exclude the legitimacy of subordinate authorities, just as judges have power under the king's final authority. Power to determine membership of a particular church does not exclude people from 'the church of Christ'. But Wesley also maintained that it is not only legitimate but a duty commanded in Scripture to be subject to religious and secular authorities in 'things indifferent'.[36] Having, as he believed, settled the issue of principle, Wesley claimed that it was unnecessary to deal with Towgood's detailed criticisms of Anglican worship, which echo those of earlier Puritans and Dissenters. This was perhaps convenient in view of his own recently expressed doubts.

How far Wesley was being consistent or fair here will be considered in the conclusion to this essay.

A third controversy was with Dr John Taylor of Norwich. Here the issue was purely theological: a fundamental threat to the traditional doctrine of salvation by Christ's atoning death and resurrection as the indispensable remedy for human fallenness resulting from inherited original sin.[37] Taylor argued that the Fall only resulted in the 'sorrow, labour and death' of humanity. Though denying the full divinity of Christ, Taylor claimed that he had obtained resurrection for us by his righteousness and obedience. We have free will and power to develop a righteous life. Predestination to heaven or hell cannot be upheld because it would be unjust of God to hold us guilty if we were unable to accept the gift of grace. Wesley saw Taylor's teaching as a threat to Methodist belief and as posing a choice between Christianity and heathenism, for it takes away 'the scriptural doctrine of redemption or justification and that of the New Birth, the beginning of sanctification.'[38] Yet Wesley had a delicate task in answering Taylor. His *Doctrine of Original Sin*, which drew on Isaac Watts and other Dissenters, painted the traditional dark picture of fallenness; but, like Taylor, he rejected predestination in favour of salvation being open to all. We have free will to accept or reject the offer, but he avoided Taylor's 'heathen' dependence on human effort by claiming that free will is not a 'natural' attribute of humankind but a universal gift of God's grace.

One other controversy with a Dissenter, the Baptist Caleb Evans, was of a different character since it did not concern Dissent as such, but rather Wesley's controversial views on the conflict and war with America in the 1770s. Evans charged Wesley not only with inconsistency and plagiarism from Dr Johnson's attack on the Americans, but also with wrongly claiming that he had not recommended a pro-American book to his publisher Walter Pine and friend James Rouquet.[39] It has been claimed that there is a relationship between Wesley's and John Fletcher's anti-Calvinist theology and their political loyalism and between their opponents' Calvinism and pro-American 'republicanism'. But this seems open to doubt, since there is no consistency between the theological and political loyalties of individuals on either side.[40]

Borrowings and Influences

Given the markedly high church and Nonjuror influences on Wesley's pre-conversion thinking, followed by his conversion under Moravian tutelage, surprise has been expressed at the large proportion (over one third) of 'Puritan' authors in his collection of 'practical divinity', *The Christian Library* (1749–55).[41] Exactly how and where he acquired this knowledge has never been fully explained. It is frequently claimed to be due to the advice of Philip Doddridge, in a letter which Wesley published years later.[42] But, as Monk points out, hardly any of Doddridge's recommendations were included in the *Library* and none by Wesley's Dissenting contemporaries.[43] It seems likely that Wesley was seeking Doddridge's advice about a different need. Their correspondence in March–June 1746 preceded the first references to the plans for the *Library* and Wesley was apparently asking for advice on reading for 'young preachers' with a 'practical' bias.[44] At the first two Conferences in 1744 and 1745 a desire was expressed for a 'seminary for labourers' but a tutor was lacking.[45] Meanwhile, Wesley produced an ambitious preachers' reading list, not confined to 'practical' theology, and in 1745 an even more comprehensive collection, including philosophy and science, to be available 'for our own use' in London, Bristol and Manchester. It looks as though in 1746 he was asking Doddridge for a more strictly 'practical' list, but Doddridge's reply arrived too late for the 1746 Conference. It is surely significant that the minutes of that Conference contained a short, purely 'practical' list for preachers' reading. Doddridge's delayed letter contained a comprehensive list of secular, biblical, theological and practical works, including a number by contemporary Dissenters. It probably reflected the curriculum for his Academy, but hardly suited the leisure and capacity of most Methodist preachers. It was published thirty years later in the *Arminian Magazine*, significantly entitled 'A Scheme of Study for Clergymen'.

Wesley drew mainly on modern Dissenters for his *Notes* on the Old and New Testament, though for the New above all on the Pietist Bengel. This may seem surprising, as the most recent study of Wesley's approach to the Bible says, quite plausibly, that it 'was that of an eighteenth-century high church Arminian [anti-Calvinist] Anglican'.[46] Characteristically, in using the Dissenter Matthew Henry for the Old Testament, Wesley says that what Henry 'wrote in favour of particular redemption [predestination] was totally left out.'[47] Wesley's use of Watts for his work on *Original Sin* has already been noted.

On worship the situation is more complex. Wesley expressed a characteristically Anglican admiration for the Book of Common Prayer: 'I believe there is no liturgy in the world... which breathes more of a solid, scriptural, rational piety than the Common Prayer of the Church of England.'[48] He also claimed that Methodists needed Anglican worship since their own assemblies lacked the full range of public prayer.[49] Furthermore, he found 'more life in the church prayers than in the formal extemporaneous prayers of the Dissenters' and he warned against the Calvinism of Dissenting sermons.[50] Yet he could be critical of the sloppy conduct of Anglican worship compared with Methodist reverence, when they used Common Prayer. He also acknowledged that he supplemented the liturgy with extempore prayer and defended this as legitimate.[51]

But this and other irregularities seem to owe little to Dissent and rather to need, experience and his claim that the needs of the gospel take priority over formal church order.[52] Of the special Methodist meetings only the Covenant service originated in Dissent as an adaptation from the seventeenth-century Alleines to become a corporate rather than individual observance.[53] But Wesley did make early use of Isaac Watts's hymns, some surviving into the *Hymns for the Use of Methodists* of 1780.[54]

Yet, despite his love of the Book of Common Prayer, in 1755 (as we have seen) Wesley acknowledged that he recognised faults in it and could not now subscribe to it as completely conforming to Scripture. His 1784 service book for the American Methodists involved much more substantial omissions and alterations from the Book of Common Prayer than he acknowledged in his preface. Though the alterations are obvious enough, the reasons and possible sources for them have excited marked differences of opinion. Frederick Hunter claimed that Wesley closely followed the Puritan Savoy Conference proposals of 1661 and A.E. Peaston that Wesley echoed all the seventeenth-century Puritan complaints.[55] J.F. White, in his edition of Wesley's book, claimed that he was familiar with, and drew on, all the proposals of every kind appearing in the seventeenth and eighteenth centuries. That is to say, Puritan, Nonjuror, anti-Trinitarian (a frequent eighteenth-century type) and others.[56] In contrast with these claims that Wesley consciously drew on specific sources is Frank Baker's view. He allows that Wesley was aware of the Puritan proposals 'in a general way' but was unlikely to be influenced by the anti-Trinitarian proposals. What really influenced him, Baker claimed, were the needs of the Americans and his 'personal predilections', reflecting criticisms of the Common Prayer felt for many years past. Furthermore, Baker argued, Wesley's known methods of abridging books suggest that he simply supplied a copy of the Book of Common Prayer to his publisher, marked with omissions and alterations.[57]

Although lack of space and expert knowledge preclude a detailed assessment of these rival claims here, some cautionary observations are in order. Apart from the very limited (and misleading) claims in his preface of the limited nature of his alterations, Wesley gives no further clues to his motivations or possible sources. There is only direct evidence for his knowledge of two previous revision proposals. In 1750 he read John Jones's *Free and Candid Disquisitions* (1749) with little appreciation. In 1754 he read Calamy's *Abridgement of Mr. Baxter's History*, without commenting on the details it contained of the Savoy Conference. But in his address to the 1755 Conference against separation he listed objections to the Book of Common Prayer and to Samuel Walker noted that they resembled those made by Puritans a century before.[58] These are the only sources for Prayer Book revision he records (apart from the very different early Nonjuror influences). These explicit references come from years before 1784 and it should be noted that his objections to the Prayer Book were his own and (always an important consideration) those of other Methodists. They were clearly not borrowed from the Puritans (as sometimes seems to be implied). He merely recalled that they had had similar criticisms. Nor is there any direct evidence in diaries, journals or letters of when or how he made the revision, unlike references to his other writings and editing. All the theories about sources and reasons for changes come from the indirect evidence of apparent resemblances to other revisions and speculations about Wesley's motives. Two further comments are in order. Baker's picture of Wesley slashing and amending a copy of the text accords with his known practice and busy life better than systematic comparison of numerous texts. There is also no trace of the Nonjuror adaptations of the Prayer Book he used in Georgia. On the whole, though not consistently in the sacramental services, this seems a 'low' rather than 'high' revision, though some copies of the book show inclusion and others omission of the manual acts in the eucharist and the sign of the cross in baptism which have been variously explained.[59]

On church organisation there is little to record. We have seen that the suggestions in 1744 about consulting 'the kirk' and Quakers were not followed up, though it is thought that the Quarterly Meeting pioneered by John Bennet in 1748 may owe something to the Quakers.[60] Although Wesley claimed that he was not founding a church, his strenuous attempts to control his relatively centralised 'connexional' system implied a much tighter ecclesiastical polity than that of most churches of his day. His ordinations certainly owed nothing to Dissent. In his own eyes they followed the example of Scripture and the 'primitive church' for Americans providentially set free from the limitations of hierarchical Anglican episcopacy. He exercised his alleged right to ordain as a presbyter, claimed long before in 1746.[61] The form of ministry he saw as 'primitive' resembled the Anglican version in being three-fold: deacon, presbyter or elder and superintendent. But the last term is significant. On his argument the superintendent is not a separate, superior 'order' of ministry, but exactly what it says – a supervisor or overseer. It is significant that he objected violently to the American Methodists' adoption of the title of bishop.[62] Charles Wesley claimed that his brother had turned 'Presbyterian'. So did Dr Whitehead in his biography of Wesley, hostile to the ordinations and blaming the preachers' influence. Here, too, there is talk of the 'Presbyterian plan', though also of 'a hodge-podge of inconsistencies'.[63] It is understandable that ordinations by a mere presbyter and without a superior order of bishop being involved would seem 'Presbyterian', though it in no way resembled, for example, the Scottish model. In Wesley's eyes it was surely a 'primitive' episcopacy owing nothing to Presbyterianism.

Conclusion

Although, as we have seen, Wesley's stiff exclusive churchmanship had been modified by experience and expediency after his conversion, his treatment of Dissenters was characterised by a mixture of appreciation of some individuals with suspicion of Calvinists and anti-Trinitarians. He acquired a taste for the 'practical divinity' of seventeenth-century Puritans and Dissenters, though purged of Calvinism, but thought Dissenting worship and its localised church polity seriously defective. It remains difficult to determine whether he was fair or even consistent in his attitude to contemporary Dissent and conformity to the church.

Thus in the sermon on 'The Catholic Spirit' and elsewhere he allowed for friendly and cooperative relationships grounded on a common basic Christianity and agreement to differ on 'opinions' or 'things indifferent' like worship and church polity.[64]

By contrast, the 1755 address to Conference and letter to Towgood appeared to assert that the church not only has the right to lay down rules on 'things indifferent', but also that church members are bound by Scripture to obey them.[65]

Different again was Wesley taking the high ground of principle. To 'John Smith' he claimed that the demands of the gospel take priority over 'church order', which will emerge satisfactorily if the gospel is faithfully preached. In the midst of the 1755 Conference assertion of the church's right to enforce rules he states that the Methodists do not separate from the church but submit to its governors and laws 'in all things not contrary to Scripture'. They 'dare not submit' to dropping preaching in all places, using extempore prayer, organising societies and allowing lay preaching.[66]

Perhaps the first two positions are compatible if the 'Catholic Spirit' argument only applies to relationships between churches or individual members of different churches; maybe also to Methodists as conforming to different denominations yet cooperating in the common pursuit of holiness.⁶⁷ The problem, as the disagreement with Gilbert Boyce showed, was that one person's 'opinion' was another's scriptural command. The argument about the church's right to enforce rules on 'things indifferent' appears to apply to members of the Church of England, but logically to any organised church. If so, presumably Towgood had no ground for separating from Anglicanism as disobeying Christ's law. But this also seems to destroy Wesley's claim to distinguish between those who were forced out in 1662 and those who left voluntarily. The church, on his argument, had every right to enforce conformity on dissentients who in any case should not dispute on 'things indifferent'. Nor could they opt at that time for a more congenial church, though this was open to them after the Toleration Act of 1689. But Wesley's third position rises above these positions to justify Nonconformity on things not 'indifferent' but 'contrary to Scripture.'

In reality Wesley appears in practice to be asserting a right to a fourth position. This seems to combine the freedom to differ on 'opinions' with the necessity of promoting the gospel at the cost of violating Anglican rights to enforce conformity on 'things indifferent' while remaining within that church. To justify this, while appealing to high principle, Wesley appeared to use a variety of legalistic and opportunistic arguments: the Conventicle Act does not apply to religious societies; the Canons are of doubtful legality and we cannot reform them or the church courts. But other Anglicans also dislike them and do not separate. There are faults in the Book of Common Prayer but we 'can leave the evil and keep the good' and are not required to subscribe to it. We can take advantage of the Toleration Act to protect preachers and preaching houses without describing ourselves as Dissenters. (It was indeed found difficult to interpret and apply the law to Methodism.)⁶⁸

Wesley, then, appeared to claim that Methodists could remain within the church without being obliged fully to conform to it. While this was ostensibly based on the high ground of obeying Scripture and not disobeying what he acknowledged as the church's right to enforce rules on 'things indifferent', the distinction appeared to be applied so as to suit what he wished to achieve. His critics understandably simply saw him as violating Anglican 'order'. For Dissenters, whatever the defects of Towgood's basic argument, their numerous criticisms of Anglican worship were felt to be matters of principle rather than 'opinions'.

Whatever one's judgement on these arguments, two final points can be made about Wesley's conduct which seem fairly clear. One is that he could only have survived within the Church of England in eighteenth-century conditions. In the 1660s he would surely have been prosecuted for Nonconformity. In terms of the traditional derogatory view of the eighteenth-century church his survival might seem evidence of Anglican slackness. In terms of recent revisionism, perhaps as a sign of a certain flexibility in response to need.[69] The second point illustrated here is that what usually conditioned Wesley's encounters with Dissenters was less hostility to them as such than the threats their beliefs posed to Methodists' health and the risk of seducing them from attachment to the Church of England. One important element in this concern was to secure the advantages of Methodism's peculiar position as neither fully conforming to Anglican norms nor formally separating. This avoided the legal, social and practical limitations of life fully confined within the Toleration Act, as well as the localised churches and ministries which would have destroyed Wesley's connexional polity and undermined his control of it.

Notes

1 Wesley (1779) in *Arminian Magazine*, 2, pp92-95.
2 For Wesley and Puritanism see especially Newton, J.A. (1968, 2002), *Susanna Wesley and the Puritan Tradition in Methodism*. London, Peterborough: Epworth Press; R.C. Monk (1966, 1999), *John Wesley. His Puritan Heritage*, London: Epworth Press, Metuchen: Scarecrow Press. For the continuing problem of defining Puritanism, recent essays in Copping, J. and Lim, P.C.H. (2008), *Cambridge Companion to Puritanism*, Cambridge: CUP.
3 Baker, Frank (1962/63), 'Wesley's puritan ancestry'. *London Quarterly and Holborn Review*, pp187, 180-86.
4 Wesley, John (ed F. Baker et al) (1975), *Works of John Wesley* (Bicentennial Edn), Oxford: Clarendon Press, later Nashville: Abingdon Press, 21, pp513–18 [hereafter, *Works* (BE)]. Wesley, John (ed Telford, J.) (1931), *Letters of John Wesley*, London: Epworth Press, 5, p76 [hereafter *Letters*].

5   List in Green, V.H.H. (1961), *The Young Mr. Wesley*, London: Arnold, pp305–19; Heitzenrater, R.P. (1972), 'John Wesley and the Oxford Methodists (1725–35)', unpub. PhD, Duke University, pp495-527.
6   Rack, H.D. (2002), 'The Wesleys and Manchester', *Proceedings of the Charles Wesley Society*, 8, pp6-23; Hammond, G. (2007), 'Restoring primitive Christianity. John Wesley and Georgia, 1735–37', unpub. PhD, University of Manchester.
7   Details in Rack, H.D. (3rd Edn 2002), *Reasonable Enthusiast. John Wesley and the Rise of Methodism*, Peterborough: Epworth Press, pp293-96, based on Minutes of Conference 1744–47 detailed in note 10, below.
8   Wesley, *Works* (BE), 18, pp463 (diary); 19, p356 (diary), p428 (diary); 19, p381 (diary) ; 20, p89 (journal).
9   Wesley, *Works* (BE), 26, p16.
10 Richard Viney's MS journal, 1 June 1744, copy in John Rylands University Library, Manchester, MS Eng, 965; Minutes for 1744 in *John Bennet's Copy of Conference Minutes for 1744, 1745, 1747, 1748 and John Wesley's for 1746* (1896), London: Wesley Historical Society Publications.
11 'Thoughts upon a late phenomenon' (1788) in Wesley, John (ed T. Jackson) (1872), *Works of John Wesley*, London: Wesleyan Book Room, 13, p266 [hereafter *Works* (1872)]; Wesley, *Works* (BE), 9, p70.
12 *Farther Appeal to Men of Reason and Religion*, Pt. III in Wesley, *Works* (BE), 11, p250. He described the distance of Dissent from the Church of England as increasing from Presbyterians, to Independents, to Baptists and farthest to Quakers.
13 Wesley , *Works* (BE), 20, p112; Baker, F. (1970), *John Wesley and the Church of England*, London: Epworth Press, pp145-46 [hereafter Baker, *John Wesley*]; Wesley, *Letters* , 7, p20.
14 Wesley, *Works* (BE), 11, pp319-20.
15 Wesley, *Works* (BE), 26, p231; 20, p162.
16 Wesley, *Works* (BE), 2, p86; Wesley, *Letters*,, 5, p22.
17 Wesley, *Works* (BE), 26, p421.
18 Wesley, *Works* (BE), 26, p203.
19 For a discussion and one remarkable exception see Rack, *Reasonable Enthusiast*, pp309-12.
20 Wesley, *Letters*, 6, p26.
21 Wesley, *Works* (BE), 23, p40.
22 Lenton, John (2009), *John Wesley's Preachers*, Milton Keynes: Paternoster Press, p316.
23 Wesley, *Works* (BE), 21, pp454-61; Wesley, *Letters*, 4, pp235-39.
24 Baker, *John Wesley*, pp133-35 for the claim and examples; compare *Farther Appeal* in *Works* (BE), 11, pp250, 351, 254.
25 'Ought we to Separate?' in Baker, *John Wesley*, 338-39; Jackson, T. (ed) (1849), *Journal of Charles Wesley*, London, Wesleyan Methodist Book Room, 2, p137.
26 Wesley, *Letters*, 6, p346.
27 Baker, *John Wesley*, pp316-19.
28 Wesley, *Letters*, 2, pp116-28; Wesley, *Works* (1872), 10, pp177-88.
29 Wesley, *Works* (BE) 26, pp418-19, 444-47, 425.
30 Originally Anon. (1746), *The Dissenting Gentleman's Answer to… the Rev. Mr. White's….Letters*; later as Towgood, M. (1753), *A Dissent from the Church of England*….
31 Wesley, *Works* (BE), 21, pp9-10.
32 For details and copies of the address, Baker, *John Wesley*, pp165, 326-40.

33. Baker, *John Wesley*, p331; Wesley, *Works* (BE),26, p594.
34. Wesley, *Works* (BE), 21, p134.
35. Wesley, *Works* (BE), 21, p76; Wesley, *Letters*, 3, pp221-26 especially 223; Ward, W.R. in Wesley, *Works* (BE), 21, p120 note 68 , following Tyerman, Luke (1872), *Life and Times of John Wesley* (2nd Edn), London: Hodder and Stoughton, 2, p281, mistakenly identified Walker's letter of November 1755 as being in October 1757 and as referring to the Conference of that year. Correct date in Wesley, *Letters*, 3, p144 and *Works* (BE) 26, p613.
36. Wesley, *Letters*, 3, pp250-56.
37. For a discussion of Taylor's (1735-36) *Scripture Doctrine of Original Sin* and Wesley's (1757) *Doctrine of Original Sin* in his *Works* (1872), 9, pp196-444, see Eddy, G.T. (2003), *Dr Taylor of Norwich: Wesley's Arch-Heretic*, Peterborough: Epworth Press.
38. Wesley, *Letters*, 4, p67.
39. For the context see Wesley, *Letters*, 6, pp170, 188-89, 194-95; Rack, *Reasonable Enthusiast* , pp376-79; and for a critical account of Wesley's conduct Abelove, H. (2000), 'John Wesley's plagiarism of Samuel Johnson and its contemporary reception', *Huntington Library Quarterly* , 59(1), 75-79 to whom I am indebted for a copy.
40. For the claim see Semmel, B. (1974), *The Methodist Revolution*, London: Heinemann, especially chapter III.
41. Monk (1966), *John Wesley*, p42,.
42. Baker, *John Wesley*, p134 and in Wesley, *Works* (BE), 26, p190 note.
43. Monk (1966), *John Wesley*, pp255, 39-40.
44. Only Doddridge's letters have survived: Wesley, *Works* (BE), 26, pp190 and note, 191, 195-99.
45. Bennet, *Conference Minutes* (above, note 10) 29 June 1744, questions 11,14; 3 August 1745, questions 6, 13; 14 May 1746, questions 14,15; *Arminian Magazine* (1778), 1, 419-25; Tyerman, *John Wesley*, 1, pp515–17 also interpreted the request as for the preachers' needs.
46. Bullen, D.A., (2007), *A Man of One Book? John Wesley's Interpretation and Use of the Bible*, Milton Keynes: Paternoster Press, p xxviii.
47. Prefaces to the *Notes* in Wesley, *Works* (1872), 14, pp235-39, 246-53.
48. White, J.F. (ed) (1991), *John Wesley's Prayer Book. The Sunday Service of the Methodists in North America (1784)*, Cleveland OH: OSL Publishers, p2 of facsimile.
49. *Minutes of the Methodist Conference from 1744* (1862), London: Mason. 1, pp58-59.
50. Wesley, *Letters*, 6, p326.
51. Wesley, *Letters*, 3, pp226-28; Wesley, *Works* (BE), 18, pp502, 233; 9, pp187-88.
52. To 'John Smith' in Wesley, *Works* (BE), 26, pp205-206.
53. Rack, *Reasonable Enthusiast*, pp412–14 and Tripp, D. (1969), *The Renewal of the Covenant in the Methodist Tradition*, London: Epworth Press.
54. Wesley, *Works* (BE), 7, p31.
55. Hunter, F.E. (1941-42), in *Proceedings of the Wesley Historical Society (PWHS)*, 23, pp124-33 with comments by J.E. Rattenbury, pp133-35; Peaston, A.E. (1964),*The Prayer Book Tradition in the Free Churches*, London: James Clark, pp35-65.
56. White, *John Wesley's Prayer Book*, Introduction, pp5-8.
57. Baker, *John Wesley*, pp242-43.
58. Wesley, *Works* (BE), 20, pp357, 485; Baker, *John Wesley*, p331 in 'Ought we to separate?'; *Works* (BE), 26, p612.
59. Swift, W.F. (1953) in *PWHS*, 29, 13–16; Barton, J.H. (1960) in *PWHS*, 32, 97-101 (with comments by Swift; George, A.R. (1976) in *PWHS*, 40, 137-44.

60 John Bennet, MS Letter book C81 in diaries box, John and Grace Bennet, Methodist Church Archives in John Rylands University Library, Manchester, folios 29,31; Baker, F. in Davies, R.E. and Rupp, E.G. (eds) (1965), *History of the Methodist Church in Great Britain*, London: Epworth Press, 1, p239.
61 Wesley, *Letters*, 7, p21.
62 Wesley, *Letters*, 8, p91.
63 Tyson, J.R. (ed) (1989), *Charles Wesley. A Reader*, Oxford: OUP, pp430, 61; Baker, F. (1948), *Charles Wesley as revealed by his Letters*, London: Epworth Press, p138; Whitehead, J. (1793-96), *Life of John Wesley and Charles Wesley*, London: S. Couchman, 2, pp418, 420.
64 Wesley, *Works* (BE), 2, pp79-96.
65 Baker, *John Wesley*, pp29-31; Wesley, *Letters*, 3, pp250-56.
66 Wesley, *Works* (BE), 26, pp205-206; 'Ought we to Separate?' describes these actions obliquely (Baker, *John Wesley*, p328) but to Walker of Truro explicitly: Wesley, *Works* (BE), 26, p595.
67 'Thoughts upon a Late Phenomenon' in Wesley, *Works* (BE), 9, pp536-37; compare Wesley, *Letters* 7, p190 and early *Rules of the United Societies* in Wesley, *Works* (BE), 9, p70.
68 See discussion with Bishop Gibson in Charles Wesley, *Journal*, 1, p133 (date corrected to 20 October 1738 in Wesley, *Works* (BE), 19, p359 (diary); Anon [Gibson, Edmund] (1744), *Observations...Upon...the...Methodists*, London: E. Owen, p4; Wesley, *Letters*, 8, pp230-31; Wesley, *Principles of a Methodist Farther Explained* in *Works* (BE), 9, pp186-96. For the legal and practical problems of prosecuting Methodists, Hempton, D. (1996), 'Methodism and the Law' in his *The Religion of the People*, London: Routledge, pp145-61.
69 For excellent and original discussions of the Wesleys from this point of view see Gregory, J. (2005), '"In the church I will live and die": John Wesley, the Church of England and Methodism' in Gibson, W. and Ingram, R. (eds), *Religious Identities in Britain 1688–1832*, Aldershot and Burlington NJ: Ashgate, pp47-78; Gregory, J. (2007), 'Charles Wesley and the Eighteenth Century' in Newport, K.G.C. and Campbell, T.A. (eds), *Charles Wesley: Life, Literature and Legacy*, Peterborough: Epworth Press, pp18-39.

The Rise of Methodism in Southern England[1]

John Vickers

The area covered by this article comprises a broad triangle with its apex on the high chalk plateau of Salisbury Plain and almost the whole of the counties of Hampshire and Dorset to the south-east and south-west. It is interesting that this coincides quite closely with the ancient kingdom of Wessex, and with one of C.B. Fawcett's proposed 'provinces', which he defined as 'the natural region of which the Hampshire basin is the central area', describing it as 'a well-marked natural region' despite the absence of any obvious provincial capital and 'the most distinctive province of the south-eastern half of the English lowland'.[2]

More immediately pertinent is the fact that it represents the extent of the original Salisbury Wesleyan Circuit and that it was one of the areas in which Methodism was noticeably slow to take off. Both features invite closer examination. The 'Wiltshire Circuit', formed from London in 1758, was divided ten years later into 'Wiltshire North' and 'Wiltshire South'. The latter was renamed the 'Sarum' or 'Salisbury Circuit' in 1781 and as such remained intact until within a year of John Wesley's death in 1790. Even then, the main argument for dividing it must have been its wide geographical extent and the scattered nature of its comparatively few societies – in fact, an argument from weakness rather than from strength, providing a contrast to the early proliferation of Methodism in areas as diverse as Cornwall and the north of England.

Wesley remained reluctant to divide circuits where growth was slow, declaring as late as March 1790: 'I am in no haste to multiply or to divide circuits. Most of our circuits are too small rather than too large. I wish we had no circuit with fewer than three preachers in it or less than four hundred miles' riding in four weeks.'³ Salisbury Circuit was extensive enough, but it remained one of slower than average growth. In its first year, 1768, it represented only 1.41% of the connexional membership, and by 1790 this had dropped to 1.1%. Wesley's reluctance to divide it was understandable.

Reasons for Methodism's slow growth and continuing weakness in this part of the south are not far to seek. The region was predominantly rural, with the coastal ports of Portsmouth and Southampton as the only urban areas of any size. Its two cathedral cities, Winchester and Salisbury, were no more than market towns, as was Chichester just to the east.⁴ Communication and travel remained poor until the later rise of the toll-road and the railways. Agriculture was still the most widespread source of employment; and such industries as were to be found were small-scale, localised and traditional in nature. The main centres of the old woollen industry lay to the west. Cottage industries, still giving employment to the families of farmworkers, included pockets of glove- and button-making. There was silk-weaving around Sherborne and at Salisbury, lace-making at Salisbury, Blandford Forum and elsewhere. Stone was still quarried at Purbeck and Portland, but no longer as plentifully as before. Paper mills were to be found throughout the chalkland areas of the three counties and the usual range of rural crafts, from hurdle-making to brewing and from basket-weaving to thatching. Large-scale industrial development was not in evidence.

The Church of England dominated the religious scene. Parishes were predominantly small and nucleated rather than with a dispersed pattern of settlement.⁵ In many cases the land holdings were held by a handful of persons, including the lord of the manor, who might also be the patron of the living. In such circumstances Methodism, like the earlier Nonconformist groups, found itself up against strong opposition from the establishment, exemplified in many villages by the difficulty in finding a site on which to build a chapel.

Turning from the general scene, we must note that, compared with his incessant itinerating through the rest of the country, John Wesley was conspicuous by his absence in central southern England. Salisbury was one of the earliest places in which a Methodist society was formed. But this was not a matter of deliberate strategy, so much as an accidental result of personal circumstances. Wesley returned from Georgia in 1738 to find his mother living with her daughter Martha and her son-in-law Westley Hall in Fisherton. The little society that Hall founded there in 1740 came to grief as a result of Hall's highly unstable character and flagrant immorality. It took years for it to outlive this inauspicious beginning.

Meanwhile, there is little evidence that Wesley found himself in any other part of the area that was later to become the Salisbury Circuit. It was not until July 1753 that he visited Portsmouth, and even then it was as a port of call on his way to the Isle of Wight.[6] He stayed long enough to preach on 'an open part of the Common' to a 'large and well-behaved' congregation. Noting that the population of the town was now probably half that of Bristol, he added: 'So civil a people I never saw before in any seaport town in England.' The sting of that comment is no doubt in the qualifying word 'seaport'. All the same, the evidence suggests that the citizens as a whole came out of it better than did the minority of evangelical Christians in the town. The 'little society' he found already established there was weakened and 'wellnigh destroyed by "vain jangling" they called "contending for the faith."' Returning later in the year he again described them as 'people who had disputed themselves out of the power, and well-nigh the form, of religion.'[7]

We have here a reminder that the Evangelical Revival was a much wider phenomenon than the Methodism directly associated with the Wesleys. The Portsmouth society was one that owed its origin to Whitefieldite preachers[8] and the disputing Wesley encountered related to the Calvinist/Arminian issue that bedevilled the Methodist movement throughout the eighteenth century. Returning to the town in 1758, Wesley preached in the Tabernacle, but it was another nine years before his next visit. This comparative neglect may be no more than a geographical accident, since his normal routes on his preaching tours still did not bring him to this part of the south coast. But it may also indicate some reluctance to grapple with what continued to be a problem society – or, at the very least, a reluctance to cultivate what seemed unprofitable soil. His own society, when it was formed, had no meeting place of its own until a room in Warblington Street was opened in 1767, with a second chapel in Bishop Street, Portsea, the following year. Tensions and disputes continued to disturb the Wesleyan society, so that for many years it remained 'a day of small things'.

Apart from the societies in Salisbury (where the first Church Street chapel was opened in 1758) and in Portsmouth, Methodism remained thinly scattered throughout the area up to and beyond the division of the widespread circuit in 1790. This is confirmed by the diary and notebook of the itinerant George Stor(e)y, which has survived for the year 1784–85, when he was stationed for a second year in the Salisbury Circuit.[9] Fifteen societies (or classes) are listed, plus one somewhere in the Blandford area which cannot be identified. Table 1 shows the membership recorded from each in Story's notebook. The societies at Salisbury and Portsmouth between them account for half the total membership, with Winchester, Newport (IoW) and Whitchurch (Hants) trailing well behind. If we are looking for factors to explain the tardy progress of Methodism in the south, one must surely be the comparative isolation of these widely scattered societies, providing little mutual support in their crucial early days.

Table 1
Salisbury circuit 1784–85: Membership figures

Portsmouth	89	Timsbury	6
Salisbury	100	Crowdhill	9
Newport	31	Fareham	9
Wilton	20	Winchester	33
Broad Chalk	9	Whitchurch	27
Morden	14	Winterbourne*	13
Damerham	8	Houghton	15
Swanage	15	[*Unidentified*	12]
		Total	**410**

*Among the many Winterbo(u)rnes in Wiltshire and Dorset, this may have been Winterbourne Earls, three miles north-east of Salisbury, where there was a small group of Methodists as early as 6 September 1750, when John Wesley preached in the village.

The existence of strong local leadership clearly played its part in these circumstances. The relative strength of the society at Whitchurch can be accounted for by the fact that the pioneer itinerant John Haime had spent his closing years there, dying as recently as August 1784. If, as happened at Hursley, the leading figure, a schoolmaster named Dodd, left to try his fortune elsewhere, Methodism went with him (in this case to Titchfield).

Winchester provides a particularly clear example of this factor at work. Here the key figure was an ironmonger named Jasper Winscom, who came under Methodist influence early in the 1760s. Reading Methodist literature brought him to the surprising discovery that their teaching was that of the Church of England and he took the first opportunity to invite one of the itinerants to visit the city and preach there. A small group began to meet in the summer-house belonging to his mother-in-law. Growth was slow and numbers remained small, boosted from time to time by the support of soldiers whose regiments were stationed in the town. Without this the cause might well have died out, especially in the face of opposition from the mob in the 1770s. But it survived, with some sort of 'preaching-house' licensed in January 1773, replaced by a semi-derelict property in Silver Hill, opened by Wesley in 1785. Although he was undoubtedly a difficult character, Winscom's leadership was clearly a crucial factor in the effort to establish a Methodist presence. Following his retirement to Whitchurch in 1787 the society suffered a period of dissension, as well as struggling with debts Winscom had incurred on their behalf and with a dispute over the legal settlement of the chapel. Unsurprisingly, the membership of thirty-three in 1784/5 had dropped to twenty by 1795.

The towns most conspicuously missing from Story's list are Weymouth and Southampton. The origins of Weymouth Methodism are somewhat obscure and not much can be deduced with any certainty. Wesley records preaching 'at the new house in Melcombe' in September 1776, and local tradition identifies this as the 'Old Assembly Room' in the yard of the King's Head Hotel. William Myles gives 1778 as the date of the first chapel. But the earliest Quarter Sessions registrations that can be identified as Methodist are for houses in St Mary Street and Maiden Street in 1792 and 1793. The first purpose-built chapel, in Conygar Street, was not opened until 1805.

The case of Southampton throws further light on the obstacles to Methodism's progress in this part of the country. Wesley twice passed through the town in 1753, but apparently without attempting to preach there. He did not revisit it until October 1767, when the mayor, no doubt under pressure from influential citizens, withdrew his consent for the use of the town hall, leaving Wesley to make do with a 'small room'. Influenced, perhaps, by this rebuff, he did not return for another twenty years. The itinerants seem to have shared his reluctance. William Ashman is on record as having refused to arrange for regular visits, saying (no doubt with the Above Bar Independents in mind), 'We shall do no good. I have been at such places before: they are all dissenters.'[10] Early records show that, between a flourishing dissenting cause and the Established Church there was not much room in a town like Southampton for Methodism to take root, though several attempts were made. By the time of Wesley's visit in 1787, a small society had been formed under the patronage of a family named Fay, who were members of the well-established Above Bar Independent congregation. Mr Fay, a pattern-maker, had probably encountered the Methodists before the family moved down from London. But in Southampton he withdrew his support when they acquired a preaching room of their own in East Street and began to meet there at the same hour as the worship at Above Bar chapel. As in Winchester, the members of this infant society were of humble social origins, some of them domestic servants, and this clearly made them less acceptable at the Independent chapel. Eventually, but not until 1799, they took over an existing chapel in Canal Walk (later known as Union Terrace).[11]

When the Salisbury Circuit was eventually divided in 1790 its membership stood at 556. The following years saw a quickening of pace, in terms of both membership and circuit proliferation. By the end of the century Southampton Circuit had been formed from Portsmouth and Blandford (later renamed Poole and then Weymouth) Circuit from Salisbury. In 1809 further Dorset circuits came into existence: Shaftesbury from Salisbury and Poole from Weymouth. Nine years later Shaftesbury in turn gave birth to the Sherborne Circuit, so that by 1818 Dorset Methodism was divided into four circuits, covering the south-east and south-west, north-west and north, with the north-east still largely untouched by Methodist influence, though nominally under the aegis of Salisbury. Similarly, in Hampshire, Gosport and Andover both achieved circuit status in 1818, though the former reverted to Portsmouth after only one year. Winchester became the head of a circuit in 1816, only to revert to Southampton two years later; it did not regain its independence until 1862. The advance was still hesitant and there is no clear correlation between circuit status and membership figures. But by 1825 there were eight circuits (plus the Isle of Wight) within the former Salisbury Circuit.

1825 is a convenient point from which to survey the scene because it was the year in which the 'Marriott Collection' of circuit plans was made.[12] The collection is all the more valuable for being countrywide in its scope, so that it provides a basis for significant comparison. Although not every aspect of Wesleyan church life is reflected in its preaching plans, we are at least nearer the grass-root realities than when relying on such connexional records as the *Minutes of Conference*.

Table 2 (see over) attempts to rank the eight circuits in central southern England in terms of their geographical extent, measured in terms of the number of preaching places and their distance from the circuit town. (What the national averages were has still, so far as I am aware, to be calculated.) The picture is modified if the staffing level of each circuit is taken into account. This varied considerably. Three circuits had three itinerants and four had two. Andover, with only one itinerant to look after its seventeen places of worship and 214 members, was on this basis the most demanding circuit. Again, the picture changes if the ratio of itinerants to members is taken as the key factor. Sherborne Circuit then rises to the top with 115 members per minister, while Portsmouth, with three times that ratio, but also far more compact, is at the other extreme.

The ratio of circuit staffing to members may go some way towards explaining the apparent neglect of the outlying societies in the Portsmouth Circuit (see further below). What is less easy to account for is the comparative over-manning of the Southampton and Weymouth Circuits and, most markedly, of the recently formed Sherborne Circuit. One itinerant per 115 members was half the connexional average. It is tempting to see these staffing levels as a

Table 2
Extensiveness of Circuits 1825

Circuit	Year of Origin	Ministers	Local Preachers[1]	Preaching Places	Chapels	Furthest Preaching Place	Members	Members per minister	Index of Geographical extent[2]
Southampton	1798	3	21	23	12[3]	20m (Mitcheldever)	486	162	201 : 67
Salisbury	1768	2	27	29	16[4]	15m (Chitterne)	615	307	178 : 89
Poole	1809	2+1[5]	21	22	8[6]	14m (Edmondsham)	530	212	202 : 81
Weymouth	1794	3	13	19	4	18m (Winterbourne Houghton)	420	140	159 : 53
Shaftesbury	1809	2	13	22	7	16m (White Cross)	500	250	156 : 78
Andover	1818	1	16	17	2	19m (Basingstoke)	214	214	114 : 114
Sherborne	1818	2	13	16	2	10m (Wincanton)	230	115	92 : 46
Portsmouth	1790	3	14	13	6	15m (Petersfield)	1040	347	39 : 13

function of the ability to afford ministerial stipends. This was probably a significant factor in the case of Southampton and Weymouth, but that of Sherborne Circuit was rather different. Here was a real growth point, as the Conference of 1823 recognised when it appointed a second minister despite local inability to meet the cost unaided. The appointment made it possible to extend and consolidate the work in and around Yeovil. Similarly, Andover did not long remain a 'single station', but in this very year, 1825, was given a second preacher, despite having the smallest circuit membership in the area. This had no immediate effect (by 1831 the membership was down slightly, from 214 to 207); but the following two decades were a period of steady advance, despite the arrival of the Primitive Methodists.[13]

Whatever the basis of computation used, Portsmouth Circuit, with its three preachers, its high proportion of urban causes and its limited extent but high membership figures, stands out as the exception in a predominantly rural area.[14]

Salisbury Circuit remained more typical, with the highest number of chapels and other preaching places despite the periodic creation of new circuits from it.

Notes to Table 2

1. Local preachers *on trial* are not included.
2. Index of geographical extent: a) the sum of the distances in miles from the circuit town to each out-of-town preaching place; b) this sum divided by the number of ministers. NB. Where two adjacent places are coupled together and treated as one preaching appointment (e.g. Stoke and Wonston in the Southampton Circuit), these are counted as one.
3. Eleven places marked on the plan with a 'C' plus King's Somborne, known from other sources to have a chapel by this date.
4. Fourteen places marked on the plan with a 'C' plus two others, Idmiston and Pilton.
5. Poole was the only circuit in this area to have a Supernumerary Minister, James Alexander, named on the circuit plan. (The six listed as 'supernumeraries' on the Salisbury plan as preaching 'occasionally' appear to have been retired *local preachers*). For the purposes of this calculation I have counted Alexander as half a preacher in this Table.
6. Seven places marked with a 'C', plus Binegar.

Table 3
Ministerial Deployment 1825

Circuit	Preaching Places	Chapels	Served only by Ministers	Served only by Local Preachers	Chapels with the Sacrament
Salisbury	29	16	1	11	5
Portsmouth	13	6	0	7	6
Southampton	23	12	0	9	11
Weymouth	19	4	2	7	6
Poole	22	8	0	11	8
Shaftesbury	22	7	0	14	7
Andover	17	7	0	9	2
Sherborne	16	2	0	6	2

One apparent consequence of the variation in staffing was that patterns of ministerial deployment varied widely (Table 3). As Alan Rogers found to be the case in Lincolnshire,[15] the full-time circuit preachers concentrated their attention on the well-established preaching places, which, in most cases, already had a chapel of some kind. In each circuit between one third and a half of the preaching places had no Sunday services conducted by ministers; they were served, therefore, entirely by local preachers. In contrast to this, the Weymouth chapel never saw a local preacher in its pulpit, despite having three services each Sunday; nor did R.C. Brackenbury's Portland chapel in the same circuit. Similarly, at Salisbury the morning and evening services were conducted entirely by ministers, though in this case laymen were sometimes appointed to take the afternoon services.

The number of places where the Lord's Supper was administered varied widely, as did the frequency of administration. The existence of a chapel seems to have played a part in this, as might be expected; but by no means every chapel had even one sacramental service in the quarter. Thus in the Salisbury Circuit sacramental services were held in only five of its sixteen chapels; and in Andover Circuit, in only two out of seven. Weymouth, on the other hand, had the sacrament not only in its four chapels, but also in two other places, the villages of Owermoigne and Dewlish. Portsmouth, Poole and Shaftesbury

Circuits, with one or more sacramental services at each of their chapels, but none elsewhere, seem to represent the norm; as does Sherborne Circuit, with the sacrament administered only in Yeovil and Sherborne, where its two chapels were situated.

Turning to the frequency of the sacramental services, there is, as we might expect, some correlation between frequency of administration on the one hand and staffing levels on the other. In the Andover Circuit, with its single minister responsible for seventeen places of worship, in twenty-two weeks the sacrament was administered only twice, once at Andover and once at Whitchurch. Yeovil and Sherborne societies, with two ministers in the circuit, had the sacrament twice as often, i.e. once a quarter. A quarterly sacramental service seems to have been the custom also in the chapels of the Weymouth Circuit; but the main chapels in the Salisbury, Southampton, Poole and Shaftesbury Circuits had two each quarter. The comparatively compact and well-staffed Portsmouth Circuit enjoyed the most frequent administration – five times in nineteen weeks in the chapels at Portsmouth and Portsea and four times in two other places. This was in addition to a number of love-feasts.

Love-feasts are found on the plans of only four of the eight circuits: Portsmouth, Weymouth, Poole and Andover.[16] Their frequency varied. With two in twenty-two weeks the Andover chapel had twice as many love-feasts as sacramental services. Portsmouth chapel had two love-feasts in nineteen weeks, one of them on Good Friday, but more frequent celebrations of the Lord's Supper. No love-feasts are listed on the Salisbury, Southampton, Shaftesbury or Sherborne plans; nor, for that matter, are Watchnights or Fast Days. In fact, according to the plans, only Portsmouth Circuit still observed a quarterly Fast Day and also had occasional Watchnight services in the two town chapels.

Some indication of the direction in which matters were developing during this period may be derived from a comparison of surviving Weymouth Circuit preaching plans for 1825 and 1829–30. By 1829 the Dorchester society, having acquired a regular preaching place, had joined Weymouth and Portland in having only ministerial appointments, except for one Sunday in the quarter when the third minister was planned at Bere and Bere Heath. In the meantime the villages of

Owermoigne and Dewlish had lost the occasional ministerial appointment (and therefore also the sacramental service) which they had enjoyed in 1825. This left fourteen places on the circuit plan served on Sundays entirely by local preachers.

Among the preaching plans we have been examining from southern England, only the one from Portsmouth Circuit gives details of weekday as well as Sunday appointments. Once again, the restricted sphere of ministerial activity is highlighted. Back in 1795 James Crabb had found the circuit quite extensive enough. He records walking between three and four hundred miles in one six-week period and notes in his diary that in twelve months he had walked 1,300 miles and ridden 800 miles, besides covering another hundred in crossing to and from the Isle of Wight.[17] Here was an embodiment of the early Methodist ideal of an itinerant ministry as set out by Wesley in a letter to Jasper Winscom: 'No preacher ought to stay either in Portsmouth or Sarum, or any other place, a whole week together. That is not the Methodist plan at all. It is a novel abuse.'[18]

'Methodist plan' or not, by 1825 the situation in the (now much smaller) Portsmouth Circuit was very different. There were two places in the town itself (Union Road and Greenwich Place), served on Sundays entirely by local preachers, but with ministers planned to take weeknight services. But no ministerial appointments at all were listed at the outlying places (Titchfield, Stubbington, Ewer Common, Portchester and Petersfield) on either Sundays or weekdays. One is left wondering when and how pastoral oversight was exercised. Not, it seems, by the full-time pastors. The 'pastoral office', seen at this grassroots level, looks rather different from the theory propounded at connexional level by men like Jabez Bunting and Richard Watson.[19]

The Census of Religious Worship conducted in 1851 provides a wealth of statistics from the mid-century, but cannot be adequately examined here. Instead, it is time to ask how far the situation in these southern circuits was, by 1825, typical of the connexion as a whole. David Hempton refers to 'the decline of rural itinerancy, the virtual disappearance of the circuit horse, the financial reliance on big urban chapels with their wealthy clientele' and sees these as a result of the economic recession that followed the Napoleonic wars.[20] The 1825 circuit plans leave us in no doubt that the picture at national level was very similar to that in the south. An examination of the first twenty circuits in the Marriott collection (which is arranged alphabetically) reveals no churches served exclusively by ministers; but in the collection as a whole there is a significant number where the pulpit of the main church (or occasionally churches) was never occupied on Sundays by local preachers. These were usually places where Methodism had been established long enough to gain a degree of respectability – and in some cases, perhaps, a share in the relative sophistication of the local community. The examples include Bath, Exeter, Liverpool (both Mount Pleasant and Leeds Street chapels), Durham and Leicester.

On the other hand, virtually every circuit had many village causes served entirely by local preachers. In the sample of twenty circuits, 191 of the 398 preaching places never had a ministerial appointment on a Sunday; and many of these same chapels saw only local preachers during the week. The situation in Portsmouth Circuit outlined above was by no means unique.

Alongside this may be noted the decline of such 'occasional' means of grace as Watchnight services and love-feasts. Both had been characteristic features of eighteenth-century Methodism, but by 1825 they were in widespread decline. According to Frank Baker, in earlier days the love-feast had commonly, though never universally, been a monthly event, with men's and women's and 'general' love-feasts alternating. But (to quote Baker):

> *by 1780... the quarterly, half-yearly, or annual general love-feast was in most places the only survival... Throughout most of the nineteenth century, from the evidence of circuit plans, love-feasts continued to be arranged quarterly, though this was increasingly restricted to the leading churches only.*[21]

This general picture is largely confirmed by the evidence from central southern England in 1825. Nor was the love-feast in any sense a lay version of, or a substitute for, the Lord's Supper. Whatever congregational participation may have survived (e.g. in the form of testimony), the love-feast seems to have invariably coincided with a ministerial appointment.

Finally, there is evidence that much of the initiative for missioning new areas had passed from the itinerants to local preachers. Local examples of this include Augustus William Marblestone, a Swedish immigrant in Portsmouth and Portchester, James Crabb of Wilton after he had left the itinerancy on health grounds, William Sanger of Salisbury and Harry Noyes of Thruxton, both of whom became associated with the Tent Methodists.[22] Each of these stepped in to fill gaps created by ministerial neglect or inertia. It is difficult to avoid the conclusion that by 1825 the 'itinerant system' had already been fundamentally modified throughout the Wesleyan connexion, though, as the Religious Census of 1851 would show, it survived in the non-Wesleyan offshoots, especially the Bible Christians and Primitive Methodists, as one token of their attempt to return to Methodism's eighteenth-century roots.

Notes

1. This essay draws on material from my doctoral thesis, 'Methodism and Society in Central Southern England 1740–1851' (Southampton, 1987).
2. Fawcett, C.B (1919, Revised Edn 1960), *Provinces of England: A Study of some Geographical Aspects of Devolution*, London: Hutchinson, pp119, 126.
3. Letter to Jasper Winscom, 13 March 1790 in *Letters of John Wesley* (ed) Telford, John (1931) VIII p206.
4. The whole of Sussex was a Methodist desert, ignored by Wesley apart from the towns on the Kent border which he visited from London during the winter months and where he had local supporters. On the one occasion when he rode through the county from west to east, in October 1758, he does not appear to have paused anywhere long enough to preach until he got to Rye.
5. In the West Riding the average size of a parish was over 13 sqm, whereas in all three southern counties it was below the national average of 5.15 sqm: in Dorset, as low as 4.18 sqm. Similarly, the average population of parishes in the Salisbury Diocese was 715 compared with 1,236 in the diocese of York. Ignoring the concentration of inhabitants in Portsmouth and Southampton, the figures for the Winchester diocese were much the same. For a detailed analysis of the effect of types of settlement on religious Dissent, see Everitt, Alan (1972), *The Pattern of Rural Dissent: the Nineteenth Century*, Leicester.
6. The Isle of Wight has been excluded from this survey because of its relative isolation. In the earliest decades it was part of the mainland circuit, sometimes visited rather reluctantly by the itinerants from Portsmouth, but never very closely related to the mainland.

7   Journal of John Wesley, 8 July 1753 and 5 October 1753.
8   Their meeting place was characteristically known as 'The Tabernacle'.
9   The diary and notebook are now in the William R. Perkins library at Duke University, NC. There are minor discrepancies between the membership figure in the two sources, reflecting the volatile membership in that early period.
10 John S. Stamp, MS 'History of Methodism in Hampshire' in Methodist Archives Centre, John Rylands Library, University of Manchester.
11 Built by a local bricklayer, probably as a speculation, it measured a mere 42ft by 40ft. All but one of its trustees were artisans. Enlarged in 1823, it was not replaced until 1850 (by a chapel in East Street).
12 The Marriot collection is now at Drew University, New Jersey. More extensive use of its evidence would contribute significantly to comparative studies of the growth and other features of Methodism in different parts of the country.
13 Membership rose to 292 in 1841 and 373 in 1851. Then a steady decline set in.
14 The furthest preaching place was Petersfield, fifteen miles away, an isolated cause which briefly gained circuit status in 1826, but lost it in 1836. At the time of the 1851 Religious Census it was in the Guildford Circuit.
15 Rogers, Alan (1979), 'When City Speaks for County' in Baker, D. (ed), *The Church in Town and Countryside*, Oxford: WileyBlackwell, pp335-42.
16 Their absence from the plan does not, however, indicate that none took place. James Dredge (1833) refers to love-feasts held in private homes at both Salisbury and Alderbury about ten years earlier, but these would not feature on the circuit plan. See his *Biographical Record* (privately printed) pp42, 63.
17 Rudall, John (1854, 2009), *Memoir of the Rev. James Crabb*, London, p36.
18 Letter of 8 November 1788 in Telford, John (ed) op. cit. VIII p104.
19 See especially Bowmer, John C. (1975), *Pastor and People: A Study of Church and ministry in Wesleyan Methodism from the death of John Wesley (1791) to the death of Jabez Bunting (1858)*, London, Epworth. It is not entirely unfair to suggest on the basis of Dr. Bowmer's study that although responsibility and authority were seen as two sides of the ministerial coin, it was the latter which was the chief concern of pastors and members alike during the first half of the twentieth century. The power of admitting and expelling members seems to have loomed much larger than the need to nurture them.
20 Hempton, David (1854), *Methodism and Politics in British Society 1750-1850*, London: Hutchinson, p110.
21 Baker, Frank (1957) *Methodism and the Love-Feast*, London: Epworth Press, p41.
22 Registration certificates of preaching places by both Sanger and Noyes at the time of the incursion of the Tent Methodists into the area are preserved at the Wiltshire and Hampshire Record Offices. Though Tent Methodism did not long survive, the Primitive Methodists found the ground prepared for them a decade or so later. Similarly, Crabb's missioning of New Forest villages 'buried in moral darkness' which the Wesleyan authorities had declined to support, was followed up by the Primitive Methodists. Cf Rudall op. cit. pp82-96.

Two Preachers at St Mary's: Wesley and Newman

Mervyn Davies

In 1990, at an ecumenical centenary service to mark John Henry Newman's death held in St Paul's Cathedral, London on 23 November, the sermon was preached by the Revd Dr John Newton, Free Church President of Churches Together in England.

. . . .

The University Church of St Mary the Virgin in Oxford's High Street has known many famous preachers but few, if any, can rival John Wesley and John Henry Newman for their impact on the Church in this country as well as overseas, as they sought, in different centuries, to revive the Christian religion in their time, particularly through the medium of preaching, which both of them undertook well into their eighties. Though preachers and pastors, both men published their sermons and wrote extensively, including many letters, journals and diaries. They were formed intellectually by their Oxford experiences as well as by other influences, including what they read, which overlapped considerably, although Wesley perhaps was the more eclectic of the two. Classical literature, the Eastern Fathers of the Church, the Reformers, the English Divines, Law, Aristotle, Locke, Butler and Hume are only examples of a great range of common sources.[1] Indeed, much of the European religious and philosophical thought that preceded them had its part to play in their intellectual formation, albeit in differing ways. Many other influences, especially those of Wesley's mother Susannah and Newman's mother Jemima, shaped their personal piety and spirituality. Wesley himself was also influenced by some Catholic writings, notably Thomas à Kempis, as well as by Moravian teaching.

Like Wesley, Newman also had a conversion experience of an Evangelical nature when he was aged fifteen, through the influence of the Revd Walter Mayers, but it was less an event than a process, as far as we can tell, which may also be true of Wesley. Mayers was the 'human means of this beginning of divine faith in me'.[2] Newman acknowledged his debt to Evangelicalism when he wrote that it 'had been a great blessing for England; it had brought home to the hearts of thousands the cardinal and vital truths of Revelation'.[3] They both shared a dislike of Calvinism; although Newman had been affected by it as a young man he later found that it would not square with his parochial experience.

Each of them modestly denied that they were theologians in the sense that was understood at that time. This would be especially true today, which sees the role as purely academic, unconnected with personal faith. Arguably theirs was a theology arising out of faith, coupled with a sense of the needs of the time. The unity of their preaching, pastoral work and the place of faith, reason and the heart were common factors as they sought to awaken and nourish the religious mind of Church and nation.

The University Church which the Wesley brothers knew was rather different inside from what it was in Newman's time or today. The present pulpit and furnishings were installed by the university in 1827 and galleries were erected on the north and west walls, creating in the nave a space which can seat a large congregation. The Wesley brothers were regular worshippers there as undergraduates and Charles as well as John later preached before members of the university and local people as occasional preachers appointed by the university. It is not clear how often John Wesley preached in Oxford, but it seems as if he was the university preacher at St Mary's at least a dozen times and, unusually, three times in close succession in 1733, as well as preaching in college chapels.

Newman began preaching there in 1828 on taking up his appointment as Vicar and continued to do so until he resigned his living in 1843, being by that time already in semi-retirement at Littlemore, the little hamlet outside Oxford, a poor parish attached to St Mary's where he had converted some old stables that had provided horses for the London coaches. Almost a hundred years earlier, John Wesley had preached his last sermon at St Mary's, entitled 'Scriptural Christianity', on 24 August 1744, with its scathing critique of complacent Christian living in the university, and was never invited to preach there again. This was not the first time that Wesley had pursued this theme in a sermon at St Mary's: he preached on 'The Almost Christian' there on 25 July 1741, for which he was also famous. Newman himself was equally demanding, preaching 'The Ventures of Faith' there on 21 or 28 February 1836. Both preachers admonish their hearers for their lack of Scriptural Christianity and their unpreparedness to risk all for Christ. Indeed it was a theme that underpinned all that they said.

For Wesley and Newman, Christianity was a revealed religion and their task as pastors was to guide people on the path to heaven. If the university authorities could ignore Wesley by not inviting him to preach again, Newman was a more difficult target as the incumbent of St Mary's, so the colleges changed their time for dinner to coincide with the 4pm Sunday sermons to discourage undergraduate attendance. Students thus had to choose between a hot supper and a different form of nourishment. Nevertheless, some have estimated that attendance at the sermons numbered about 500 or 600 at the height of his influence. Newman had decided upon this system, whereby he, as parish priest, would preach each Sunday to complement the visiting preacher system, which was the norm in the mornings, in order to give his hearers a more rounded and systematic exposition of the Christian faith.

If, as preachers, Wesley and Newman had much in common in terms of the content of their sermons, there are also some important differences. Wesley usually preached *extempore* for an hour or more and records in his Preface to his published sermons that what we have is largely the 'substance' of what he preached[4]. The sermons were obviously delivered several times and would be adapted and filled out to suit the occasion, so what we have is a distillation of what was said or a basis for it. On the other hand, Newman's published sermons are largely the actual text of what he preached as, unusually, he read his sermons, and these tended to follow the liturgical year and would last for about forty-five minutes. However, he does not use them, by and large, to promote explicitly Tractarian positions. Wesley's distinction between the purposes of oral and written sermons, recorded by Outler, is helpful in understanding their differing intentions. Oral sermons are chiefly for proclamation and invitation, written sermons for nurture and reflection, although the distinction is not absolute since some of the sermons of Newman's which most closely parallel those of Wesley have the same sense of challenge.[5] Nurture and reflection, however, aptly sum up the main purpose of Newman's preaching.

One of the many distinguishing features of Newman's sermons, apart from their roots in patristic writings and the lectionary, was their extensive use of Old Testament passages with which to illuminate the New Testament texts. Wesley's use of these was also similar. The sources that had informed them were subtly interwoven in ways of which they may not have been totally aware, so steeped were they in what they had read. Newman's several sermons on the 'Offices of Christ' are good examples of this and of patristic typology. Both in many ways wore their learning lightly. Interestingly, Newman abandoned the practice of reading his sermons when he became a Catholic, although he prepared notes and often a partial text, of which many have survived. Many more of Newman's sermons survive than those of Wesley, of which the *Parochial and Plain Sermons* are the most famous. Others are in the process of being published, as Newman only made a selection from those that he had preached, seemingly disposing of very few of his notes or texts, which fill many boxes in the Birmingham Oratory Archives.[6]

The danger of not having a text is, of course, that of descending into garrulity or anecdotes, or being simply colloquial, and this was one complaint levelled at Wesley when he was obviously not at his best, according to some contemporary hearers. Clearly when he was 'on form' his sermons must have been inspirational to attract such huge crowds of people, often after a long journey. He also often preached more than once in a day. We can only be amazed at the achievement of this itinerant revivalist preacher, whose success was not so much due to any eloquence of style, but rather to the content of his message. Indeed, Outler records that Wesley was by no means the most eloquent of preachers of his time, but that his impact lasted longer than any other comparable preacher of the eighteenth century.[7]

Newman's immediate congregation was much more restricted and regular, although his influence as a preacher was nationwide, as copies of his sermons circulated throughout the country, being reprinted several times. It would be wrong to think, however, that he was used to preaching only to educated congregations – members of the university or High Street shopkeepers. His first appointment as a deacon in 1824 was to one of the poorest parishes in Oxford, St Clement's, which had an elderly and infirm incumbent, Mr Gutch, so that much of the pastoral work fell upon him, including preaching. Attached to St Mary's, by a quirk of history, was Littlemore, where Newman built a church and a school, at times spending more time there than he did at St Mary's in preaching and pastoral work. When he moved to Birmingham, after his conversion to Catholicism, Newman acquired a former gin distillery in Alcester Street to catechise and preach to the many poor Irish immigrants who were coming to the city. Nevertheless, it is true to say that Newman regarded as his primary target the educated population of the country because he knew that through the educated classes, the Church could influence the direction in which society was going, a matter of considerable concern to him. In many ways Wesley and Newman perhaps exemplify the difference between the work of the itinerant preaching friars, especially the Dominicans and Franciscans, and that of the parish priest in the mediaeval period. For Wesley, like the friars, the world *was* his parish. Newman reached the world *through* his parish and his educational work, which to him was a 'special pastoral office' and a kind of missionary work, rejecting the secular view of the world that was becoming prevalent in the nineteenth century.[8]

Both Wesley and Newman rejected the use of florid or elaborate language in sermons that had become common in some Protestant and Catholic circles after the Reformation. This might seem surprising in the case of Newman, widely regarded as an exemplar of English prose poetry. In his Preface, Wesley expressly advises his preachers to use 'plain language for plain people' and to avoid 'all nice and philosophical speculation', 'all perplexed and intricate reasonings', 'all words which are not easy to be understood', 'all which are not used in common life', and 'in particular, those kinds of technical terms that so frequently occur in Bodies of Divinity' which 'to common people are an unknown tongue', while recognising that he himself might occasionally 'slide into them unawares'.[9]

Newman's sermons were also regarded as having something of this character. Dean Church remarked that they were 'The most practical of sermons, the most real in their way of dealing with life and conduct, they are also intensely dogmatic'.[10] They were 'plain, unpretending, earnest sermons' based on the Prayer Book.[11]

According to eyewitness accounts, Newman's style had many of the features recommended by Wesley. Principal Shairp records how Newman preached in a simple service, with little pomp or ritual. What struck the hearer was the silver intonation of Newman's voice as he read the lessons and preached. But, he says, 'a stranger was not likely to be much struck, especially if he had been accustomed to pulpit oratory of the Boanerges sort. Here was no vehemence, no declamation, no show of elaborate argument'. If you came expecting that, Shairp says, you would come away disappointed and he adds that if Newman had preached like that in Scotland he would have been regarded as a 'silly body'. Shairp recalls that Newman spoke each sentence of short paragraph quite rapidly with very clear intonation punctuated by very long pauses, sometimes up to half a minute before continuing. He adds:

> *As he spoke, how the old truth became new! How it came home with a meaning never felt before! He laid his finger – how gently, yet how powerfully! on some inner place in the hearer's heart, and told him things about himself he had never known till then. Subtlest truths which it would have taken philosophers pages of circumlocution and big words to state, were dropt by the way in a sentence or two of the most transparent Saxon.*[12]

Many tributes have been made to the extraordinary influence and beauty of Newman's preaching, but one recollection is different from all the others, by an Anglican Vicar of Staines, Charles Wellington

Furse (1821–1900) and exists in the Birmingham Oratory Archives. Furse describes the effect of Newman's sermon as being like 'vivisection' in which each paragraph, as it were, nailed the hearer down until he was completely impaled. The effect was not paralysis but rather that of being 'quickened in every fibre into a more vivid sensibility' and that he achieved this without being 'hard-hitting' or 'exaggeration' or transcendentalism.'[13]

If Wesley avoided the extravagances of Calvinist 'gospel preachers', he was probably on occasions more animated than Newman and more varied in pitch, to which an *extempore* sermon, especially one preached outside, would lend itself. Newman invariably preached in a church and preferred to do so to people with whom he was familiar, disliking 'set piece' sermons for special occasions.[14]

Like Wesley, Newman also had advice for the would-be preacher, suggesting that a great deal of preparation was needed to preach and advising him to have 'the subject distinctly before you; to think it over till you have got it clearly in your head'.[15] The sermon should be known by heart rather than preached *extempore*, and he advised against a proliferation of topics, arguing for one subject or topic only. Wesley and Newman seem to speak together when Newman writes:

> *Humility, which is a great Christian virtue, has a place in literary composition – he who is ambitious will never write well. But he who tries to say simply and exactly what he feels ands thinks, what religion demands, what Faith teaches, what the Gospel promises, will be eloquent without intending it, and will write better English than if he made a study of English Literature.*[16]

And Wesley:

> *Nay, my design is, in some sense, to forget all that ever I have read in my life. I mean to speak, in the general, as if I have never read one author, ancient or modern (always excepting the inspired). I am persuaded, that, on the one hand, this may be a means of enabling me more clearly to express the sentiments of my heart while I simply follow the chain of my own thoughts, without entangling myself with those of other men; and that, on the other, I shall come with*

fewer weights upon my mind, with less prejudice and prepossession, either to search for myself, or to deliver to others, the naked truths of the Gospel.[17]

The fact that Newman's hearers were largely the same each week meant that the scope of the topics that he chose to preach on could be wider, following the liturgical year and celebrating and exploring the meaning of the Christian festivals. He was able to expound the doctrines of the Church more frequently than Wesley, who preached to a great variety of audiences as a result of his many journeys. Newman's other motivation in doing this was his feeling that the Evangelicals of his time were neglecting the dogmatic element in religion. It was this quality of being able to breathe new life into these doctrines that was remarked on by many of his hearers. As a high churchman, however, Wesley was no dogmatic minimalist, sharing many of Newman's doctrinal concerns, but more focused in his aim to meet a particular need in his preaching.

Newman and Wesley can be seen to be at their closest in their preaching and writing on salvation and the need for holiness. At the core of this were the doctrines of Justification and Sanctification. In this Wesley seems to have been largely faithful to the Lutheran position, whereas Newman seems to have undergone an evolution from an Evangelicalism slightly tinged by Calvinism to a more mature position, represented by his *Lectures on Justification* given in the Adam de Brome chapel at St Mary's in 1828, in which he not only tried to reconcile the Reformation position (as he understood it – not always entirely correctly) with the Catholic position of the Council of Trent, but also to give the doctrine a more ecclesial dimension. However, we should not assume that Wesley left this out of account, for in his sermon on 'The Catholic Spirit' he emphasises his belief in the Episcopal tradition and urges membership of some church or congregation as being essential, but says that he no longer feels that anyone should *have* to be a member of the Church of England and worship 'in the particular manner which is prescribed by that Church'.[18] There are various ways of worshipping God, he felt. Newman would not have been so happy with this, more with what Wesley had to say about the means of grace: sacraments, especially the Eucharist, prayer, reading, hearing and meditating on the Scriptures and his stress on these being subservient to the real spirit of religion.[19]

In some ways, Wesley had anticipated Newman in the way he brought together justification and sanctification, refusing to see justification as merely extrinsic, but as bringing about a genuine renovation of heart. In Newman's day, Charles Simeon would have been a good example of an Evangelical in the Lutheran tradition, Thomas Scott of Sandford of one in the moderate Calvinist position. Both Wesley and Newman come together when they argue for the importance of an inner righteousness which is not really ours but is nevertheless within us. From the Evangelical tradition, Newman took his strong emphasis on the work of the Spirit, which features in many of his sermons; because he saw that it was here that there was a real chance of a *via media*.

In his *Sermons on Several Occasions,* Wesley was clear that we must attribute, firstly, creation as such and then whatever righteousness that may be found in humans to the free grace of God, an important conjunction of ideas. He strongly denies any atoning value to human works for 'Only corrupt fruit grows on a corrupt tree', whereas 'Grace is the source, the faith the condition of salvation'.[20] The faith that Wesley discussed here is emphatically not mere belief in propositions, but rather trust and confidence in Christ which accepts that he has redeemed us from eternal death and that without his saving grace we are nothing. The justification of each person is 'by Christ formed in his heart'.[21] The believer is thus 'born again of the Spirit unto a new life'. Good works are inextricably linked to this, for Wesley argued that he speaks of a faith which is necessarily 'productive of all good works, and all holiness'.[22] He then went on to point out that good works are brought about by God working within us so that 'he giveth us a reward for what he himself worketh'. Those who stress the importance of godliness and holiness do not realise that good works *follow* justification rather than preceding it. Wesley was following the tradition of the High Anglican Divines when he wrote:

> *God hath willed and commanded that all our works should be done in charity, in love, in that love to God which produceth love to all mankind. But none of our works can be done in this love, while the love of the Father (of God as our Father) is not in us. And this love cannot be in us till we receive the "spirit of Adoption, cry in our hearts, Abba, Father."*[23]

We cannot obey the moral law while we are in sin, but only after Christ's coming so that we are justified without the deeds of the law. Faith is the necessary condition of justification, for it is by faith that we cast ourselves onto the mercy of God and thereby destroy our pride. Wesley personalised salvation in many passages by stressing that Christ 'hath died for *thee*, a perfect cleansing of *thy* sins'.[24] It is when we are justified that Wesley held we are treated as if we are guiltless and righteous, but true faith brings forth fruit, which is why Wesley stressed the importance of sanctification: of becoming what we now are. Newman talks about a 'spiritual gift or presence in the heart'.[25]

Like Newman, Wesley stressed the importance of the Spirit and has much to say about the Spirit's role in the Christian life after justification. It is the Spirit of God who conforms the believer to Christ so that 'His very body is a "temple of the Holy Ghost"' and a 'habitation of God through the Spirit',[26] all phrases that fall from Newman's lips also.[27] One of Wesley's favourite phrases is to 'walk in the Spirit', which enables the Christian to 'love of God and their neighbour, to be 'led into holy desire', to 'holiness of conversation', to 'show forth in their lives the genuine fruits of the Spirit of God' giving 'full proof to all mankind, that they are actuated by the same Spirit "which raised up Jesus from the dead."'[28]

Wesley and Newman were well aware that sin persists even in those who have turned to Christ, hence their emphasis on sanctification. Wesley granted – and he was surely basing this on experience – that 'there are two contrary principles in believers, – nature and grace, the flesh and the Spirit' and reminds us that St Paul's 'directions and exhortations' are based on the supposition that 'wrong tempers or practices' will be found in believers still but exhorted them 'to fight and conquer these, by the power of the faith which was in them'.[29]

For Newman, reflection on this led him to abandon his mild Calvinism and the doctrine of final perseverance, which can be dated from about 1822. In his *Autobiographical Writings* Newman recalled how Hawkins, later Provost of Oriel but then Vicar of St Mary's, used to criticise his sermons. Newman had showed him a sermon entitled 'Man goeth forth to his work and to his labour until evening', which seemed to imply a denial of baptismal regeneration. He says:

> *Mr Hawkins, to whom he showed it, came down upon it upon this score. The sermon divided the Christian world into two classes, the one all darkness, the other all light, whereas, said Mr Hawkins, it is impossible for us in fact to draw such a line of demarcation across any body of men, large or small, because difference of religious and moral excellence is a matter of degree. Men are not either saints or sinner; but they are not as good as they ought to be, and better than they might be – more or less converted to God, as it may happen.*[30]

Newman was trying to reconcile what he had hitherto believed with his experience as a young curate visiting in the parish of St Clement's and adds:

> *I found many who in most important points were inconsistent, but whom yet I could not say were altogether without grace. Most indeed were in that condition as they had some spiritual feelings, but weak and uncertain.*[31]

Hawkins gave him Sumner's *Apostolical Preaching Considered in an Examination of St Paul's Epistles* to read, which led him further to abandon Reformed doctrine (as he understood it) but which also sowed the seeds of doubt about imputed righteousness, and led him to emphasise still further the need for grace through the Church and its sacraments.

Newman came to see that his Evangelical principles need not be abandoned but rather complemented and completed. He set out his understanding of the difference between Calvinists and Catholics in the *Apologia*.[32] Calvinists argue, he says, that the elect and the world are separated, but go on to assert that the converted and the unconverted can be discerned by man, and the justified can be conscious of their justification and that the regenerate cannot fall away. Catholics maintain that there are different degrees of justification and between sin and sin and that there is no knowledge given to anyone that they are saved. All can fall away. Luther and the other Reformers held a doctrine of imputed righteousness by which we are treated by God as if we were just even though still sinners: 'simul justus et peccator'. In his early years as a preacher, Newman was still very influenced by Thomas Scott of Sandford, the most significant Evangelical theologian of the early nineteenth century, whose emphasis was less on the total depravity of humankind than on the personal transgression of individuals who bear the image of God. Scott was no antinomian, but he did not compromise the gratuitousness of salvation. Justification is the state of sinner who has found acceptance with God leading to forgiveness of sins and a renewed life. Regeneration is a change brought about by the Holy Spirit in the understanding, the will and affections of the sinner and the commencement of a new kind of life. However, Scott said there was no intrinsic connection between baptism and regeneration.[33] Newman began to doubt Scott's position on this in about 1821. At this point he adopted a very Lutheran position.

Newman was to admit in his *Autobiographical Writings* that the views he held at this time failed to evoke a spark in his experience and he began to think, from 1822, of salvation as both instantaneous and progressive with six stages: a sense of God's holiness and our own vileness; sorrow for sin; belief in Christ as saviour of the world; justification and adoption as sons of God in Christ; peace with God and faith working by love; good works. He was clear, however, about the necessity of conversion and a radical change of heart, a 'revolution of sentiment' as he was to put it. Justification is different from regeneration, he thought at this stage. Baptism confers privileges but is only an accidental adjunct of regeneration. Holiness is that to which regeneration aims, however. Holiness requires good works and is a lifetime process, but it is foreign to our natures and its seed has to be planted there by God.

1825–27 was the definitive period of change for Newman. He was also by this time reading Butler's *Analogy of Religion* and received two principles from him which were to be hugely influential: probability is the guide of life; and the visible world is a sign of the invisible world, which is opened to us by faith and hence is in a sense unreal. The visible is an instrument of the supernatural.

These principles persuaded Newman to move in a much more Catholic direction over sacraments and the theology of the Church. Sacraments and the Church now become means of grace, especially through baptism, which gives us the principle of holiness within us. The word 'regeneration' now becomes more or less equivalent to the word 'sanctification'. In an unpublished sermon he produces a remarkable formula: 'Grace caused our salvation, Christ effected it, baptism conveyed it, the Spirit applies it, faith evidences it, and hope is the character of it'.[34] It is through baptism that we are pledged and sealed in the fellowship of the Holy Spirit who is the source of all moral goodness.

In March 1828 Newman was instituted vicar of St Mary's, which was the beginning of a new era. It was in Adam de Brome's chapel (at that time walled off from the main church) that he was to lecture on the *Prophetical Office of the Church* and also on justification, but it was some time before his views finally matured. He was still preaching justification by faith but using the term 'faith' in a two-fold sense: as a kind of knowledge when connected with regeneration, but as a confession of sinfulness and helplessness before God when speaking of justification itself.

He continued to stress the instrumentality of the Church against what he felt to be the excessive individualism of the Evangelicals, being convinced that the visible and invisible church are one, like body and soul, and that the sacraments are the indispensable means of grace. The Church is a continuation of the incarnation, a body drawn out of the world to train us up for heaven. It is the concrete expression in time of God's election. Admission to the Church is thus admission to a state of grace and favour. More and more he saw salvation in terms of a process, even sometimes preferring regeneration to justification. Regeneration is the communication of a new principle rather like leaven, opposing any idea of salvation by the mere fact of conversion. He then came to see his own conversion aged fifteen not as the beginning of something, but as an added grace. At this point, for Newman, soteriology becomes clearly associated with ecclesiology. The Church is not just a visible group of believers, but a society with a God-given structure which is transformative of those who belong.

In a series of sermons on faith at this time Newman attacked two illusory kinds of faith: the cold faith of the mere intellect, which is consistent with the supreme devotion to the enjoyments of this world; and the hot and feverish faith of mere emotion, which is powerless to work a change in the heart. There is much in Newman's thought here that was anticipated by Wesley in such sermons as 'The Almost Christian' as he explores the nature of true faith. Both of them share this distaste for what they call 'Enthusiasm', Wesley in Sermon 37 'The Nature of Enthusiasm' and Newman in such sermons as 'Religious Worship – the remedy for excitements' (PPS I Sermon 23) or 'Sudden Conversion' (PPS VIII Sermon 15). Newman's view was that while enthusiasm can lead people to a genuine conversion, all too often it does not:

> *They look upon the turbid zeal and feverish devotion which attend their repentance, not as in part the corrupt offspring of their own previously corrupt state of mind, and partly a gracious natural provision, only temporary, to encourage them to set about their reformation, but as the substance and real excellence of religion. They think that to be thus agitated is to be religious; they indulge themselves in these warm feelings for their own sake, resting in them as if they were then engaged in a religious exercise, and boasting of them as if they were an evidence of their own exalted spiritual state; not using them (the one only thing they ought to do), using them as an incitement to deeds of love, mercy, truth, meekness, holiness.*[35]

Wesley describes the kind of enthusiasm Newman has in mind as 'undoubtedly a disorder of the mind' which 'shuts the eyes of the understanding'. He claimed that this is no part of real religion, which is 'the spirit of a sound mind'.³⁶ Wesley listed some of these aberrations: those who imagine they have grace and redemption when they do not; a form of self-deception. Then there is the fiery zealot for the opinions and modes of worship of religion of which he approves, and those who imagine themselves Christian but are not, or who think they have gifts from God which they do not have, or who claim they are influenced by the Spirit in prayer or preaching or in their private lives and are not. There are also those who expect to be directed by God in an extraordinary manner by visions, dreams or other influences on the mind, and who look for other answers or direction than those contained in Scripture. Others imagine things to be due to the providence of God and that they are really some kind of heavenly favourites. It is a devastating list.

When Newman returned from his travels abroad in 1833 (during which time he wrote 'Lead, Kindly Light'), the Oxford movement was beginning to be under way with the *Tracts for the Times*. At first Newman tried to enlist the aid of Evangelicals against the rising tide of what he saw as Liberalism, but they detected too much popery in his writings. His strong sacramental theology developed a firm view that sacraments are not mere outward signs but 'effluences of grace' by which the effects of the cross and resurrection are applied to us. The 1822 Newman would not have said this. Now baptism is elevating or, following the Eastern Fathers, 'divinising', because of the presence of the Holy Spirit. The peculiar blessedness of the Christian is to be a partaker of the Divine Nature through a divine indwelling. In similar language to Wesley Newman described what he meant:

> *The Holy Ghost, I have said, dwells in body and soul, as in a temple...He pervades us (if it may so be said) as light pervades a building or as a sweet perfume the folds of some honourable robe; so that in Scripture language, we are said to be in Him and He in us. It is plain that such an inhabitation brings the Christian into a state altogether new and marvellous, far above the possession of mere gifts, exalts him inconceivably in the scale of beings, and gives him a place and an office which he had not before.... This wonderful change from darkness to light through the entrance of the Spirit into*

the Soul, is called Regeneration, or New Birth; a blessing which, before Christ's coming, not even the Prophets and righteous men possessed, but which is now conveyed to all men freely through the sacrament of baptism.[37]

Newman's final position was thus that justification and regeneration consists in the sacred presence of the Spirit of Christ in soul and body. Not so much a moral change but a gift, the spirit of adoption. This a far cry from the doctrine of imputed righteousness that he had held in 1822.

Newman sets out in the *Lectures on Justification* what he thinks are the Roman Catholic and Lutheran positions on Justification, but in fact we now know that he was not relying so much on primary sources for Lutheran and Calvinistic position, as on his experience of Calvinism and Lutheranism in his contemporary scene. In fact his exegesis of Luther is questionable, but what is more important is what his understanding led him to say. While he acknowledged the Lutheran position on faith as trust, he felt that this could exist without loving faith, which manifests itself in holiness of life. In fact Luther really meant 'loving faith'. Like Wesley, Newman was anxious to establish an intrinsic connection between justification and regeneration, which to his reading can be interpreted as accidental in Calvinism and Lutheranism if the doctrine of imputed righteousness is accepted. Thus for him justification has two parts: acceptance and renewal.

He was anxious on two counts: the first is that if faith alone is the instrument of justification, then this marginalises the role of baptism and the Church (a feature of his day among some). The second issue is in what way faith is related to love, since they are distinguished as virtues. Newman preferred the Roman Catholic position, which says that justification consists in renewal of heart and a spirit of obedience, but then Wesley also argues for this. If we have been declared righteous then we have also been given the gift of righteousness. Newman's account in fact perpetuates a Roman Catholic misunderstanding of Luther that was common at and after the Council of Trent, although to be fair, Luther changed his mind about this and his language is not always clear, being polemical rather than systematic.

If Newman and Wesley are very close in their preaching and teaching on justification and sanctification, their concern for holiness, for the real spirit of religion, the dangers of wealth and mere conformity to Christian living, the nature of faith, grace and many other topics are explored in their preaching in a remarkably similar vein, especially if we take the whole corpus of their published sermons and papers into account. A full comparative study of their sermons has yet to be done, but perhaps Newman's words might serve to sum up the achievement of them both:

> *We must witness and glorify God, through evil report and good report; but the evil and good report is not so much of our own making as the natural consequence of our Christian profession.*[38]

Prophets are rarely containable within the community in which they are called. If Newman and Wesley found themselves in tension with that part of the Church to which they belonged, it is perhaps because both should be seen as gifts to the universal Christian Church as voices for their own and our own time.

Notes

1. Outler, Albert C. (ed) (1984), *The Works of John Wesley*, Nashville: Abingdon Press, Introduction, Volume 1 pp66ff. All references are to this edition. Cf Newman (1888) *Apologia pro Vita Sua*, London: Longmans, Green, and Co., Ch 1.
2. *Apologia*, p4.
3. Tristram, Henry (ed) (1956), *Autobiographical Writings*, London and New York: Sheed and Ward, p79.
4. Rack, Henry (1992), *Reasonable Enthusiast* (2nd Edn), London: Epworth p343.
5. *The Works of John Wesley*, Introduction, Volume 1 p14f.
6. Further collections are now being published in four volumes.
7. Rack (1992), pp343-4.
8. Neville, W.P. (ed), *Addresses to Cardinal Newman and His Replies*, p184.
9. Preface to *Sermons on Several Occasions* in Outler, Albert C. (ed) (1984), *The Works of John Wesley*, Volume 1 para 3.
10. Church, R.W. (1897), *Occasional Papers II*, London and New York: Macmillan, p457.

11 Church, R.W. (1891), *The Oxford Movement*, London: Macmillan, p21. However, Dean Church there records that Newman disliked the 'fierce intolerance' of what he regarded as the more 'questionable' features of Methodism and Calvinism at that time, which condemned any deviation from 'its formulas and watchwords' (ibid).
12 Quoted in Ward, Wilfrid (1913), *The Life of John Henry Newman*, London: Longmans, Green and Co, Volume 1, pp64-5.
13 Quoted in Chavasse, Paul (2007), 'Newman the Preacher' in Lefebvre, P. and Mason, C. (eds) *John Henry Newman in His Time*, Oxford: Family Publications, p125.
14 Dessain, C. et al (eds) (1961), *The Letters and Diaries of John Henry Newman*, London: Nelson, Vol. XII p198.
15 *The Letters and Diaries of John Henry Newman* (1978), Oxford: OUP, Vol. XXIV p44.
16 Ibid.
17 Outler (1984), Vol. 1, p104.
18 Sermon 39 'The Catholic Spirit' in Outler (1984), Vol. 2, pp84-5.
19 Sermon 16 'The means of Grace' in Outler (1984), Vol. 1, pp381ff.
20 Sermon 1 'Salvation by Faith' in Outler (1984), Vol. 1, p381. Compare also Newman's unpublished sermon at the funeral of Walter Mayers: 'The just man shall live by faith – in all ages and in all countries faith will save a man and (as far as we know) faith alone. Now I will tell you what faith is: – simply this: to feel ourselves to be nothing, and God everything. It is the Spirit of self-renunciation, and self-abhorrence, self-denial.' Birmingham Oratory Archives A-50-5: 163.
21 Op. cit. p124.
22 Ibid.
23 Sermon 5 'Justification by Faith' in Outler (1984), Vol. 1, p193.
24 Op. cit. p194.
25 *Lectures on Justification* (1892), London: Longmans Green and Co., IX p214–15.
26 Sermon 13 'On Sin in Believers' in Outler (1984), Vol. 1, pp322-3.
27 Cf *Parochial and Plain Sermons* (1891), London: Longmans, Green and Co, Vol. II, Sermon 19 passim.
28 Cf Sermon 8 'The First Fruits of the Spirit' in Outler (1984) Vol. 1 passim.
29 Sermon 13 'On Sin in Believers' p163.
30 Tristram (1956), p77.
31 Op. cit. p206.
32 *Apologia*, pp6 ff.
33 Scott, Thomas (1822), *Works*, London, Vol. II p237.
34 Birmingham Oratory Archives A-50-2: 162 12 March 1826 on 'Infant Baptism'.
35 *Parochial and Plain Sermons* (1891), Vol. I Sermon 13 passim.
36 Sermon 37 in Outler (1984), Vol. 2, pp49ff.
37 *Parochial and Plain Sermons* (1891) Volume II Sermon 19 'The Indwelling Spirit'.
38 *Parochial and Plain Sermons* (1891) Volume I Sermon 12 'Profession without Ostentation' p163.

PART TWO

Ecumenical Theology

Now and Then: Ecumenism over time

Frances Young

To write in honour of John Newton, a great ecumenist and a historian, is a privilege. I hope that those interests of his, as well as our common association with the Ecumenical Society of the Blessed Virgin Mary, are reflected in this contribution.

What I want to suggest is that it may be fruitful to think of 'tradition' as a kind of 'ecumenism over time'. Responsible historical awareness of the 'otherness' of the past is necessary, so that the kind of listening, respectful dialogue learned in ecumenical encounter becomes the stance adopted towards tradition. To respect 'otherness' means proper differentiation. However stable and fixed it may appear, particularly to those churches that put a premium on the preservation of tradition, Christianity is always being 'incarnated' in the particular, in different eras, in different societies, with different cultural norms. Ecumenism over time is a concept that allows a hermeneutic of differentiation, as well as assimilation to the family likeness, so deepening Christian identity as well as enabling us to see tradition as dynamic, vital, living. The aims of this paper, then, are to suggest:

- That as Methodists we need to take tradition more seriously, recognising that we have an identity which stretches back beyond the eighteenth century – that we are part of something bigger than ourselves;
- That in ecumenical dialogue we, together with our ecumenical partners, need a shift in perspective on the subject of tradition. There can be no simple appeal to precedent, because institutions, actions and words carry different meanings in changed cultural contexts. Yet respectful dialogue with our forebears in the faith can offer creative and renewing possibilities for the future.

To substantiate these suggestions and illustrate what might be involved in ecumenism over time, I will tackle four topics – the relationship of scripture and tradition, the place of Mary, typology and ordination, and the value of virginity.

1. The Relationship of Scripture and Tradition[1]

The Reformation set scripture and tradition in opposition to one another. The Reformation watchword, *sola scriptura*, had some justification, as did the challenge to traditions that could not be found in the New Testament. However, those of us in the Protestant tradition need to take tradition more seriously because in the end scripture is inseparable from it, as one soon discovers if engaged with the work of Irenaeus, often regarded as the first Christian theologian. He articulated at the end of the second century the outlines of what would become 'mainstream' Christianity in the face of the challenges of his time. He lived through persecution, and opposed those promulgating 'knowledge falsely so-called' (I Tim. 6.20) – the heretical groups which would subsequently be named 'Gnostics'. So his world was poles apart from ours, there are features of his theological position from which many of us would now need to differentiate ourselves, and his long disputes with his opponents most of us would hardly find congenial bed-time reading. Yet he has significant things to say to us if we engage in respectful ecumenical dialogue across the centuries.

In Irenaeus' time, the books honoured as inspired scripture were the 'prophetic' volumes that the church had taken over from the Jews, together with other 'apostolic' texts which showed their fulfilment in Christ. There was no single Bible – it was technologically impossible to copy all the texts into a single roll or codex; still less was there, as yet, complete agreement as to which books belonged to the sacred canon of scripture. Irenaeus was possibly the first to imply that the books of the old covenant had a counterpart in books of the new covenant, Gospel and Apostle mirroring Law and Prophets. Against opponents who either used only one Gospel or appealed to various others (now regarded as apocryphal), he insisted on the fourfold gospel: Matthew, Mark, Luke and John, justifying the fourfold-ness with arguments we would hardly find convincing; but he also took apart their hermeneutical approach, and how he did this is what we need to take seriously.

As far as Irenaeus was concerned his opponents had upset the whole structure and meaning of scripture. It was just as if there was a beautiful representation of a king made in a mosaic by a skilled artist, and someone altered the arrangement of the pieces into the shape of a dog or a fox, and then asserted that this was the original representation of a king.[2] They played with the text like those who wrote 'centos' of Homer: what they did was to take selected lines of Homer's epic out of context and string them together to make a new poem, but as Irenaeus said, 'anyone who knew Homer would recognise the lines but not accept the story'.[3] The heretics thus 'stitch together old wives' tales, and wresting sayings and parables... from the context, attempt to fit the oracles of God into their myths'.[4]

Now sometimes it was possible to show from the immediate context that their reading upset the flow of the text; the one subject of the Johannine Prologue, for example, should not be broken up into a multiplicity of subjects, which is what happened when the Gnostics found there their *plērōma* of aeons: *Archē* (First Principle = Beginning), *Logos* (Word), Christ, *Zōē* (Life), *Phōs* (Light), *Sōtēr* (Saviour), *Monogenēs* (Only-Begotten) – all separate beings. But in the end Irenaeus could not justify his reading of scripture without appeal to the apostolic tradition. The person who has in mind the Rule of Truth which he received at his baptism will immediately recognise names, quotations and parables, but will not accept their blasphemous system as scriptural, nor mistake the fox's portrait for the king's, he asserts.[5] In a number of places Irenaeus rehearses what he calls the Rule of Truth, a loose summary of Christian belief, which never appears exactly the same, though always takes a threefold form, like the later creeds. In other words it is not straightforwardly a summary of the plot of scripture taken overall: there is nothing about the history of Israel, nothing about Abraham and the patriarchs, nothing about Exodus or Exile. Rather it focuses on the one God who made heaven and earth, on Jesus Christ and on the Holy Spirit which inspired the prophecies of Christ. In other words it is a particular *tradition* of construing scripture to which Irenaeus resorts when challenging a system he regards as false.

The discovery of a number of original Gnostic texts, notably at Nag Hammadi, has illuminated the kind of interpretation Irenaeus was up against. Essentially Gnostics tended to read Genesis 'upside-down': the Demiurge, or Creator-God, was a fallen being who trapped spiritual beings in the material world; the serpent was the saviour, the embodiment of wisdom who brought knowledge. It is no wonder that the members of one Gnostic sect were known as Naasenes or Ophites (using the Hebrew or Greek word for 'snake'). However absurd this might seem to us, steeped as we are in another tradition of reading Genesis, the idea was not entirely implausible. In that world the serpent represented wisdom – figurines of the goddess of wisdom have snakes in their hands, and even in the Gospels we find the saying, 'Be wise as serpents'. Against that background we can understand why Irenaeus' theology focuses so firmly on Adam and Eve, on their free choice to disobey and its reversal in the obedience of Christ.

Now this theory of 'recapitulation' lies at the root of traditional Christian theology, as does the idea of the fulfilment of prophecy in Christ. Both were essential to Irenaeus' defence against the wrong-headed interpretations of scripture found among the Gnostics. Yet in our context they are both ideas with which we may have difficulties. Evolutionary theory challenges the story of Adam and Eve; historical readings of the biblical texts challenge their straightforward reading as prophetic – they had a meaning in their original context rather than pointing forward to a future in Christ. To enter dialogue with Irenaeus in an ecumenical spirit is to acknowledge difference – his context was different from ours, his challenges, problems and questions different. Our way of understanding 'Fall and Redemption' can hardly be identical with his.[6]

But to say that is to acknowledge the potential significance of having a respectful debate over matters of difference, while allowing ourselves to be challenged. The watchword *sola scriptura* has been problematic, spawning both fundamentalism and the tendency of Protestantism to be fissiparous. In the 'post-modern' period there has been a reaction against the historico-critical method of scriptural interpretation, and, amongst other things, a critique of its analytical outcomes has been offered by 'canon-criticism', the idea being that rather than dissecting scripture into its sources we should seek the meaning acquired by the texts of scripture in their final form, the meaning that is to be found when the whole of the biblical context is taken into account. But Irenaeus reminds us that it is not this endeavour that will yield a common Christian reading. Such an ecumenical reading will depend, not on canons of interpretation offered by scripture itself, nor simply a sense of context within the flow of an over-arching narrative history, but rather on a sense of God's plan of salvation as passed down in the *kerygma* or gospel received from the apostles – in other words, on a framework belonging to the community of the church which designates these particular books as authoritative and provides the interpretative key in the Rule of Faith enshrined in the creeds. We need to reintegrate scripture and its interpretation into tradition. It was after all the tradition of the church which established what belonged to scripture, as well as how to construe it 'Christianly'.

2. The Place of Mary[7]

Why might Mary be important for ecumenism over time? After all, most Methodists only think about Mary at Christmas, and are somewhat sceptical about the devotion offered to Mary in Catholic and Orthodox circles. The Reformation is responsible in this case also; with some justification, devotion to the saints in general and Mary in particular was treated as unscriptural and potentially idolatrous. But Mary already figured large in Irenaeus' overarching scheme of salvation, and that introduces the first of three reasons for taking Mary more seriously in our theology.

(i) Mary and the incarnation

The earliest theological reflection on Mary draws a parallel between Mary and Eve. Paul had associated Adam and Christ (Romans 5.12-17; cf. 1 Corinthians 15.45-9), and suggested that in Christ we are a new creation (2 Corinthians 5.17). At the end of the second century, Irenaeus expressed this in terms of 'recapitulation': humanity was bound to death through Adam's disobedience, then released from sin and death through the obedience of Christ. To accomplish this, the Word took flesh from a virgin, paralleling Adam's formation from the virgin earth. Those who suggest Christ took nothing from Mary are far astray, suggests Irenaeus: for if he did not take the substance of flesh from humanity, he did not become human. Then, just as Adam fell through a disobedient virgin, so humanity received life again by means of a virgin who obeyed God: for Mary responded, 'Behold the handmaid of the Lord'. So Adam was recapitulated in Christ and Eve in Mary.[8] Two significant points emerge from this:

- The true humanity of Jesus depends on his birth from Mary;
- Salvation comes from reversal of what went wrong for both women and men.

This parallel between Eve and Mary became standard in reflection on redemption and Christology. Holding Christology and Mariology together prevents any interpretation of the biblical stories of the virgin birth as analogous to pagan myths; Christ simply cannot be conceived as a divine-human hybrid. Matthew and Luke present us with stories pointing to the fulfilment of prophecy and the new creation; Luke echoes Genesis when he speaks of the Holy Spirit overshadowing the Virgin Mary, implicitly suggesting the parallel with the virgin earth. Mary's role ensures that this is not a novel act of creation, but a renewal of our very own, true humanity. However we may now conceive the realities behind the Adam and Eve story, the heart of the gospel lies in the role of Jesus and his mother, who are both involved in God's act of restoration. Ecumenism over time may help us to reclaim such insights. Mary is essential to salvation, part of the logic of incarnation – Christology is impoverished by the Protestant neglect of Mary.[9]

The true humanity of Christ is a fundamental Christological principle: what is not assumed is not healed. This humanity is Mary's gift to God on behalf of humankind, enabling the incarnation. It is therefore profoundly important that she remains truly human, suffers pain and grief, and dies. In the spirit of ecumenical dialogue, we may want to express reservations about some later developments on the very grounds that the reality of the incarnation is paramount. Such ideas as Mary's assumption to heaven, or the suggestion that Mary's virginity was intact even after Jesus' birth, or that she felt no birth-pangs, might appear to threaten her true humanity and so undercut her crucial role. But these too had a kind of theological logic, as we see when we turn to the second reason for attending to her role.

(ii) Mary as redeemed

It is true that scripture has little to say about Mary, and Catholic exegesis of what there is goes beyond the plain meaning of the texts: neither her perpetual virginity nor her assumption to heaven has concrete scriptural support, and some texts (notably Mark 3.31-5 and John 2.4) seem to imply tension between Jesus and his mother when read most straightforwardly. Many features of Mariology, found both in Eastern icons and Western art, have their origin in a second century apocryphal work, the *Protevangelium of James*, as do many surviving Christmas traditions which have no basis in the canonical Gospels.

In this apocryphal work we find imaginative story-telling filling in the gaps in the scriptural narrative, creating *midrash* by using material from the Old Testament as prophecies to provide details, some of which were impossible in a purely Jewish context. Thus, Mary is dedicated to the Temple, but in Hebrew tradition that could not happen in the case of a girl, still less her entry into the Holy of Holies. Mary and other virgins spin and weave a new veil for the Temple; these 'undefiled daughters of the Hebrews' seem suspiciously parallel to the vestal virgins in Rome, and the girls of Athens used to make the new veil or robe for the statue of the virgin goddess Athena.[10]

The text is again foreign to Jewish tradition in its focus on establishing Mary's absolute purity and perpetual virginity:

- Joseph is presented as an old widower who accepts 'the virgin of the Lord' as his ward;
- proofs are offered before priests that neither he nor she had intercourse;
- the story of Salome is told to show that Mary was still a virgin after the birth of Jesus – she doubts; her hand is consumed by fire when she touches Mary to confirm her virginity, and then is healed by touching the Christ-child.

None of this is scriptural, yet it must be acknowledged that the traditions in this text are very ancient, and have scriptural roots. There is biblical precedent in the dedication of the child, Samuel, to the Temple – here is a special child with a special call, no matter that she is female. Her mother, Anna, is clearly modelled on Hannah, and Mary's birth reads like a typical biblical story of a miraculous birth to a barren couple. A typological parallel between Mary and the Ark of the Covenant seems to be implicit in the story of Salome, who suffers for touching her as Uzziah did when he touched the Ark.

So why is Mary's purity important, and why does it figure so large so early? The underlying logic derives from what has already been said about the incarnation and our redemption. Mary had to be pure, just as Christ had to be sinless, for the sake of our salvation. There are other inner biblical resonances also – the Holy Spirit overshadowed the Ark of Covenant and the Holy of Holies, as Mary was overshadowed at the annunciation; while the burning bush mediated the Divine presence as does the mother of Emmanuel, God with us. So profound reflections on scriptural resonances appear in story-form in the *Protevangelium*. The ikons representing these stories, however apocryphal they may be, convey the specifically Christian sense of Mary's holiness, rather than some kind of pagan mother-goddess or fertility-myth. The important implication of this insistence on Mary's purity is the notion that she was the first to be redeemed by Christ, providentially prepared as a suitable human vessel to receive God's presence and very self. According to Genesis pain in child-bearing was Eve's punishment; is it any wonder that Mary, the redeemed one, was thought to have borne the Redeemer without pain? As the first to be redeemed Mary's humanity is and is not our fallen humanity – she anticipates the fact that in Christ we are a new creation. Our ecumenical dialogue over time challenges us to think again.

(iii) Mary as 'type' of the Church

This leads to another deep tradition in Mariology – that as the first to be redeemed she is a 'type of the church'. Vatican II placed Mariology within the statement on ecclesiology. The connection between Mary and the church is evident in the Eastern Orthodox ikons of Pentecost and the Ascension, where Mary has a central position among the disciples, and in the *Deesis* ikon, where John the Baptist represents those of the old covenant while she leads the intercessions of those under the new covenant.

The church appears as a woman early in the second century; in the *Shepherd of Hermas*[11] Irenaeus suggested that Mary was 'prophesying on behalf of the church' when she sang the Magnificat.[12] Clement of Alexandria wrote:

> *The universal Father is one, and one the universal Word; and the Holy Spirit is one and the same everywhere, and one is the only virgin mother. I love to call her the church... She is at once virgin and mother, pure as a virgin, loving as a mother. And calling her children to her, she nurses them with holy milk, the Word for childhood.*[13]

Tertullian said that, just as from the side of Adam Eve was formed, so from the wounded side of Jesus the church, 'the mother of all living', arose.[14] Cyprian famously stated that 'he who does not have the church as mother cannot have God as Father.'

Mary explicitly becomes a 'type' of the church in Ambrose,[15] and in Augustine we find:

> *Imitate Mary, who gave birth to the Lord.... If the church, then, gives birth to the members of Christ, then the church greatly resembles Mary.*

But Augustine resisted over-valuation of Mary:

> *Mary is holy. Mary is blessed, but the church is better than the Virgin Mary. Why? Because Mary is part of the church, a holy member, an outstanding member, a supereminent member... If she is a member of the whole body, the body is undoubtedly greater than one of its members.*[16]

Indeed, saying that Mary is a 'type' of the church is not to suggest that we are 'in Mary' in the same sense as we are in 'in Christ' or members of the Body of Christ. Rather it is to express the notion that she is an exemplar of redeemed humanity, one for believers to imitate or follow. Commenting on Gregory of Nyssa, Verna Harrison wrote:[17]

> *Notice that an essential feature of Mary's virginity and also that of the Christian soul is receptivity to God. Her purity and integrity open a place within her where God can enter, where Christ can be formed, and from which he can come forth.... [Mary's] receptivity is intrinsic to her creaturehood; like all human persons, as Gregory understands them, she lives by participation in God and is not the source of her own life... For Gregory the virginal soul, like Mary receives the entrance of God and brings forth Christ, though spiritually, not physically.*

This idea is still found in Erasmus at the time of the Reformation:

> O *Virgin Mother, may your Son grant us that in imitation of your most holy life we may conceive the Lord Jesus in our innermost soul and once conceived may we never lose him.*[18]

So in the spirit of ecumenism over time, maybe we Protestants need to recognise both the antiquity of such traditions and the Christian theological insight that lies at their root. This might encourage us to insist on Mary's humanity, implying some critique of certain Marian developments. We might become inclined to confess her as the human Mother of God the Son, the human daughter of God the Father, the Creator, and the human Temple of God the Holy Spirit, while perhaps feeling some caution with respect to the 'Queen of Heaven'. We might honour her purity and her reception of grace, but feel that the notion of the Immaculate Conception is in danger of removing her from common humanity, as are ideas about her painless birth and intact virginity afterwards. But Mary's humanity is in fact at the heart of what our ecumenical partners affirm. Her pilgrimage of faith is acknowledged in the Vatican II statement, and the fact that her response developed has been explored in Catholic reflection on Mary as the first disciple, and a model to transform today's church.[19] Jean Vanier[20] speaks of her as a woman who has done nothing extraordinary apart from love: to enter the world, he writes, the Word of God needed a mother – he needed her to nourish him as an infant, and to give him love. In the Eastern tradition we find the ikons of lovingkindness (*eleousa*). All this puts proper emphasis on her humanity, and perhaps indicates that all traditions are implicitly engaged in the kind of critical reflection involved in ecumenism over time.

3. Typology and Ordination[21]

The current situation with regard to women's ordination presents us with a great irony. The ordination of women is historically a novelty, yet it has been largely embraced by the churches of the Reformation, who owe their existence to a desire to reach back beyond tradition to scripture;[22] whereas those churches, both Catholic and Orthodox, which have historically appealed to tradition over scripture, so entertaining the possibility of developments beyond scripture, have refused to countenance a development with no precedent. One reason why post-Reformation churches have found it easier to make the move is their insistence on the priesthood of all believers – ministers are easily treated as having a functional role, proper to the ordering of the church and representative of the priesthood of the community, but not ontologically different from any other believer. The specific connotations of priesthood, as distinct from presbyterate or eldership, came into the tradition through typology.

Typology is many-faceted. Within the Bible itself we find stories told in ways that mirror one another: Elijah and Ezekiel bear the marks of a new Moses, the stories of Abraham 'typify' the exodus.[23] In early Christianity the notion that past narratives foreshadow, or prefigure, the future is implicit: so, Jesus brings manna in the desert as he miraculously feeds the crowds, and as the blood of the Passover lamb saved the Israelites from the angel of death, so Christ's blood saves from death and the devil; and in Hebrews, the covenant, the Temple and the whole sacrificial system is reinterpreted as fulfilled in Christ. Another kind of typology emerges in early Christian preaching as Biblical characters become 'types' of virtues to be imitated, Job, for example, typifying patience. Though the association of presbyters and deacons with priests and Levites is already found earlier (*I Clement*), the key moment for church order comes in the third century with Cyprian, who inherited and developed the tradition that saw persons of the Old Testament as prophetic pre-figurations of Christ, while persons in the church may become what we might call 'post-figurations'.

In Epistle 63 Cyprian[24] speaks of Christ being prefigured in the priest, Melchisedek: so, in Genesis, 'the image of sacrifice clearly constituted in bread and wine is already present proleptically. Fulfilling and completing this reality, the Lord offered bread and the cup mixed with wine'. As Melchisedek pre-figures, so the eucharistic president post-figures:

> For if Christ Jesus our Lord and God himself is the High Priest of God the Father and first offered himself as a sacrifice to the Father, and commanded that this take place in his memory, that

> *priest indeed truly functions in the place of Christ who imitates that which Christ did, and consequently offers a true and complete sacrifice in the church to God the Father.... the Lord's passion is the sacrifice we offer. (Ep. 63.14, 17)*

Such typology lies at the root of objections to women's ordination.

The hermeneutics of typology, therefore, is the crucial issue. What I want to suggest is that the claim that no woman can be a type of Christ is an extraordinary misunderstanding of the dynamics of typology. Even Cyprian regards anything in creation as potentially a type of Christ, and the one who puts on Christ in baptism is a living type of that new creation in Christ, humanity refashioned in God's image. Above all the martyrs are types of Christ, expressing 'to the fullest the common vocation of all Christians to live typologically the *passio* of Christ'.[25] There were in Cyprian's time famous women martyr-saints. There is, then, nothing to stop a woman being a type of Christ – gender is irrelevant; it is simply not the point of comparison. Types of Christ are like ikons – they represent not as literal portraits, but function as symbols that bear the presence of Christ. The eucharist is not something like a passion-play with the priest acting out the role of Christ at the Last Supper. The Body of Christ is the gathered church; and the whole sacrament is a representation of the one perfect and sufficient sacrifice made by the priest Christ in offering his own body for the sins of the whole world.

So far my argument challenges the 'literalising' of typology in terms of gender representing gender. Now, however, I wish to offer a positive typological argument for including women among those who may act as priests at the eucharist, an argument which builds on the Catholic understanding of Mary as type of the church.

The Orthodox theologian, Elisabeth Behr-Sigel, makes exactly this move. She graphically describes the omnipresence of Mary, the Birth-giver of God (*Theotokos*), in Orthodox devotion and liturgy, emphasising that 'her glory reflects on all humanity, and the Mother of God reveals mankind's (*sic*) highest vocation'.[26] 'She is the archetype and the guide of those men and women who aspire to give birth to Christ in their hearts'.[27] Behr-Sigel concludes that 'in the Orthodox vision Mary is not seen mainly as the model for women or as the archetype of womanhood in the banal or sociological meaning of the term'. Rather the 'signification of Mary is both unique and universal, both cosmic and eschatological'. 'It is of no small consequence, however, that this new creation, having Mary as its human root, has a woman's face'.[28] Mary is a figure of the church, of the Body of Christ, of which men and women both are members.[29] In her writings Behr-Sigel repeatedly insists that tradition should not be identified with precedent, but be living; and eventually reaches the conclusion that the priesthood of the church could properly be represented by a man or a woman.

I suspect she could have gone further. For in Orthodox feasts and their ikons there is much that appears to place Mary in a priestly role. Many ikons show her in the *orans* (praying) position: at the Ascension she is there *orans* at the centre of the group of the Apostles; in the *Deesis* she leads the saints of the new covenant in intercession. Leading the church in intercession is surely a priestly role. Could it not further be said that this priestly role is expressed symbolically in the feast and icon of her presentation in the Temple, Mary becoming typologically the archetypal high priest who enters the Holy of Holies? The hymnography of these Feasts celebrates Mary as the Ark of the Covenant, the place of God's presence, the Temple of the Holy Spirit and the Tabernacle of the Word of God. So she mediates God to the world in Christ, as the living Temple. She is all-holy, her purity from contamination making possible the incarnation, and so our purification. Again we may speak of a priestly role. In the preface to the original French edition of Behr-Sigel's book, Anthony Bloom wrote:

> *Twice Mary had a properly priestly ministry: once when she carried her son who was destined to be sacrificed to the Lord, and once when, at the foot of the cross, she completed the offering by uniting her will, in heroic abandoning of self, to the will of the heavenly Father and to that of the Son of God who by her had become the Son of Man and the sacrificial Lamb.*

If it can be acknowledged that Mary has a priestly ministry, then through that typology priesthood can surely not be withheld from women, particularly when it is set in the broader context of Mary's role as 'type' of the church.

Recent Roman theology contrasts the apostolic-petrine tradition with the Marian tradition:

> *The fact that the blessed Virgin Mary, Mother of God and Mother of the Church, received neither the mission proper to the apostles nor the ministerial priesthood clearly shows that the non-admission of women to priestly ordination cannot mean that women are of lesser dignity, nor can it be construed as discrimination against them. Rather it is to be seen as the faithful observance of a plan to be ascribed to the wisdom of the Lord of the Universe.*[30]

But John Wijngaards, in *The Ordination of Women in the Catholic Church*,[31] cites mediaeval precedents for honouring Mary as the priest *par excellence*. Ecumenism over time might allow a more creative dialogue between divided churches about the implications of precedent and possibilities for the future.

4. The Value of Virginity

A distinguished Methodist once commented in my hearing that you could understand why celibate priests were devoted to Mary – she enabled the sublimation of erotic desires. Be that as it may, Mariology certainly developed alongside the monastic movement, and the notion of her perpetual virginity clearly provided a model for the ideal of celibacy. The goals of the ascetic movement, including the repression of sexual urges, is one way in which our cultural attitudes are diametrically opposed to those in the church of the early centuries. But once again, if we are prepared to listen carefully and respectfully in an ecumenical spirit, we may find useful things to learn. Scholarship has increasingly shown how old the ideal of sexual abstinence was in the life of the early church.[32] From the fourth century, however, the monastic movement, taking various forms in different parts of the Roman Empire, made it the more insistent – indeed, Elizabeth Clark has shown how profoundly it affected the interpretation of scripture.[33] But it was not just that 'virginity' (celibacy) became the ideal; reaching vision of God, and attaining likeness to God, came to be associated with *apatheia* (passionless-ness).

The Protestant Reformation challenged these ideals – after all, the Bible celebrates marriage, and humanity is told to be fruitful and multiply. The clergy of post-Reformation churches have married. The conjugal bliss of Adam and Eve in Paradise Haydn celebrated in his oratorio, *The Creation*. Romanticism gripped European culture, and after Freud people have begun to worry about the effects of repressing emotion and sexual urges. Our culture regards it as important to let it all out – whether anger or love, it must be expressed. And in our preoccupation with the problem of suffering we resist the notion that God is *apathēs*, assuming that such a notion implies indifference – only a suffering God can help, we say, pointing to Christ's suffering on the cross to demonstrate that God is love and that love necessarily involves suffering.

Ecumenism over time might allow us to come to a more sophisticated understanding of *apatheia*, and a more balanced view of our emotional urges. Space hardly permits a full exploration of this, but it is perhaps significant that interest is burgeoning in the work of the desert ascetic, Evagrius, along with appreciation of his diagnosis of the human heart, struggling against 'thoughts' or fantasies.[34] He may express this at times in terms of a battle with 'daemons', and in various other ways we need, as in our earlier examples, to differentiate ourselves from some of his assumptions. Yet there is a wisdom here that could be fruitful in terms of our spiritual journeying. Evagrius is actually concerned with the schooling of emotion, recognising that feelings are the driving force for our action. All too often our motivations are skewed, and until we are freed from our own deep anxieties and needs, we cannot really love. Constantly we try to possess the object of our love, and make them conform to what we want, refusing to let go and lovingly accept them as who they really are. *Apatheia* means that inner peace, that release from irritation, from guilt and self-concern, that self-acceptance, which alone allows full attention to be given to the needs of others; in other words, true compassion. *Apatheia* is the condition of true love and joy. It is becoming what God is.

The fear of God strengthens faith, my child, and abstinence in turn strengthens fear of God, and perseverance and hope render abstinence unwavering, and from these is born impassibility (apatheia) of which love is the offspring; love is the door to contemplation,[35] which is followed by theology and ultimate blessedness.[36]

Conclusion

To spend time in one of the great mediaeval cathedrals of England, or the chapel of St Peter's-on-the-Wall at Bradwell, Essex – probably the earliest surviving place of Christian worship in England – is to be drawn into a depth of time far deeper than one ever senses in a Methodist church. Here generations of our forefathers prayed, and the stones seem saturated with it. History is even more enveloping if one visits the catacombs in Rome or St Katherine's monastery in the Sinai desert. That some of our ecumenical partners value tradition is not surprising. That sense of being earthed in deep historical continuity is clearly of profound significance.

For Methodists tradition is more ambivalent, for a number of reasons:

- our evangelical heritage tends to mean we adopt the Protestant position, giving scripture priority;
- our mission perspective makes us open to fresh enculturation of the gospel in a pluralism of cultures, so encouraging a tendency to sit light to inherited baggage;
- appeals to tradition or precedent which deny validity to our sacraments, or press us to adopt episcopacy and the apostolic succession, or challenge innovations such as the ordination of women, make us suspicious.

Yet our claim to be part of the universal church means not only acceptance of the historic creeds, even if they are frequently dropped in our actual worship practices, but also, whether we like it or not, engagement with a past which is larger than New Testament origins and John Wesley. The notion of 'ecumenism over time' might give us a way of embracing tradition gladly. As we listen to our contemporaries from different denominations, so we might engage with the past, not simply seeking the lowest common denominator, but rather learning how to respect, honour and celebrate difference, to embrace 'otherness', acknowledging the realities of diversity and historical change.

Notes

1. This section derives material from a number of my previous publications, such as *The Art of Performance* (1990), London: DLT; and the Prelude to *The Cambridge History of Christianity: Origins to Constantine*, Mitchell, Margaret M. & Young, Frances M. (eds) (2006), Cambridge: CUP.
2. *Against Heresies* I.8.1.
3. *Against Heresies* I.9.4.
4. *Against Heresies* I.8.1.
5. *Against Heresies* I.9.4.
6. Though modern theology, in reaction against the Augustinian view that Adam and Eve were perfect, has sometimes retrieved the 'Irenaean theodicy', whereby Adam and Eve are treated as children who needed to grow into moral maturity – notably Hick, John (1966) *Evil and the Love of God*, London: Macmillan.
7. This section is derived from my article, 'The Church and Mary', in *Ecclesiology* 5.3 (2009), 276-98.
8. *Demonstration of the Gospel* 31-3; *Against Heresies* III.22.
9. Yeago, David (2004) 'The Presence of Mary in the Mystery of the Church' in Braaten, Carl E. and Jenson, Robert W. (eds), *Mary, Mother of God*, Grand Rapids MI: Eerdmans.
10. Benko, Stephen (1993) *The Virgin Goddess: Studies in the Pagan and Christian Roots of Mariology*, Studies in the History of Religions LIX, Leiden: Brill.
11. Benko (1993), pp229-30.
12. Benko (1993), p231.
13. *Paed.* 1.6. Cf. *Paed.* 1.5: the mother draws the children to herself; and we seek our mother the church; and *Paed.* 3.12: Let us complete the fair face of the church; and let us run as children to our good mother. See Benko (1993), pp231-2, including footnotes.
14. *De Anima* 43. See Benko (1993), p232.
15. *Exposition of Luke* 2.7. See Benko (1993), p234.
16. Augustine quoted by Beattie, Tina, 'Mary in Patristic Theology' in Boss, Sarah Jane (ed) (2007), *Mary: The Complete Resource*, London: Continuum.
17. Harrison, Verna (1966), 'Gender, Generation and Virginity in Cappadocean Theology', *JTS* NS 47, pp38-68.
18. Quoted by Boff, Leonardo (1983, 2005), *Praying with Jesus and Mary*, ET Maryknoll NY: Orbis Books, p172.

19 Azzarello, Marie (2004), *Mary, The First Disciple: A Guide for Transforming Today's Church*, Ottawa: Novalis.
20 Vanier, Jean (2001), *Visages de Marie*, Nouvelles Editions Mame.
21 This section is drawn from my paper, 'Hermeneutical questions: the ordination of women in the light of biblical and patristic typology' in Jones, Ian, Wootton, Janet and Thorpe, Kirsty (eds) (2008), *Women and Ordination in the Christian Churches: International Perspectives*, London: T&T Clark.
22 There is, of course, a conservative tradition among Protestants which argues against the ordination of women on two grounds: (1) the Pauline texts prohibiting women to speak or have headship over men, and (2) the supposed order of creation established in Genesis. See discussion in Edwards, Ruth (1989), *The Case for Women's Ordination*, London: SPCK.
23 A range of different kinds of typologies is traced in the Hebrew Bible by Fishbane, Michael (1985), *Biblical Interpretation in Ancient Israel*, Oxford: Clarendon, pp35-79; for further discussion see my *Biblical Exegesis and the Formation of Christian Culture* (1997), Cambridge: CUP, pp192-201.
24 My discussion of Cyprian owes much to Laurance, John D. (1984), *'Priest' as Type of Christ: The Leader of the Eucharist in Salvation History according to Cyprian of Carthage*, New York: Peter Lang, though he should not be held responsible for all the conclusions drawn. The following paragraphs draw upon my lecture 'Presbyteral Ministry in the Catholic Tradition or Why shouldn't women be priests?' (1984), The Methodist Sacramental Fellowship.
25 Laurance (1984), pp193-4.
26 Behr-Sigel, Elisabeth (1991, 1999), *The Ministry of Women in the Church*, ET Stephen Bigham; republished Crestwood NY: St Vladimir's Seminary press, p189.
27 Behr-Sigel (1991), p207.
28 Behr-Sigel (1991), p210.
29 Plekon, Michael and Hinlicky, Sarah E. (eds) (2001), *Discerning the Signs of the Times: The Vision of Elisabeth Behr-Sigel*, Crestwood NY: St Vladimir's Seminary press, p112.
30 From his *Apostolic Letter on Reserving Priestly Ordination to Men Alone*, quoted by Schüssler Fiorenza, Elizabeth (1994), *Jesus: Miriam's Child, Sophia's Prophet*, London: SCM Press, p163.
31 (2001) London: DLT. This book I found after developing the above argument; I was intrigued to find that I had been anticipated by a Roman Catholic.
32 The classic study was Brown, Peter, *The Body and Society*, but it has been followed by many important works on the subject, too many to list here.
33 Clark, Elizabeth (1999), *Reading Renunciation: Asceticism and Scripture in Early Christianity*, Princeton: Princeton University Press.
34 For a discussion which puts Evagrius in relation to our culture and spiritual needs, see Tilby, Angela (2009), *The Seven Deadly Sins: Their origin in the spiritual teaching of Evagrius the Hermit*, London: SPCK.
35 'Natural knowledge' is an important term for Evagrius, implying the understanding of God and divine providence that comes from contemplation of created things. I have attempted to capture this by substituting 'contemplation' in the translation.
36 *Praktikos* 8.

Conference *Episcope*: History and theology

Brian E. Beck

The claim has often been made over the last few decades, in ecumenical discussions of episcopacy and more generally in Methodist ecclesiological writing, that while British Methodism lacks the office of bishop it does possess *episcope*, exercised by the governing Conference, and by individuals and groups under the Conference's authority. While the claim is justified it conceals significant variations both in practice and in understanding. In current understanding Conference *episcope* represents corporate oversight of the church by a representative body, shared collaboratively by ordained and lay. It has not always been so. Of course oversight has always been exercised in Methodism since the days of John Wesley, but where it has been exercised corporately it has not always been shared, and in so far as it has been shared it has not always been seen as oversight in the fullest sense.

The use of the anglicised Greek word *episcope* for the English 'oversight' is relatively recent and is intended to distinguish between the exercise of personal oversight in the office of bishop, 'episcopacy', and the ministry or function of oversight in itself, however exercised. At the same time it gives the notion of oversight a theological undergirding, protecting it from misrepresentation in purely secular managerial terms. The earliest use of it I have discovered in Methodist writing is in an exchange of articles in the *Proceedings of the Wesley Historical Society* beginning in December 1956, when it was evidently already a familiar term. But the English alternatives, 'oversight', 'superintendence' and 'watching over' are much older in Methodist use.

It is, understandably, in ecumenical dialogues, between British Methodism and the Church of England and internationally between the World Methodist Council and the Roman Catholic Church, that *episcope* comes to be employed, from 1963 in the one case and from 1976 in the other. But it is important to note a shift in emphasis in successive reports, from functions of *episcope* exercised in some respects by individuals and in others by the Conference in the earlier dialogues, to its overall exercise by the Conference which authorises individuals to act on its behalf in the later ones, and from a concentration on collective ministerial oversight to a recognition of oversight as a gift to the whole church, shared by lay and ordained alike, which only comes to full expression in the Methodist-Roman Catholic document *Speaking the Truth in Love* in 2001.

Two recent Conference reports set out what British Methodism currently understands by *episcope: Episkopé and Episcopacy* (2000) and *The Nature of Oversight* (2005). It is comprehensively defined as 'the function of ensuring that the church remains true to its calling'. It includes governance, management and leadership, and involves pastoral care, discernment of God's will, leadership in mission, interpretation of doctrine, the admission, ordination, appointment and oversight of presbyters and deacons, general ordering of the church's constitution, concern for its unity, and the exercise of authority and discipline. It is exercised primarily by the Conference, but also under its authority, by presbyters and deacons, by district synods and a range of circuit and local church bodies and by lay individuals throughout the church. It is only in the collaboration of ordained and lay that oversight is fully exercised. Such a definition easily bears comparison with ecumenical statements.[1]

Certain features of it are important for our discussion. While presbyters have a significant part in the oversight of the church, it is not their exclusive province. Oversight is shared between ordained and lay leaders throughout the church, and by ordained and lay in more or less equal numbers in the Conference. It is also a holistic concept. All aspects of the church's life and mission come within the Conference's purview and are embraced in *episcope*, including finance, property, publishing and general organisation.

The Methodist Conference

There is no doubt John Wesley functioned, in effect, as Methodism's bishop, although he eschewed the term, and was furious when the title was adopted by the Methodists in the United States. It is also undisputed that after his death in 1791 the British Conference assumed the authority that had once been his. The more interesting questions are whether that was what he intended, and whether the authority his successors exercised over the Methodist Societies was as securely grounded as they claimed. In time they grounded their claim theologically in the doctrine of the pastoral office, to which we shall return shortly, but they also assumed that it had a legal basis in the Deed of Declaration which Wesley executed in 1784.

Forty years earlier, in 1744, Wesley had gathered a group of five sympathetic clergymen and four lay preachers to confer with him about doctrine, discipline and practice. It was the first of an unbroken and continuing succession of Methodist Conferences. Two aspects of it are important. It was a mixed gathering in which ordained and lay shared, although not in equal numbers or influence, and it was advisory. Whether in later years its members all considered it so we may doubt. In practice it was a barometer for Wesley of opinion among the preachers and from time to time a means by which internal disagreements could be resolved, but he always insisted on its advisory status. It was an instance of what might now be called 'bishop in council'. It is also significant that its minutes were published. Its conversations were in effect a set of directives for the preachers and for the wider Methodist membership.

Wesley's hope in 1769, in a letter to the preachers of 4 August, was that after his death the preachers would elect a committee of between three and seven, each of whom would be moderator in turn, and who together would take over Wesley's functions of proposing preachers for trial, admitting and excluding them, stationing them and fixing the date of the next Conference. What is interesting is that these duties were to be carried out by a committee, not by the preachers in Conference, reflecting his view of the Conference as no more than advisory. But what was his intention in 1784?

In that year, in the vacuum created by the absence of ecclesiastical authority after American Independence, Wesley conducted his first ordinations, of Richard Whatcoat and Thomas Vasey, for the Methodist societies there. He gave the Americans 'full liberty simply to follow the Scriptures and the Primitive Church', but he did not delegate any specific powers to their Conference. He also laid hands on Thomas Coke, who was already ordained, and appointed him and Asbury joint superintendents in America. The best interpretation of this is that he was delegating his own supervisory authority to Coke, to be shared in turn with Asbury. The conclusion must be that he expected the American Conference, like the British, to be advisory. In the event, however, Asbury refused to accept appointment as superintendent until it had been ratified by the vote of the preachers in the Conference, and thereby significantly shifted the balance of authority, although in subsequent decades it became apparent that there were conflicting interpretations as to whether the 'general superintendency' exercised by the bishops was subordinate to the General Conference that elected them or co-ordinate with it and not subject to its control.[2]

Subsequently, when Wesley began to ordain preachers, first for service in Scotland and later for England, he ordained Alexander Mather, as he had Coke, as superintendent. That suggests he anticipated a similar arrangement in Britain after his death as had obtained before it: a superintendent in his place and an advisory Conference. It was certainly the fear of this that led to the often-quoted decision taken in 1791 that they would not have another 'king in Israel', but an annual president instead. One reason cited for their decision was that it would be in conflict with the 1784 Deed. Careful attention to the terms of the Deed, however, suggests that in that respect they misunderstood its scope and supports the view that Wesley intended that his place should be taken by an individual.

As the opening recitals make clear, the explicit purpose of the Deed was to secure the chapels for the use of Methodist preachers. The standard form of trust deed for the chapels specified that they were for the use of preachers appointed by John Wesley and after his death by the Conference, with a proviso about the doctrine to be preached. Wesley had been advised that the reference to the Conference was insecure, and the 1784 Deed therefore gives the Conference a legal identity, empowers it to enrol and deploy the travelling preachers and provides for its continuation in perpetuity. There is no suggestion in the recitals that the Deed was intended in any wider sense to provide for the future governance of the Methodist people.

The main part of the Deed begins by referring to the situation obtaining in 1784 when it was drawn up. The Conference is declared at that date to be advisory. The only functions attributed to it are the admission of preachers on trial and into full connexion, their expulsion and their stationing. These functions are then assigned to the future Conference. They are precisely the functions mentioned by Wesley in 1769, and are those necessary for identifying which preachers might occupy the chapels. Apart from that there is nothing in the Deed to suggest that the Conference ceases to be advisory. No mention is made of the wider oversight of the Methodist societies or the formulation of rules for them. By no means all of the societies had chapels, so the powers the Deed provides are of limited scope. Nor is there any mention of the local preachers, as distinct from the itinerant preachers, or of the funds which by this date featured in the annual minutes. The Deed achieves what it sets out to do: establish the Conference and guarantee its powers over the trustees to decide who should preach in the chapels.

During Wesley's lifetime affairs in the local societies were regulated in part by the various sets of rules that he published, and in part by the periodic visitations conducted by himself or the itinerant preachers appointed, notionally by the Conference, in reality by Wesley himself. It was the preachers, and in particular the 'assistants' (later called 'superintendents'), who on Wesley's behalf determined who should be admitted as members, continued in membership or struck off. It is in keeping with this that the annual published minutes, and the periodic summaries of them known as the 'large minutes', were cast in the form of instructions to the travelling preachers about the exercise of their ministry. This national extra-parochial system of pastoral oversight was only possible, however, because in every local society Wesley entrusted day-to-day care of society members and the management of their financial affairs to lay class leaders and stewards. Although they were accountable to him, and were appointed or removed from office by him or the itinerant preacher, they represent a sharing of oversight by lay people that has remained an important feature of Methodism.

After Wesley's death all this continued, but now the preachers no longer acted in his name, but their own. And with the change came subtle differences. They were mostly laymen, but because of the role they played in the oversight of the societies, they had all along had a quasi-ministerial relationship to the members of the societies, and now they began to see themselves in ministerial terms. The custom began of an annual letter from the Conference to the societies. The annual minutes began to lose their character as a record of conversations between preachers about the conduct of their ministry and to take on the tone of legislative pronouncements for the general membership, a process driven by the need, in the years following Wesley's death, to resolve disputes about worship and relations with the Established Church. The notion quickly took hold that the 1784 Deed gave a legal foundation for all the powers that the Conference exercised.

The basis of it, however, was established custom, not legal entitlement – custom and consent. The Methodist connexion was a voluntary association, as Wesley himself and subsequent writers were fond of stressing, and it would only hold so long as its members consented to its arrangements. That custom was soon to be challenged and the consent, by some at least, withdrawn. It is worth underlining the fact that some of those who did so, in 1797 and subsequently, argued that the 1784 Deed gave the Conference authority only over the preachers and not over the societies and circuits. On the face of it they were right. Later Wesleyans were in the habit of quoting the statement of the Vice-Chancellor in his judgement in the Court of Chancery on the Warren case in 1835 that 'The Conference has been the supreme legislative and executive Body since the death of Mr Wesley', but that was an observation based on what was admitted by both sides in the dispute, not a ruling;

in legal terms the remark was *obiter*. The scope of the Conference's powers over the whole connexion was never tested in the courts.

The Conference identified by the 1784 Deed was a conference of one hundred of the travelling preachers, and although in respect for Wesley's wishes other preachers attended and joined in the debates, there was no provision for participation by representatives of society members. In an age of rising democratic aspirations that was bound to be questioned. The Methodist New Connexion separated in 1797, in part over the issue of relations with the Established Church, and in part over the composition of the Conference. Their constitution provided for an equal number of travelling preachers, in later terminology ministers, and lay representatives in the membership of the Conference, and for lay members also to share in government at district and more local levels.

Other breakaway movements in the period 1800–1850 went further. The Bible Christians ensured that every five years at least there would be an equal number of ministers and lay members. The Primitive Methodist Conference consisted of two lay persons to every minister, while the United Methodist Free Churches instituted an Assembly with fewer powers over the local churches, constituted by free election, ordained or lay, from the quarterly meetings of the various circuits. The details of these arrangements matter little for the present discussion; what is important to note, however, is that these Conferences, however constituted, and whatever the extent of their authority, exercised a supervisory role in which no distinction was made between 'spiritual' and 'temporal' affairs.

Meanwhile, the Wesleyan Methodists began to develop a theological rationale to underpin the exclusively ministerial membership of their Conference and the manner in which it exercised its authority, the doctrine of the pastoral office. Shepherds, according to their reading of the New Testament, were divinely appointed to preach, to teach and to rule, and in consequence to relinquish the power of government to others in the church would be a betrayal of a sacred duty. Lay people might be consulted on various matters, locally on the admission or exclusion of members, or in district and conference committees on 'temporal affairs' (specifically money), but the final decision on such matters continued to be reserved to the ministers. It was central to the Wesleyan position that one could not be held accountable (to God or to one's peers) for oversight that one could not enforce; but this was to take an excessively disciplinary view of *episcope* to the detriment of the aspects of encouragement and nurture.

The modern reader is struck by the emphasis on rules and discipline in the literature of the period. In essence it goes back to Wesley's conception of a network of religious societies dedicated to the pursuit of holiness. 'Ruling' the flock meant ensuring that each member's manner of life conformed to the faith he or she professed, and that they observed the rules requiring regular attendance at weekday class meeting and Sunday worship. Otherwise they were removed from membership, and the final decision on that was jealously reserved to the ministers.

It is not surprising that in the early decades of the nineteenth century this authoritarian and inflexible stance caused widespread resentment and was the cause of major schisms, culminating in the loss of one-third of the Wesleyan membership in the 1850s. It is more surprising today that so many lay Wesleyans supported it for so long. Even so it could not survive. Change had begun with the appointment of 'mixed committees' of ministers and lay people (not strictly representatives, but chosen by the ministers) reporting to the Conference, the earliest being in 1803. From 1819 district meetings of ministers included lay officials from the circuits to discuss financial matters. Gradually a series of national committees were set up to deal with the various connexional funds and business related to them. Most of these met on the eve of the Conference itself and reported to it, so that the same business would be discussed within the space of a few days by two overlapping groups. It was largely for reasons of economy, therefore, that in 1878 the Conference was opened up to lay representatives, no longer chosen by the ministers but elected by the lay members of the district committees or by the mixed session of the Conference itself.[3]

Ministerial authority remained entrenched in two respects, however. The 'Legal Hundred' identified as the Conference in John

Wesley's 1784 Deed continued to operate and had to confirm all decisions taken by the larger gathering. Moreover, the business of the representative session, comprising ministers and lay people, was restricted to what were considered to be 'temporal' affairs. All matters relating to the selection, admission, oversight and discipline of the ministers, the discipline of lay members on appeal, the supervision of publications and the conduct of public worship (effectively therefore all doctrinal matters), and pastoral supervision generally were reserved to the pastoral session comprising ministers only. The developments of 1878 do not represent *episcope* shared by ordained and lay alike.

Throughout the second half of the nineteenth century attempts were made to reintegrate divided Methodism and the first fruit of it was the union of the Methodist New Connexion, the Bible Christians and the United Methodist Free Churches in 1907 to form the United Methodist Church. Its annual Conference was composed of equal numbers of ministers and lay persons, continuing the tradition of the New Connexion, and its authority over all aspects of the church was given legal basis by Act of Parliament in the same year.

The union of this body with the Wesleyan and Primitive Methodists in 1932 was the subject of protracted negotiations because of the differences involved. There is no need here to go into the details, but it is important to note the outcome. As in 1907 the Conference was given legal foundation by the Methodist Church Union Act 1929 (now superseded by an Act of 1976). The Wesleyan tradition was continued: a representative session, with elected ministers and lay representatives in equal numbers, and a ministerial session, with additional ministers. To the ministerial session were reserved all matters relating to the selection, oversight and discipline of ministers and the final decision as to their stationing, the annual pastoral address to the churches, pastoral consideration of the state of the church and pastoral efficiency, and 'all ministerial and pastoral subjects of like nature'. No definition was offered of the word 'pastoral'. Reception of ministers into full connexion with the Conference (effectively their licensing) was reserved to the representative session, but the decision to ordain, and the ordination service itself, were acts of the ministerial session. In practice this arrangement meant that a number of issues were brought to both sessions, particularly matters of doctrine and ecumenical relations. In many respects the distinction between temporal and spiritual was retained, and there was no mechanism by which conflicting decisions by the two sessions on the same issue could be reconciled. This could, and did, lead to difficulty and effectively to a ministerial veto.

As a result a major revision of the Conference was adopted in 1988–89. This now clearly locates the authority of the Conference in its representative session, at least one half of whom must be lay. Apart from oversight of those in training for the ordained (presbyteral) ministry and acting as a final court of appeal in the discipline of ministers, all the decisions of the ministerial session are recommendations reported to the representative session, although in relation to ministerial candidature, ordination and retirement that session cannot act without such a recommendation. The ministerial session now meets essentially as a professional gathering, concerned not only with the maintenance of professional standards, but also with the general life of the church, about which it can express its views to the representative session. Similar provisions were introduced in 1998 for the order of deacons, whose representatives now meet as a committee of the Conference.

Thus, although the Wesleyan tradition continues in the existence of a separate gathering of presbyters for the discussion of Conference business, it is true to say that as at present configured the Conference, comprising ordained and lay in more or less equal numbers, exercises oversight over the whole life, 'temporal' and 'spiritual', of the Methodist Church, but it has been a long journey to reach this point, and earlier statements, prior to 1990, about Conference *episcope* have to be understood in the light of the distinction then obtaining between the authority of ordained presbyters and that of lay members.

Theological rationale

What theology or theologies can be said to underlie these attitudes to the Conference? The answer is not always apparent. Because the Conference in the 1790s was driven by circumstances into a legislative role, it is the language of government rather than pastoral oversight that dominates all sides in the polemical literature, even though in practice all the Conferences of divided Methodism would continue to comment on the spiritual state of their societies. But when the Wesleyan ministers came to defend their exclusive jurisdiction it was to theology, and specifically to Scripture, that they turned.

We have seen the understanding of the pastoral office upon which they grounded their practice. Following the line taken by John Wesley himself they held that the New Testament made no distinction between presbyters and bishops and that consequently all powers of oversight resided in the travelling preachers who were responsible for the welfare and progress of the connexion, including authority to select and admit (ordain) new members to their ranks.

As we have seen, the changes in 1878 were not driven by a change in theological conviction. If they had been, negotiations for the 1932 union would have been less difficult. The theology of the pastoral office, although now restricted in scope, remained. Ministers retained their own session and held half the seats in the other.

What of the non-Wesleyan bodies? Considering the political atmosphere of the period 1790–1850, it is not surprising that there was much talk of 'liberty' and the right to self-government. There were ecclesiastical precedents to hand, too, in congregationalism. But it would be mistaken to think those were the only influences. Apologists appealed to the New Testament to show the involvement of the whole church in its government. Government, however, as for the Wesleyans, was the key concept. The wider, pastoral, language of oversight is hard to find in their writing about the Conference.

Surprisingly, little use seems to have been made by them, in print at least, of 'the priesthood of all believers'. They regarded the Wesleyans as exercising 'priestly domination' and 'popery' comparable to that which obtained at the Reformation, and asserted against it the freedom and right of every member of the church to exercise whatever ministry God might from time to time call them to, and to take an equal share in decisions about the church's governance, but they do not seem to have expressed this in the theological language of universal priesthood.

By the twentieth century, however, it was certainly being discussed and at the union of 1932 it was incorporated into the statement of doctrinal standards of the united church and was instrumental in allaying non-Wesleyan fears about the status of the ministry:

> *Christ's ministers in the church are stewards in the household of God and shepherds of his flock. Some are called and ordained to this sole occupation and have a principal and directing part in these great duties but they hold no priesthood differing in kind from that which is common to all the Lord's people and have no exclusive title to the preaching of the gospel or the care of souls. These ministries are shared with them by others to whom also the Spirit divides his gifts severally as he wills.*
>
> *The Methodist Church holds the doctrine of the priesthood of all believers and consequently believes that no priesthood exists which belongs exclusively to a particular order or class of men [sic] but in the exercise of its corporate life and worship special qualifications for the discharge of special duties are required and thus the principle of representative selection is recognised.*

Significantly, the first of those paragraphs was lifted almost verbatim from a statement adopted by the Wesleyan Conference in 1908, and shows how far that body had come by that time. Earlier, Wesleyan writers such as W.B. Pope had acknowledged universal priesthood as a Reformation doctrine, but made little application of it. However, there is still in these paragraphs a reference to the 'principal and directing part' taken by ordained presbyters, which was the theological undergirding for the reserved powers still assigned to the ministerial session of the Conference in 1932.

What of the changes in 1988–89? Both practical and theological factors were involved. The exclusive authority of the ministers over their own ranks was gradually being eroded. Lay people were becoming involved in the selection of candidates and in various committees dealing with their oversight. Slowly the conviction was taking hold that lay people had insights and experience that were relevant in such cases. There was also the difficulty of conflicting decisions taken by the two sessions, to which we have referred.

Perhaps more important, however, is the fact that in 1932 the uniting church had included a significant proportion, about 40%, of members and ministers who had been steeped in the non-Wesleyan traditions, and who might as a matter of practice accord ministers a 'principal and directing part', but would continue to appeal to the priesthood of all believers to insist that in principle the exercise of all forms of ministry is open to those whom God calls and equips, whether ordained or lay. Often that appeal was in negative terms, about individual 'rights', and lacked the rich corporate and liturgical content of the New Testament references and the classic expositions of Reformation writers. But that non-Wesleyan tradition persists, and was for many a driving force behind the changes to the Conference introduced in 1988–89.

The principal factor, however, in 1988–89 was a wider ecumenical shift in theological understanding placing greater emphasis on the 'people of God'. It is no coincidence that another report presented to the 1988 Conference was entitled *The Ministry of the People of God*. Greater stress was being placed on the calling of every Christian individually, and of all Christians collectively, to take responsibility for the life and mission of the church. It came to be recognised that all Christians are 'lay' in that they belong to the one *laos* of God, and that the differentiation between ordained and unordained is a differentiation between specific callings and gifts. One stimulus to this had been the structure of the 1964 Dogmatic Constitution on the Church of the Second Vatican Council (*Lumen Gentium*), which discusses church and ministry in the context of the calling of the People of God. A similar emphasis can be seen in World Council of Churches publications of the period. This was more than a reaffirmation of the priesthood of all believers as understood earlier. That tended to concentrate on rights. Now the stress could be on gifts. Every member, as a member of the Body of Christ, had a contribution to make towards its well-being and a share of responsibility for the quality of its life. The implication was that oversight, *episcope*, is a responsibility in which all share.

Such an emphasis resonates well with Methodist experience. Ever since John Wesley had instituted the office of class leader lay people have exercised oversight in their local situation. Underneath the conflicts over governance in Methodism's history lies a frustration that lay people, called to and entrusted with oversight, were only entrusted so far. For most people the exercise of that responsibility will be in the local church of which they are members, for some, in the wider sphere of the circuit or district. Those who are office holders will have particular perspectives and exercise specific responsibilities, but none in principle can abdicate. In the governing Conference, where oversight responsibility for the faith and order, worship and mission, spiritual well-being and material maintenance of the church ultimately resides, *episcope* is shared by ordained and lay on terms which acknowledge that while some are particularly called and ordained to a ministry of oversight, and are consequently more strongly represented proportionately to their overall numbers than lay people, they have no exclusive voice, and no over-riding veto, in the process of discerning and executing God's will for his church.[4]

Personal, collegial, communal

Recent ecumenical discussion of *episcope* has distinguished three ways in which it may – indeed should – be exercised: personally, collegially and communally. The personal aspect may be exercised not only by those designated bishops but by others, ordained or lay, who have leadership responsibilities. 'Collegial' refers to the collective action of those having personal oversight who consult together, agree on common policies and so act in concert. The communal dimension refers to the involvement of the whole body of believers in consultation.[5] These definitions leave unclear the precise relation between the first two and the third. Are those with personal oversight subject to the communal authority, or is the communal gathering simply advisory? Of course the problem may be resolved by assigning separate spheres of authority to each, but the often-used phrase 'bishop in council' fails to provide for the situation where the two disagree.

Personal *episcope* is exercised in Methodism in many ways, by the President of the Conference, district Chairs, circuit Superintendents and other ministers in their various appointments and by lay officers and pastoral assistants. But all are accountable through the appropriate oversight bodies ultimately to the Conference, from which all exercise of *episcope* is delegated, by ordination or appointment. There are various contexts in which collegial oversight is exercised, for example in circuit staff meetings which may often include both ministers and lay officers.

But what of the Conference? As we have seen, for John Wesley the Conference was advisory. Oversight resided in him and those to whom he delegated it, including not only the travelling preachers but also local stewards and class leaders. For the New Connexion and Bible Christians, authority lay with the Conference; for the Primitive Methodists in the early days, partly with the Conference and partly with the district synods, later with the Conference; and for the United Methodist Free Churches with the Conference for connexional (nationwide) matters, such as the deployment of ministers, and with the relevant society and circuit meetings for all local matters. Representative ministers and lay persons were involved in all of these and there were no special powers reserved to individuals, so oversight in these traditions was truly communal. The case with the Wesleyans and with Methodism post-1932 is more complex.

We have already seen that in the early nineteenth century the Wesleyans developed a doctrine of the pastoral office. The logic of this position was that oversight resided, not in the Conference per se, but in its members, and was derived from their divine calling and consequent recognition as pastors (after 1836 by formal ordination with laying-on of hands). The Conference represented their 'united counsels', ensured consistency of oversight throughout the connexion and reinforced the authority of each minister. The Conference did not delegate authority to the ministers, they imparted their own authority to it. In 1829 Richard Watson could write, 'The sum of [the Conference's] power is nothing more than the power which is essentially vested in each Minister, by the very duties which he is under scriptural obligation to perform.' Each was 'received' by the Conference into connexion with it on condition of observing its rules. They were accountable to each other and were regularly interrogated in the annual Conference and district meetings. The outcome was collegial episcopacy in all but name.

The adjustments made in 1878, when lay people were included alongside ministers in a representative session, introduced a communal element but dealt with the tension between personal-collegial and communal by splitting the responsibilities. The communal body essentially dealt with 'temporal' matters while the collegial body of ministers retained oversight over the 'spiritual' (and legally authority still lay with the collegial 'Legal Hundred', established by the 1784 Deed, who had to ratify all decisions). This arrangement was essentially carried over at Methodist Union in 1932 without the potential veto of the Legal Hundred. The ministerial session retained a collegial responsibility for its own membership and to some extent for the wider church. It is only with the changes of 1988–89 that Conference *episcope* became truly communal. Such collegial ministerial oversight as remains, in the sense of retaining a final decision, is confined to recruitment and final appeals over discipline. For the rest it processes business for final ratification elsewhere and acts as a gathering for mutual support. The same may be said of the order of deacons, with the exception that being also a religious order there is collegiality in the annual Convocation.

Thus a Conference exercising *episcope* over the church has been a feature of Methodism since John Wesley. Its composition and powers, so far as Britain is concerned, and its theological rationale, have changed over the years. The language of *episcope*, introduced by ecumenical discussion, is recent, but the exercise of oversight, collectively and individually, has always been present. It is ironic that what now obtains, oversight over the whole life of the church shared by lay and ordained on equal terms, was first introduced by the Methodist New Connexion in 1797 (without any separate ministerial gathering). It has taken a long time to return to that point. But it now rests on broader theological foundations. It is appropriate that the story should be rehearsed in a tribute to Dr John Newton, who chaired the commission that produced the proposals enacted in 1988–89.

Notes

1 For example *The Nature and Mission of the Church* (2005), Faith and Order Paper 198, Geneva: World Council of Churches, paras.90-98.
2 The story is set out in Kirby, James E. (2000), *The Episcopacy in American Methodism*, Nashville: Kingswood.
3 See, e.g. Bunting, T.P. (1871), *Laymen in Conference?* London: Elliot Stock.
4 More recently the attempt has been made to link shared oversight to the relational aspects of the doctrine of the Trinity, but it has not been very fully developed. See *The Nature of Oversight*, section 4.7.
5 See *The Nature and Mission of the Church*, para.96, and earlier, *Baptism, Eucharist and Ministry*, p26 para.26.

A Methodist Re-Reading of St Paul

Neil G. Richardson

Some years ago I undertook a survey of commentaries on the Epistle to the Hebrews. The survey was to be presented to the British Catholic–Methodist Committee, of which I was then a member. Predictably, perhaps, the commentaries I studied reflected, in varying ways, the Christian tradition to which the author belonged.

In this paper I offer a Methodist re-reading of St Paul, with particular reference to his letter to the Romans. In the first section, 'Religion and Faith', I look at Paul's teaching on justification and the law in the light of recent scholarly debates about Paul and of Wesley's sermon 'The Almost Christian'. In the second section, I shall seek to relate the lack of binary opposites in Romans (and in Paul's other letters), to another of Wesley's sermons, 'The Catholic Spirit'. A short concluding section will draw out of some of the contemporary implications of the argument.

1. Religion and Faith in St Paul and in Wesley

The publication in 1977 of E.P. Sanders's *Paul and Palestinian Judaism*[1] was a watershed in Pauline studies. Although some of his arguments had been foreshadowed in various ways by earlier scholars,[2] Sanders presented a massively detailed argument that salvation by works was not, and never had been, the *credo* of Judaism, contrary to what many Christian scholars and preachers had thought. Ever since, New Testament scholars have rightly been more sensitive to the danger of misrepresenting Judaism and what Paul has to say about it. Such caution, however, should not obscure the searching implications of Pauline teaching. The canonical status of Romans for Christians gives it a universal significance which transcends its original context, and so Paul's critique of both Jewish and Gentile religion in this letter extends to all human religion, Christianity included. All religion is easily distorted, becoming, in its distorted form, a divisive and even destructive force in human life. (My working definition of 'religion' will become clear in the ensuing discussion; religion can be identified by its 'fruits').

In Paul's opening salvo against idolatry (Romans 1.18-32), he has, contrary to the received view, both Jewish and Gentile idolatry in his sights; he refers to 'all human (*anthropon*) ungodliness and wickedness' (v.18), not 'all Gentile ungodliness'; in v.23, for example, there is a clear echo of the golden calf story in Exodus.[3] So God's own people are not excluded from the charge of idolatry, Christians as well as Jews. (I note how Paul, in 1 Corinthians 10.1-13, relates the experience of Israel to the Church).

In the apostle's critique of religion, the word *sarx* (lit. 'flesh'[4] is especially important. No single word or phrase in English adequately conveys the meaning of *sarx* in the negative sense in which Paul often uses the word.[5] However, the observations of two scholars take us a long way towards understanding it. Ernst Käsemann notes that the word is used in the Old Testament and in Judaism to denote the difference between the creating God and the creature, in the sense not only of weakness, but also of resistance to the Creator.[6] More recently, Leander Keck has defined *sarx* in its negative sense as 'the physical or phenomenal when it inappropriately exercises power'.[7]

Some illustrations may indicate that these definitions are not as far removed from contemporary church reality as they might at first seem. For example, when the use, maintenance and financing of its premises dominates the life of a local church, 'the physical' is exercising inappropriate power. When a local church is dominated by one group or one family, marginalising and excluding others, that, too, constitutes life *kata sarka*, 'according to the flesh'. When Sunday worship is dominated by the contribution of the choir, because that's what the choir has always done, again, *sarx* prevails over spirit. In fact, it should be obvious from some of Paul's other letters that religion distorted by 'fleshly' considerations can be found in a church, as well as in other religions. Of the Galatians Paul asks, 'Having started with the Spirit, are you now ending with the flesh (*nun en sarki epiteleisthe*)?' (Galatians 3.3b).[8]

One characteristic of living 'according to the flesh' is its divisiveness. That much is clear both from what Paul says to the church at Corinth (1 Cor.3.3, cf. 1.11-13), and also from his criticisms of the Galatians (5.13-15, cf. vv.16-21). The divisiveness of fleshly living is implied also in the downward spiral of Romans 1.18-32: human idolatry dehumanises people, leading both to immorality and social fragmentation.

So Paul's language shows that 'flesh' and 'Spirit', cannot be simply identified with Jewish and Gentile religions on the one hand and Christian faith on the other. The real antithesis is not 'Jewish' and 'Christian'. This would be not only a serious misreading of Paul, but, in the first century, anachronistic too. Paul's use of *sarx* points up the universality of human failure and weakness in all religion, Christianity not excepted. And one of the hallmarks of such failure is division.

It is time to turn to Wesley's sermon, 'The Almost Christian', preached at St Mary's Oxford in 1741.[9] In the first part of the sermon Wesley asks what is implied in being almost a Christian, and in the second part what is involved in being altogether a Christian.

The profile of 'the almost Christian' begins with what Wesley calls 'heathen honesty' and justice, including love and practical assistance, or, at least, 'the assistance anyone could give another without prejudice to himself'.[10] From this modest beginning, the profile becomes increasingly religious. The 'almost Christian' has a form of godliness, abstains from wine 'wherein is excess', does not seek revenge when wronged, lives by the 'golden rule', 'does not confine himself to cheap and easy offices of kindness', but 'labours and suffers for the profit of many'.[11]

There is still more in Wesley's portrait of the 'almost Christian'. Such a person uses all the means of grace, 'and at all opportunities', coming to church not lightly, but with real sincerity – a word Wesley is careful to define as 'a real, inward principle of religion', which includes a genuine wish to serve God and do his will.[12]

At this point, Wesley wisely anticipates the question forming in the minds of his hearers/readers: how can a person be and do all these things, and still only be 'almost a Christian'? Not surprisingly, he proceeds to cite his own experience, before going on to offer a profile of one who is 'altogether a Christian'.

Wesley begins this second profile by quoting the two great commandments, to love God and our neighbour, but then goes on to speak of the faith which is 'the ground of all': the faith which 'works by love' (Galatians 5.6).[13] As the sermon moves towards its climax and its final appeal, Wesley says this (once again echoing Paul's Letter to the Romans):

> *The great question of all, then, still remains. Is the love of God shed abroad in your heart? Can you cry out, 'My God and my all?' Do you desire nothing but him? Are you happy in God? And is this commandment written in your heart, 'that he who loveth God love his brother also?'*[14]

In quoting Wesley at length, I do not thereby accord him canonical status. Nor do I wish to endorse a kind of doctrine of infallibility. Wesley was a fallible human being, as recent studies have shown well enough.[15] The question we need to ask here is simply whether Wesley's argument is Pauline. Even when we allow for the way in which his own experience has so clearly shaped the sermon, I think we have to say it is. The leading characteristics of the 'almost Christian' are sincerity, commitment, and a dutiful concern to do the right thing. What is missing in Pauline terms is 'life in Christ', or life *en pneumati*, ('in the Spirit'). How are they to be gauged? Here the Wesleyan answer is also the Pauline answer: 'the faith which works by love'.[16] So we return to Paul.

Paul's previous religious experience, like Wesley's, doubtless influenced his theology. Two words, in particular, claim our attention: the words which, in the older translations, are rendered as 'boast' and 'zeal'. Both of them, so crucial in understanding both Paul's gospel and his critique of human religion, engender a division into 'us' and 'them'.

Käsemann claims that the verb 'boast' (*kauchomai*) serves to differentiate true and false religion.[17] While he is wrong to designate Romans 2.1-11 as 'a polemic against the Jewish tradition', he is on firmer ground in suggesting that Paul's argumentation sees Jewish reality as 'exemplary for humanity as a whole'.[18] So human religion, (*not* Jewish religion *per se)* becomes the sphere for inappropriate 'boasting'.

Once again, a literal translation of Paul can obscure the significance of what he is saying. 'Boasting' (in its Pauline context) '... is an expression of human dignity and freedom'. What is crucial is a person's 'lord': by their boasting, a person 'tells to whom he belongs'.[19] A contemporary analogy may help us appreciate what Paul is saying here. To whom do I, as a Methodist minister, belong? To whom is my first loyalty? It cannot be the Church, or even 'Christianity'. The only Pauline answer I can give is 'Christ, and him crucified':

> *May I never boast of anything except the cross of our Lord Jesus Christ, by which the world has been crucified to me, and I to the world.* (Galatians 6.14).

By contrast, Paul implicitly criticises his fellow-Jews for boasting 'in God' and boasting 'in (the) law' (Romans 2.17 and 23). What is wrong with such boasting? We need to tread carefully, in the light of Sanders's strictures of Christian stereotyping of Judaism. Jewish boasting in the law is misguided, according to Paul, because, he argues, his fellow Jews do not keep the law, and so bring God's name into disrepute (v.24). (The analogy of Christians failing to practise what they preach is not far to seek.) But there is perhaps another reason why, in Paul's view, such boasting in the law is now inappropriate. It can no longer be a basis for dividing humankind into 'Jews' and 'Gentiles', the people of God and 'outsiders'.

That may also indicate why a certain kind of boasting in God is not appropriate in the light of the gospel. If the God in whom we boast is 'our God', differentiating us from the rest of humankind who do not believe in 'our God', then we are sowing the seeds of a division which denies the gospel. Paul goes on to ask – after insisting that all grounds for 'boasting' are now precluded – 'Is God God of Jews only?' He answers his own question: 'Is he not God of the Gentiles also? Yes, of Gentiles also' (Romans 3.27-9).

We are bound to keep asking our question: does Paul's critique of Jewish boasting by implication criticise inappropriate Christian boasting as well? There is one verse in the Pauline corpus where the apostle refers to Christian boasting in God: 'But more than that, we even boast in God through our Lord Jesus Christ, through we have now been granted reconciliation.' (Romans 5.11).

Why is this boasting permissible, when the other (Jewish) boasting in God is implicitly criticised? It can only be because it is 'through our Lord Jesus Christ'. In saying this, of course, we are only a step away from a Christian triumphalism based on 'our God'. I suggest we need to interpret this verse in the light of the only other reference to Christian boasting in Paul, the one to which I have already referred: boasting in the cross of Christ (Galatians 6.14).

The cross, however, turns all human boasting upside down. The scandal and degradation of a crucifixion was the unlikeliest foundation imaginable for human dignity and freedom (Käsemann's definition of boasting). But its theological implications are as important as the 'scandalous' historical reality. The cross subverted the old distinction between the people of God and outsiders, Jew and Gentile – and, of course, other divisions which deface human society. We shall need to return to this in the next section. If Paul's question in Romans 3.29 has to be reworded, in order for us to appreciate its challenge, 'Is God the God of Christians only?', what does that imply about Christian self-understanding today?

Another characteristic of inauthentic religion, according to Paul, is zeal. This word is not always used negatively in Paul's letters, but where it is we need to recall its Jewish background, recognising that the implicit critique of a Jewish tradition (not *the* Jewish tradition) is eminently transferable to Christian traditions. Phinehas became the Jewish 'role model' for zeal because he slew the enemies of Yahweh.[20] We might reasonably conclude that this is an extreme example of religious zeal, but such zeal is often directed at perceived enemies as Paul himself well knew. In zealous religion, there is often an 'us' and a 'them'; 'new perspective' scholars have rightly noted Paul's expression '*their* (i.e. Israel's) righteousness' (Romans 10.3).

But again it needs to be emphasised that 'boasting' and 'zeal', in the senses in which Paul criticises them, are not distinctively Jewish, even though Paul's remarks are directed towards his fellow Jews. Kenneth Grayston, writing from 'the new perspective', comments as follows on Romans 7.1-6:

> *God's bond with Israel has become too closely confined by the flesh — the habits and impulses of Jewish society: Paul wishes to free it to receive the energy of the Spirit.*

But he goes on to say:

> *Devout Christian groups may recognize themselves... in particularism that denies faith and sincerity to groups that revere God differently*.[21]

I conclude that both Paul and Wesley are witnesses to a distinction vital to the gospel. It is a distinction the Church rediscovers in times of revival and renewal: the distinction between religion and faith (in its Pauline and Wesleyan sense). Paul bears witness to a religion whose hallmarks are inappropriate 'boasting' and 'zeal', with the consequent division into 'us' and 'them' which such religion always brings. Wesley, in his sermon 'The Almost Christian', testifies to a religion which is genuinely sincere, but one marked by duty rather than by 'the faith which works by love'. This distinction between such religion and 'the faith which works by love', so relevant to our day when religion and the Christian Church are under fire from many quarters, brings us to another theme in our re-reading of Romans.

2. Is There an 'Us' and 'Them' in Paul?

Most religious people, Christians included, are inclined to think in terms of 'us' and 'them' – and in various ways. At local church level, we may distinguish between those who support the church, and those who don't, those who attend, and those who don't. Those who don't attend or support the Church are often called 'outsiders'. And, of course, church life itself can be marred by divisions (those who agree with 'our' theology, preferences in worship and so on and those who don't), within local churches and across different Christian traditions. In this section we look first at the implications of Wesley's and Paul's teaching for Christian unity, before turning our attention to their wider implications.

Wesley's sermon 'The Catholic Spirit' has been much quoted in recent years. Perhaps it has been over-used, sometimes being cited in support of an inclusiveness which Wesley himself would not have owned. Space permits only a summary of Wesley's conclusions. But I quote it here in order to explore, first, in what ways it points us beyond the kind of religion which issues in an 'us' and 'them', and, secondly, whether Wesley's teaching is Pauline.

Wesley's text is 2 Kings 10.15:

> And when he (sc. Jehu) was departed thence, he lighted on Jehonadab son of Rechab coming to meet him and said, Is thine heart right, as my heart is with thy heart? And Jehonadab answered, It is. If it be, give me thy hand.[22]

I note two points about Wesley's argument: first, his searching answer to the question he poses of the meaning of Jehu's question to Jehonadab: 'Is thine heart right, as my heart is with thy heart?' Wesley responds that it means, in the first place, 'Is thy heart right with God?', but goes on to say far more: for example, 'Dost thou "know Jesus Christ and him crucified?" Does he "dwell in thee and thou in him?" Is he "formed in thy heart by faith?"' Wesley says much more about the heart that is 'right'. Here we note only his use yet again of Galatians 5.6: 'Is thy faith *energoumene di'agapes* – filled with the energy of love?'[23]

From this foundation Wesley goes on to establish what is, and what is not, a catholic spirit. It cannot be the basis for latitudinarianism, for a person of a truly catholic spirit:

> ... is fixed as the sun in his [sic] judgment concerning the main branches of Christian doctrine. Observe this, you who know not what spirit ye are of, but are for jumbling all opinions together.[24]

At the same time:

> ... while he is steadily fixed in his religious principles, in what he believes to be the truth as it is in Jesus; while he firmly adheres to the worship of God which he judges to be most acceptable in his sight; and while he is united by the tenderest and closest ties to one particular congregation; his heart is enlarged towards all mankind, those he knows and those he does not; he embraces with strong and cordial affection neighbours and strangers, friends and enemies. This is catholic or universal love. And he that has this is of a catholic spirit. For love alone gives the title to this character – catholic love is a catholic spirit'.[25]

This sermon, like Wesley's sermon 'The Almost Christian', is also, in my view, deeply Pauline. Romans 14.1-15.7 address some deep divisions in the Christian community (or communities) in Rome. The divisions are not, in Paul's view, about Christian fundamentals. But the opposing parties (as they appear to have been) may have thought they were. Whether they did or not, their attitudes to each other clearly lacked the love of which Wesley speaks, (if we are correct in assuming that Paul is describing existing conduct in Rome, rather than being merely prescriptive). Paul condemns 'despising' and 'judging' – two verbs which occur several times in this discussion (e.g. 14.3 and 10), and he goes on to insist that no-one should act in a way that damages the faith of a fellow Christian or the unity of the fellowship, and also that no one should act contrary to their conscience (14.13-23). Wesley's teaching is similar. In the sermon 'The Catholic Spirit' he emphasises that:

> ... 'give me thy hand' means neither 'Be of my opinion', nor 'Embrace my modes of worship'.[26]

I also note that Paul assumes and emphasises the common Christ-centred life for which Wesley argues (e.g. Romans 14.3, 7-9, 15.7).

Paul and Wesley, therefore, in their different contexts, argue for the unity and diversity which in their view is one of the hallmarks of authentic religion, the 'faith which works by love'. Such faith completely precludes divisions which degenerate into a destructive 'us' and 'them'. But can this Catholic spirit be extended further? There are many ways in which Christians express the distinction between themselves and others: 'believers' and 'unbelievers' for example, or, most obvious of all, Christians and non-Christians. Here I wish to explore the extent to which this distinction between 'us' and 'them', however expressed, is to be found in the letters of Paul.

Paul Meyer, an American New Testament scholar, claims that Paul's contrasting terms *pneumatikos* ('spiritual') and *sarkinos* ('fleshly') in Romans 7.14 have come to dominate our understanding of this and other passages in Paul, through the influence of St Augustine. These two words, says Meyer:

> ... are now made to differentiate two classes of humans: the religious person who is righteous, wise... re-born... and the irreligious, the ungodly and the sinner on the other... This is the language of binary opposites, used by triumphalist religion to separate humankind into two groups of people, the saved and the damned'.[27]

Is this condemnation of the religious language of binary opposites too sweeping? It is possible that Meyer's remarks have been sharpened by his observations of the religious right in America. Whether that is so or not, I propose to test the accuracy of what he goes on to say:

> ... the depth to which any reading of Paul that clings to such a division between the 'godly' and the 'ungodly' has misunderstood the apostle is sounded accurately only when one realises that the whole of Paul's epistle (sc. Romans) is but a single massive argument against the conventional uses of this distinction.[28]

So I ask: is there any basis in Paul for 'Christians', 'believers', 'the faithful', or whatever self-referential terms we use, distinguishing themselves from the rest of humankind? Or have we reverted to the very binary language which Paul, according to Meyer, sought to exclude from religion?

Paul's language is instructive. The word 'Christian' does not occur at all in his writings; at this stage it may have been a term used by the authorities of this strange new Jewish sect.[29] Instead we find several different words or phrases referring to 'Christians'. But these words rarely or never attract their opposites. We shall briefly review the evidence.

Paul regularly refers to Christians as those who are 'in Christ' or 'in the Lord'. These expressions are not one half of an opposing pair. Even in Galatians, where Paul contrasts life in Christ with life under the law or 'according to the flesh', the contrast is not between two groups of people, but between two quite different ways of religious living. To choose one of those ways – the Judaising way – would indeed take the Galatians into an 'us' and 'them' contrast: the contrast between themselves as practising Jewish Christians, and Gentiles. For Paul, there is no such contrast, only a 'new creation' (Gal. 6.15). In a similar way to 'in Christ', the expression 'in the Lord' is never used by Paul as one half of a contrasting pair.

This lack of opposites in Paul is particularly striking when we turn to his preferred way of greeting his addressees at the beginning of many of his letters. He greets or describes them as God's 'holy ones'; the intended recipients of the collection he also refers to as 'the holy ones'.[30] But only once in Paul's writings does this descriptor of Christians attract a contrasting term:

> *When any of you has a grievance against another, do you dare to take it to court before the unrighteous* (adikon), *instead of before the saints* (ton hagion)?' (1 Corinthians 6.1)

Here, however, Paul could not have articulated his argument at all without such a contrasting word as *adikon*. But it is significant that he chose that word, with its more specific meaning of 'unjust'. (Courts in the Graeco-Roman world were not renowned for administering impartial justice).

The Greek word which functions as the opposite of *adikos* is *dikaios*, variously translated as 'righteous' or 'just'. Here we might have expected Paul to use these words to contrast Christians and non-Christians. In fact, both words are infrequent in Paul, and Paul never uses them in the contrasting way which we find in some Jewish writings of this period.[31]

Another pair of words occur more frequently in Paul: *pistos* ('believing' or 'faithful') and *apistos* ('unbelieving' or 'faithless'). *Pistos* sometimes refers to the faithfulness of God (e.g. 1 Cor. 1.9), and sometimes to a specific, named Christian (e.g. 1 Cor. 4.17). Paul uses both words as a contrasting pair only in the Corinthian letters, but even here Paul's use of these words is surprising. We note, first, 2 Corinthians 6.15, which occurs in a passage where, for once, Paul's language *is* dominated by opposites:

> *What agreement does Christ have with Beliar? Or what does a believer* (pisto) *share with an unbeliever* (apisto).

Many scholars have questioned whether the section in which this verse occurs, (6.14-7.1) is Pauline on the grounds of its allegedly unpauline language and theology. If it is Pauline, its presence here may owe something to the situation at Corinth, where over-confident Christians were interacting with paganism to the detriment of others' faith, if not their own.[32]

Paul's use of *apistos* ('unbeliever') in 1 Corinthians is especially interesting. At 7.12-15 he discusses what Christians married to *apistoi* should do, concluding that they should not seek a separation unless their partner wants one. Paul gives, as a reason for staying together, the hope that through the marriage the *apistos* might be saved (v.16), having already recognised that through this marriage the unbelieving partner 'is sanctified' (*hegiastai*, v.14). Although Paul does not refer to Jesus at this point, the life of Jesus is highly relevant; Jesus did not overturn the purity laws, but demonstrated by his actions his belief that purity could overcome impurity. By contrast, the Qumran literature (the Dead Sea Scrolls), reflects a concern about the reverse process.[33]

This may help to explain the other occurrences of 'unbelievers' (*apistoi*) in 1 Corinthians:

> *If an unbeliever invites you to a meal and you are disposed to go, eat whatever is set before you...* (10.27)

This scenario suggests that the Christians of Corinth interacted freely with their non-Christian contemporaries. Indeed, Paul says elsewhere that it would be quite unrealistic to imagine that they could do otherwise (1 Cor. 5.10). Contact between Christians and their contemporaries is envisaged in a later discussion:

> *If, therefore, the whole church comes together and all speak in tongues and outsiders or unbelievers (idiotai e apistoi) will they not say to you that you are out of your mind? But if all prophesy, an unbeliever or outsider who enters is reproved by all and called to account by all. After the secrets of the unbeliever's hearts are disclosed, that person will bow down before God and worship him, declaring, 'God is really among you'* (1 Cor. 14.23-5).

The evidence of 1 Corinthians may seem to weaken the argument I am making here. But the point to notice is that Paul needs these terms when he is addressing specific problems; otherwise, this language is not prominent, and the contrast between 'believers' and 'unbelievers' does not dominate his theology at all. There is, however, one other contrast we should note. It occurs in 1 Corinthians 1.18, where the present participle of the verb 'perish' appears to be contrasted twice with the verb 'save'. (There is a similar contrast at 2 Corinthians 2.15). Yet it is significant that Paul uses the present participle (so also at 2 Corinthians 2.15), and in both passages the contrasts are not so much between two groups of people, but between (in 1 Corinthians) human weakness and divine power, and (in 2 Corinthians) between God's saving and destructive power.[34]

So Paul rarely contrasts the holy, the righteous, the believing with their opposites. But that does not mean that the response of a person to the gospel was a matter of indifference to him. That was clearly not so. But if Paul's language is not dominated by such binary opposites, in the way that some contemporary Jewish writings were, and much subsequent Christian writing has been, what does dominate Paul's letters? The briefest glance at a concordance will show that, alongside the frequently occurring words *theos* ('God'), *Christos* ('Christ') and *Pneuma* ('Spirit'), there are two which, by virtue of their frequency or the contexts in which they occur, may fairly be said to be at the heart of Paul's gospel. They are the words *pas, pantes* ('every' 'all'), and *heis* ('one'). Two passages from Paul will illustrate their theological significance.

Romans 5.12-21 is one passage where the words 'one' and 'all' are crucial to Paul's argument. Paul contrasts the deeds of Adam and Christ ('one man', vv.12, 15, 16, 17, 18, 19), and the effects of those deeds on 'all' or 'the many' (vv.12, 15, 18, 19). Karl Barth's comment on this passage takes us, I suggest, to the heart of Paul's gospel, and, at the same time, shows why his letters are not dominated by the opposing words we have examined here:

> ... *Paul does not limit his context to Christ's relationship to believers but gives fundamentally the same account of His relationship to all . The fact of Christ is here presented as something that... includes all. The nature of Christ objectively conditions human nature and the work of Christ makes an objective difference to the life and destiny of all... What is Christian is secretly but fundamentally identical with what is universally human.*[35]

The other passage in Paul which illustrates the crucial importance of the words 'one' and 'all' in Paul's gospel is 2 Corinthians 5.14-21: '... one has died for all; therefore all have died. And he died for all....' (v.14b, 15a).

Another Pauline phrase takes us to the heart of the matter: there is a 'new creation' (Gal. 6:15, 2 Cor. 5.16). This is why there is no opposing group to the *ecclesia*: it is an eschatological reality, and, as such, it is neither in competition with, nor stands in opposition to, any other human group. As the (probably) deutero-pauline Ephesians puts it: 'Our struggle is not against enemies of blood and flesh...' (6.12).

A contemporary Roman Catholic writer, James Alison, puts his finger on the fundamental reason why Paul's theology is not dominated by binary opposites. Writing of Christ, the universal victim, Alison has this to say:

The unity which is given by and in the risen victim is purely given. It is indicative of no superiority at all over anyone else. Anyone who genuinely knows the crucified and risen victim can never again belong wholeheartedly to any other social, or cultural or religious groups. He or she will always belong critically to all other groups, because all other groups derive their unity over-against someone or some other group. The only unity to which he or she cannot escape belonging is the new unity of humanity that the Holy Spirit creates out of the risen victim, the unity which subverts all other unities...'

Alison goes on to contrast this 'new unity of humanity' with the 'sectarian belonging' often created by churches – indeed, the Church – that is, 'a definable cultural group with a clearly marked inside and outside, and firm ideas as to who belongs outside'.[36]

Conclusion

I have argued here that Christian faith becomes divisive in ways quite alien to its true heart and spirit. Perhaps our problem is having too strong a church identity, and too weak a Christian one. As a result, the Church easily becomes sectarian in a way which denies what Barth called the 'universal human', which it is called to embody. Tragically, we project on to the New Testament antinomies and opposites which are not there, or which are not as central or as fundamental as we imagine. I am not ignoring in this argument important verses such as the saying of Jesus: 'Do you think that I have come to bring peace to the earth? No, I tell you, but rather division!' (Luke 12.51, cf. Matthew 10.34).

A Church which is prophetic will inevitably be divisive. But that will be a divisiveness which arises out of a costly faithfulness to the gospel (provided, of course, that such prophecy is motivated by the love which is utterly central to Christian faith). But even in such a situation of costly witness, the consequent divisions will not be the kind of binary opposites which, I have argued, are marginal in Paul's writings. In such a situation, a hard-pressed church will need to recall the Ephesians text: 'Our struggle is not against enemies of blood and flesh' (6.12).

This is not an argument which can be dismissed as dangerously 'liberal'. Paul and John Wesley both teach us that there is a breadth to authentically Christian faith which is neither a superficial inclusiveness nor the latitudinarianism decried by Wesley. Thomas Merton was a twentieth-century Christian who admirably embodied the spirituality towards which Paul and Wesley point: the closer a person draws to God, the more such a person will be immersed in the life of the world. The 'faith which works by love' will see to that.

Postscript

I was delighted to be invited to contribute to this collection of essays in honour of John Newton. John's welcome to me (as a young minister in his first appointment), and his colleagueship at Wesley College, Bristol in 1971 I have always remembered with gratitude. John himself admirably exemplifies the depth and breadth of spirituality to which I allude in my conclusion.

Notes

1   Sanders, E.P. (1977), *Paul and Palestinian Judaism*, London: SCM.
2   E.g. Stendahl, K. (1976), *Paul Among Jews and Gentiles*, London: SCM/Fortress.
3   Cf. Psalm 106.20 and Deuteronomy 4.15-19.
4   'Flesh' was the literal translation in the influential Authorized Version, and remains in the NRSV, leading to unfortunate misunderstandings of Paul.
5   *Sarx* in Paul also has a neutral sense (e.g. Romans 1.3).
6   Käsemann, E. (1980), *Commentary on Romans*, ET London: SCM, p188.
7   Keck, L.E. (2005), *Romans*, Nashville: Abingdon Press, p205. (Used by permission.)
8   Given the prominence of the physical rite of circumcision in the argument of Galatians, the literal meaning of *sarx* may be intended here. But Paul surely intended the wider meaning of the word as well (cf. also Gal. 5.16ff and 1 Cor.3.1-5).
9   Outler, Albert C. (ed) (1984), *The Works of John Wesley*, Nashville: Abingdon Press, Vol. 1, pp131-141. (All quotations from Wesley's Sermons are used by permission).
10 Op. cit. p132.
11 Op. cit. pp132-3.
12 Op. cit. p134.
13 Op. cit. p139.
14 Op. cit. pp140-1.
15 See, for example, Rowan Williams's splendid cameo of Wesley in *Open to Judgement: Sermons and Addresses* (1984), London: Darton, Longman &Todd, pp212-6.

16 Galatians 5.6
17 Käsemann, pp53f.
18 Op. cit. pp53f.
19 Op. cit. p133.
20 Numbers 25.1-13; cf. Psalm 106 30-1, and other references to Phinehas in Bockmuehl, M. (4th Edn 1997) *The Epistle to the Philippians*, London: A & C Black, pp199f.
21 Grayston, K. (1997), *The Epistle to the Romans*, London: Epworth Press, pp55-6.
22 Outler (1984), Sermons II, p81.
23 Op. cit. p94. Compare Wesley's sermon 'On the Death of George Whitfield', op. cit. pp344f.
24 Op. cit. p89.
25 Op. cit. p94. Compare Wesley's sermon 'On the Death of George Whitfield', op. cit. pp344f.
26 Op. cit. p89.
27 Meyer, Paul W. (1990), 'The Worm at the Core of the Apple', an article first published in Fortna, R.T. and Gaventa, B.R. (eds) *The Conversation Continues*, Nashville: Abingdon Press, and reprinted in Meeks, Wayne A., and Fitzgerald, John T (eds) (2007), *The Writings of St Paul* (2nd Edn), New York: W.W. Norton & Co, pp510-24. (Quotations here are taken from *Writings*).
28 Meyer (1990), p517.
29 Acts 11:26 indicates that the name *Christianos* was coined by others – perhaps local authorities, (cf. Acts 26.28 and 1 Peter 4.16, the only other occurrences of *Christianos* in the New Testament). The use of 'in the Lord' (*en kyrio*) as an 'in-house' term is particularly clear in Romans 16, where the NRSV translates the Greek phrase literally.
30 E.g. Romans 1.7 and 15.26.
31 E.g. the Psalms of Solomon 2.34f, 3.5-8 and 9-12, 4.8 and 23; 13.6ff, 14.1-5 and 10, 15.6-12. Could St Paul still have prayed these Psalms after his conversion experience? The answer, perhaps, is 'Some, but not all of them'.
32 A problem addressed by Paul at length in 1 Corinthians 8-10.
33 Cf. Bockmuehl, M. (2000), *Jewish Law in Gentile churches*, London: T. & T. Clark.
34 Thrall, M. (2nd Edn 2004), *2 Corinthians 1-7*, ICC T. & T. Clark, pp191-5.
35 Quoted in *Writings* op. cit. p391. (I have omitted the generic use of 'men' used in the English translation of Barth).
36 James, Alison (1993), *Knowing Jesus*, London: SPCK, pp90-1.

Calvinism and Arminianism – Again! : A contribution to Anglican–Methodist relations

John Munsey Turner

A recent book by Dr Herbert McGonigle (2001) – *Sufficient, Saving Grace: John Wesley's Evangelical Arminianism*[1] – has shown that the controversies in the eighteenth century between the 'Calvinists of the heart' and the 'Arminians of the heart' raised critical issues. Behind the Calvinist belief that God has elected some for salvation, and the Arminian belief that God's grace and salvation is open to all, even if they do not accept it, there lie deep questions about the very nature of God. This then raises questions about God's relationship to humanity, the role of divine grace and human free will and the possibility of the perfection of love for God, humanity and the world – new creation.

John Wesley said: 'Our main doctrines, which include all the rest are three, that of repentance, of faith and of holiness, the first of these we account as it were, the porch of religion, the next the door, the third religion itself.[2] (1746). Or as the Preface to *Hymns and Sacred Poems* put it in 1739:

> The Gospel of Christ knows of *no religion but social, no holiness but* social *holiness. Faith working by love is the length, breadth and depth of Christian perfection. (My emphasis.)*

This is a different stance from that of the Evangelical Calvinists.

But if we are to arrive there, we must look at the origins of Evangelical Arminianism and Evangelical Calvinism, which dominated the Evangelical Revival, making Wesley and John Fletcher the odd men out.

John Calvin 1509–1564

Calvin was the most notable of the second generation of the Reformers and the theologians behind what became the Reformed churches. He needs to be revisited as more than the man who believed in 'double predestination' and the 'final perseverance of believers'. *The Institutes of the Christian Religion* (final edition 1559) are a discourse on the Creeds, and in particular, a notable presentation of the doctrine of the Trinity. Predestination features in the third part, under the heading of the Holy Spirit. Calvin, like Augustine, wrote his theology as a working pastor. Diarmaid MacCulloch[3] was not far off the mark when he wrote that 'the Reformers' theology suggested a debate in the mind of long-dead Augustine'. His system is a massive Bible-centred theology – clear, logical and more than a little terrifying! But here is a theology from a man of deep faith as well as a logical French lawyer.

The starting point of *The Institutes* is not 'justification by faith', vital though that is, but the Sovereignty and Providence of God. All life is God's: 'The world is the theatre of God's glory'. This is not an irrelevant notion now with the planet at risk. Calvin asserts that God governs the universe directly. This can lead to the desacralisation of nature and hence a modern scientific world view. For Calvin, God was not a remote deity, but reveals himself to us through Nature and beauty, even if we prefer not to see him there. The role of predestination in Calvin can be exaggerated. Calvin, here, follows Augustine and Luther. His logic is that all is of God. Humans deserve no mercy as sinners. By sheer empirical observation people do not respond to God, although the gospel must be preached to all – a matter, as we shall see, that Wesley could not grasp. It must be within God's will that they do not respond. God thus gives grace and mercy to some – the 'elect'. The others are predestined to damnation. This is what Calvin called 'the awe-inspiring decree'. 'If there is election, there is reprobation. Jacob I loved, Esau I hated'. If God elects us to salvation, 'ce n'est pas pour nos beaux yeux' – it isn't because we are his blue-eyed boys, it is because he is free to do it, it is his inscrutable Providence.[4]

Calvin has to make clear human responsibility for evil, which seems to make humans both victims of necessity and responsible creatures.

Karl Marx, who saw capitalism as an inevitable outworking of the dialectic of history, yet condemns the capitalists, is on the horns of the same dilemma. Calvin's argument, like that of Marx, leads to the resolution, which enables believers to fulfil all good works, which are the visible symbols of the grace of election. Election is liberating. As T.W. Manson put it: 'they are not the pampered darlings of Providence but the *corps d'élite* of the army of the King'. The Reformed Christian could become a man or woman of great potentiality – the John Reiths, and dare one say it, the Gordon Browns of the world!

How can we view this in the twenty-first century? Not without some admiration for its logic. In an age when Darwin (read Dawkins!), Marx and Freud have shaped our outlook, it seems more realistic than Dr Samuel Johnson, who said: 'Of course our wills are free and there's an end on't'. As we shall see, few modern thinkers can stomach the 'double predestination' theory. In our time Karl Barth's massive treatment of the matter is noteworthy. Barth sees the grace of election supremely in Jesus Christ. All indeed deserve damnation, all indeed may be predestined to salvation (Romans 11:13). The various churches which make up the Church of Scotland modified, too, the harshness of earlier positions while retaining the belief in God as holy as well as loving. The whole concept of 'the Fall' and original sin needs rethinking. Yet we might recall that when Sir Lewis Namier, a Jew, and one of the great historians of the last century, was attracted to Christianity, he read Calvin's *Institutes*. Only such a system, he claimed, could hold a candle to Freud and Marx. He said: 'There is no free will in the thinking and acting of the masses any more than in the revolution of the planets and the migration of birds and the plunging of lemmings into the sea'. Cynical?

J.S. Whale[5] illustrates the debate by drawing on a Hindu analogy. There are two parties – the 'Monkey school' and the 'Cat school'. At the approach of danger the baby monkey gets on its mother's back as she jumps and is saved primarily through the mother but also by its own co-operation, and instinct no doubt God-given. When danger threatens the mother cat, she takes her kittens by the scruff of the neck. The kitten does nothing. Calvin certainly belonged to the 'Cat school' and not all the kittens were saved. John Wesley belonged to the 'Monkey school', though he would have added that the monkey's instinct to jump was God's prevenient grace, which is how, in fact, he cut the Gordian knot at least to his own satisfaction.

'Double predestination' theology, stemming from Theodore Beza (1519–1605) and in England William Perkins (1558–1602), as much as from Calvin, was famously outlined at the Synod of Dort in 1618–19.

- T.   Total Depravity
- U.   Unconditional election
- L.   Limited atonement
- I.   Irresistible grace
- P.   Perseverance of the Saints[6]

Jacob Arminius (156?–1609), the Dutchman, who refused to believe that grace was irresistible, is more to our taste:

> *A rich man gives alms to the poor and famishing beggar, by which he can support himself and his family. Does it cease to be a pure gift because the beggar stretches out his hand to receive it?*[7]

1610. The Five Articles of the Remonstrants[8]

1. *God's decree of election and his decree of reprobation are conditional upon faith.*
2. *Christ died for all yet only believers enjoy forgiveness.*
3. *Regeneration by the Holy Sprit is necessary. The Grace of God is the beginning, the progress and the end of all good.*
4. *Grace is not irresistible.*
5. *Final perseverance of believers cannot be decreed or positively asserted.*

On this division, D.M. Baillie, naughtily, quoted an American who said: 'A Methodist knows he's got religion, but he's afraid he may lose it, a Presbyterian knows he can't lose it, but he's afraid he hasn't got it'.[9] Yet predestination was primarily meant to be a doctrine of pastoral comfort, not fear. Those who are truly redeemed do not need endlessly to worry about whether they are saved or not. Energy can be given to serving the Sovereign Lord. There is a 'Calvinism of the heart' as well as an 'Arminianism of the heart'.

The late Geoffrey Nuttall. in 1967, wrote:

> *In the last decade there has been a revival of Calvinism in Europe, but a revival of Arminianism is difficult to imagine. Since Wesley we are all Arminians whether we know it or not, whether we have heard of Arminius or not. Is that not so?*[10]

Since Nuttall wrote that, the revival of conservative Evangelicalism has occurred in the world-wide Anglican Communion which, alas, is in grave danger of fissures on the issues of homosexuality, women bishops and biblical authority. Anglican Evangelicals still stress greatly the Thirty Nine Articles and do, I fear, distrust Methodism because of its apparent liberalism. Certainly Article 17 is mildly Calvinist – certainly not Arminian as Wesley thought, much as he loved the Anglican Reformation tradition. Evangelicals may think there is a failure to distinguish between what Nuttall taught us to call the 'Arminianism of the *head*', which led to Unitarianism, and the 'Arminianism of the *heart*' or Evangelical Arminianism, which Wesley inherited from his parents, especially his mother Susanna, who abhorred the doctrine of predestination as maintained by rigid Calvinists. But we must now give some summary of the conflicts within eighteenth-century revivalists, on which there has been a spate of books since Nuttall wrote.

The eighteenth century

Do Methodists still need to be reminded that the Evangelical Revival did not begin on 24 May 1738 when John Wesley 'felt his heart strangely warmed' and changed as he put it from 'the faith of a servant' doing all he could for God to the 'faith of a son' accepting what God could do for him? The Revival was a transatlantic movement well under way by 1738. Recent writing on the revival uses a 'quadrilateral' suggested by Professor David Bebbington[11] to define who is an Evangelical.

1. *The stress on conversion* – the belief that lives can be changed.
2. *Biblicism* – a particular high regard for the Scriptures.
3. *The preaching of the cross* – the sacrifice of Christ.
4. *Activism* – the expression of the Gospel in action.

John Wesley fits into that summary. His uniqueness (save for his brother Charles and John Fletcher) was his stress on the possibility of salvation for all as opposed to predestination. There was too, the necessity of growth through grace to 'perfect love' for God and human beings. The area where he split from the 'Calvinists of the heart' was over unconditional election, irresistible grace and the 'final perseverance of believers' rather than growth in spirituality. There was a freedom of the Spirit which could lead to losing salvation or, later, losing perfect love.[12] George Whitefield, who echoed Wesley in looking at all the world as his parish and acted on it, believed that preaching was the means God used to save his 'elect', a manner which Wesley saw as a means of saving *all* who responded. In his notorious sermon on 'Free Grace' (1739) Wesley said that preaching was futile if God set apart only some for salvation. Humanity was for him free to say 'No' and could fall away. In the end the 'Moderate Calvinists' and the Arminians 'put up their daggers' as Charles Simeon of Trinity Church, Cambridge put it and got on with the struggle against slavery.

Wesley himself revealed that he was not totally opposed to Calvinism. In the Minutes of the second Conference of 1745 he asserted: 'wherein do we come to the very edge of Calvinism. In denying all natural free will and power antecedent to grace. But God will grant that grace to ALL'. This is the essence of the doctrine of universal grace and the free movement of the spirit, one of the legacies of that 'radical Reformation' which alongside the tradition of Lutheranism and Calvinism was such a fruitful source of religious ideas. Wesley derived this indirectly from Arminius – though Dr McGonigle shows that he read some of his work in Latin in 1731. Wesley certainly exploited one side of Church of England tradition. Later, to John Newton, in 1765 he, again, stressed his 'both…and' view:

> *I think on Justification just as I have done any time these seven and twenty years and just as Mr Calvin does. In this respect I do not differ from him one hair's breadth. But the main point between you and me is Perfection.*[13]

Predestination is rejected too in the letter. Can you speak of a clear triangle in Wesley's thought from 1738 (if not before) to his death – the priority of God's universal love, the need for personal faith, no limitations can be put on God's grace in its effect on humanity given the limitation of living in a fallen world?

But we need to get out a big map of the eighteenth century. Gordon Rupp,[14] borrowing ideas from a French Roman Catholic M. Rondet, put it frequently in terms of:

1. *The optimism of Nature* – the Enlightenment
2. *The pessimism of Grace* – Neo-Calvinism
3. *The optimism of Grace* – Methodism

The first is the Enlightenment. We can point to a Great Britain, where there was a more moderate religious fragmentation (despite the Civil War) than on the Continent. It meant a division into mystics, moralists and rationalists. This was a time when the place of reason, the nature of authority, thinking about the character of the universe and the nature of historical evidence were creating the World of Enlightenment, or 'modernism' as we call it now in our 'post-modern' disillusionment. Despite the 'rage of party' at the time of Queen Anne, orderliness, law and reliability of reason were stressed at least in the higher echelons of society. The growth of Deism and a rational style of piety was a contrast with the intense religiosity of the previous century.

Wesley, clearly, was influenced by the Caroline Divines and the Cambridge Platonists, as well as the mystics like Jeremy Taylor (1613–62) in *Holy Living and Holy Dying*, and the inevitable à Kempis's *Imitation of Christ*, followed by William Law (1686–1761) in *Christian Perfection*(1726) and *A Serious Call to a Devout and Holy Life*(1729). The Eastern Fathers come into the picture, especially Gregory of Nyssa

(330–399), mediated to Wesley through Macarius, whose homilies are now known to be those of a fifth-century Syrian monk. Ephrem Syrus (316–373) – 'the man of a broken heart', gave a vision of perfection as the goal of the Christian life. Jean Orcibal[15] has argued that the Catholic Tradition was influenced by Wesley in its French manifestations. Pascal was an early influence, followed by de Renty, Mme Guyon and Mexican Gregory Lopez – a curious mixture! It can be argued that the ancient and Eastern traditions of holiness as *aspiring* love produced a distinctive contribution to Christian thinking.[16] Wesley had a dispute with William Law (with whom did he not sometime have a rumpus?) but he was convinced of the impossibility of being 'half a Christian'. His sermon on 'The Circumcision of the Heart', preached before the University of Oxford in January 1733, was later placed in the Standard Sermons with only minor alterations and still affirmed by Wesley fifty years later. 'Let your soul be filled with so entire a love of him that you may love nothing but for his sake' succinctly summed it up. But how was the problem he sought to solve actually solved? It was by the Moravian stress on 'new birth' or what some now call 'the Second Journey'[17] into faith, which linked Wesley with Martin Luther and recaptured the Reformation tradition of the Church of England.

Wesley was clearly influenced by the Moravians, even if he differed greatly from Nicolaus, Count Von Zinzendorf (1700–60). Reinhold Niebuhr claimed that in the debate between Wesley and the Moravians all the important issues between Reformation and perfectionist spirituality emerge in the meeting between the two.[18] Wesley is primarily intent to guard against any idea that relationship with Christ does not involve pressing onto the goal of perfect love, a lack he perceived in Reformation thinking which stressed *imputed* not *imparted* righteousness.

With the remarkable Jonathan Edwards (1703–58), in whom there has been a renewal of interest, Wesley has an interesting intellectual relationship. Edwards was a strange mixture of Calvinism and the Enlightenment. Like Whitefield, who helped him greatly in Northampton, Massachusetts, Edwards believed in predestination *and* to all, a vital assertion, which, as we have already seen, Wesley failed to understand. Edwards's *The Faithfull Narrative of the Surprising Works of*

God (1733) influenced both Whitefield and Wesley. It was Whitefield, after all, who pushed Wesley into the open air in 1739.

In Wales,[19] revival was underway with Griffith Jones (1682–1761) and, later, Howell Harris (1714–77) and Daniel Rowland (1713–80) with William Williams (1717–1791), the 'Charles Wesley' of Welsh hymnody, both in the Calvinist and Wesleyan tradition in Welsh-speaking chapels. Methodists can sing: 'Guide Me, O Though Great Jehovah' as they can sing John Newton's 'Amazing Grace' and Montague Augustus Toplady's 'Rock of Ages', even if Toplady called Wesley 'a mean and puny tadpole in divinity', accusing him of downplaying the law, and popery. Wesley called him a 'chimney sweep'! Harris tried to reconcile Wesley and Whitefield and, indeed, Wesley preached at Whitefield's funeral in 1770.

Meanwhile there were differences with James Hervey (1714–58), an 'Oxford Methodist' whose *Meditations Among the Tombs* (1746) was a bestseller! Dr Brown-Lawson and Dr McGonigle have analysed Hervey's *Theron and Aspasio* (1755) and Wesley's reply to it in 1756. Wesley accused Hervey of antinomianism. His reply illustrates his ability to analyse and make clear his viewpoint, which he believed to be firmly Anglican, although his attribution to them of antinomianism seems at times unfair. It was a sad affair between two good men, as were so many of the debates in the mid-eighteenth century.

More personal was the case of John Bennet (1714–59), a Methodist itinerant preacher, who came from Presbyterian, puritan roots. Without men like Bennet there could be no Methodist Connexion. He pioneered the Quarterly Meeting and Methodism in Bolton. There he became a moderate Calvinist, accusing Wesley of 'popery' in 1752. Even Mrs John Wesley joined in the dispute like a Hogarthian virago! Bennet split the Society, founding Duke's Abbey Independent Chapel, ancestor of the present URC Church at which I preach annually. He became an independent minister, as did not a few itinerants. Bennet, of course, had married Grace Murray, Wesley's 'last love', which added to the personal elements behind the theological 'spats'.[20]

More well-known were disputings with the Countess of Huntingdon (1709–91),[21] who firstly supported Wesley, then moved to a neo-Calvinist position. Perhaps 'Pope John' and 'Pope Joan' could not work together; a matter which came to a climax over the rather ill-conceived *Minutes of Conference* 1770, which the moderate Calvinists felt set out salvation by works if not Pelagianism. Lady Huntingdon called the Minutes: 'horrible, abominable, and subversive.' Wesley was called an apostate. He suggested the lady might use her reason!

In 1778 Wesley was, perhaps, naïve in calling his new magazine for ordinary readers *The Arminian Magazine*. Certainly, Wesley stated that 'good works' must follow justification. Both sides in these conflicts accused the other of antinomianism, although Wesley always preached 'law' as well as grace. There were crackpots on both sides, which did not help matters. The Trevecka experiment in ministerial training, which had interesting possibilities, came into great controversy with John Fletcher and the Methodist preacher Joseph Benson being suspended by the Countess. John Fletcher (1729–85), who has had a recent renaissance, with his important 'Checks to Antinomianism', sought reconciliation between Wesley and the 'Calvinists of the heart'. He said:

> *The error of rigid Calvinists centres in the denial of that evangelical liberty, whereby all men, under various dispensations of grace, may without necessity choose life. And the error of rigid Arminians consists of not paying a cheerful homage to redeeming grace, for all the liberty and power which we have to choose life, and to work righteousness since the fall. To avoid equally these two extremes, we need only to follow the Scripture – doctrine of free-will restored and assisted by free grace'.*

He also said: 'I build my faith not on my experience though this increases but upon the revealed truth of God'.[22]

On perfection Wesley was not always consistent. His view on many things changed during his long ministry. Even his *Plain Account of Christian Perfection* of 1766 did not prevent confusion. Some Methodists followed the position of growth through grace using all the 'means of grace', not least the 'class meeting', love feasts, watchnights, the Covenant Service and regular preaching services. Others saw perfection as an 'experience', parallel to conversion, a 'Second Blessing'.

Wesley clearly believed that some achieved it, although he was never too foolish as to claim it for himself. As Gordon Wakefield put it:

> *Wesley went on to claim that entry into perfection might be instantaneous like first conversion. The doctrine not only aroused opposition, it led to some scandals within the Methodist societies, extreme claims and fanatical scenes. Wesley never claimed perfection, always standing some distance from his own movement. What must not be forgotten is that for him 'perfection' was perfect love, the keeping of the great commandments. The test was whether one loved one's enemies with the heart cleansed of hatred. But who would determine these matters?*[23]

He also greatly modified his view of assurance. Melville Horne (1762–1841) – at one time John Fletcher's successor – recalls a conversation late in Wesley's life:

> *When fifty years ago my brother Charles and I, in the simplicity of our hearts told the good people of England that unless they knew their sins were forgiven, they were under the wrath and curse of God, I marvel, Melville, they did not stone us. The Methodists, I hope, know better now. We preach assurance as we always did as a common privilege of the people of God but we do not enforce it under the pain of damnation'.*[24]

Wesley seems to have forgotten when mobs did attack him!

Recently Theodore Runyon asserted that assurance is not just emotion, but evidence expressing itself in a transformed state of living, in social relationship, in the sacraments, in rational behaviour and always in looking to the future, the goal of perfect love.[25]

Finally we need to look at Wesley's definition of sin. Wesley operated on an inadequate or confusing definition of sin. His definition of sin as: 'a voluntary transgression of a known law' in the *Plain Account of Christian Perfection* can be dangerous since it appears to ignore the unconscious drives of human nature. In our post-Freudian days we know well enough that our worst sins may be those of which we are unconscious. Sin comes, in Wesley's view, to be seen almost as a rotten tooth which can be extracted by a celestial dentist. Can one say on that definition that he or she is free from sin or not? In fairness to Wesley, he has also an Augustinian view of original sin, even believing that there were no volcanoes before the Fall!

It is interesting that Wesley could engage in controversy with what we can call 'the Arminianism of the *head*' represented by the Dissenter Dr John Taylor (1694–1761), whom recently G.T. Eddy has called 'Wesley's arch heretic'.[26] Taylor in *The Scripture Doctrine of Original Sin* (1740) rejected the idea that there is a total corruption of human nature due to the sin of Adam and Eve. We all inherit death but not inbred sin. Writing in 1758 to the Calvinist Toplady, Wesley asserted: 'I verily believe no single person since Mahomet has given such a wound to Christianity as Dr Taylor. They are his books chiefly that upon original sin which have poisoned so many of the clergy and indeed the fountains thereof – the universities in England, Scotland, Holland and Germany'. Jonathan Edwards had previously voiced similar sentiments. Taylor says that sin is a matter of personal choice and regeneration is voluntary also. Wesley's reply to Taylor, *The Doctrine of Original Sin According to Scripture, Reason and Experience* (1757), states the absolute need for grace for all. As his brother put it:

> *Thy undistinguishing regard*
> *Was cast on Adam's fallen race*
> *For all thou hast in Christ prepared*
> *Sufficient, Sovereign, Saving Grace.*

Eddy takes the view that the doctrine of original sin as stated in the *Westminster Catechism*, the *Thirty Nine Articles* and by Wesley has ceased after Darwin to be credible. Wesley espouses a lost cause.[27] Modern Calvinists would, I think, disagree. Also Wesley's stress on consciousness of guilt can cause 'guilt feelings' rather than genuine guilt.

It is doubtful, too, whether a view of perfection as in any way instantaneous can be sustained. It could encourage a kind of self-appraisal on which the Congregationalist theologian P.T. Forsyth was right to say:

> *If ever we come to any such stage as conscious sinlessness (Wesley said 'sinless perfection is a phrase I never use') we should be placing ourselves alongside Christ not at his feet... It is certain that the perfect man will be the last to know how perfect he is.*[28]

Here we must leave a very complex matter which makes some of us realise that we cannot just go back to Wesley, or Calvin, as if we lived still in the eighteenth century. I have tried to state the Calvinist difficulties with Wesley, but can only end this section with the assertion that *'faith working by love'* is the real root of Methodism. 'This doctrine', he wrote in 1790 to R.C. Brackenbury 'is the grand depositum which God had lodged with the people called Methodists and for the sake of propagating this chiefly he appears to have raised us up'.[29]

Perhaps the 'Arminianism of the heart' is best expressed in what Karl Barth called 'irregular dogmatics', especially the hymns of Charles Wesley. A comparison between the *Collection Hymns for the Use of the People Called Methodists* (1780) and the *Olney Hymns* of 1779 reveals the distance and the nearness of the 'Arminianism of the heart' and the 'Calvinism of the heart'.

> *'Tis love, 'tis love, Thou diedst for me!*
> *...Pure universal love Thou art,*
> *To me, to all, thy mercies move;*
> *Thy nature and they name is love.*
>   Hymns and Psalms (HP) 434

> *O for a trumpet voice*
> *On all the World to call*
> *To bid their hearts rejoice*
> *In him who died for all!*
> *For all, my Lord was crucified*
> *For all, for all my Saviour died.*
>   HP 226

From this stems true assurance:

He owns me for his child...
I can no longer fear,
With confidence I now draw nigh
And Father – Abba – Father cry.
HP 217

And true perfection:

Thy Nature, Gracious Lord impart
Come quickly from above
Write thy new name upon my heart
Thy new best name of love.

Nineteenth-century development and official statements

After Wesley's death, Evangelicals of many styles were engaged in the battles against slavery, in world mission and in co-operation in bodies like the *British and Foreign Bible Society* and later the *Evangelical Alliance*, which included prominent Methodists. In divided Methodism – there were soon 'many Methodisms' including those in America – we can see more divergences over the meaning and experience of sanctification. Is 'perfection' primarily an experience as well as an aspiration followed by growth in love? The greatest Wesleyan theologian W.B. Pope (1822–1903) of Didsbury College, Manchester, certainly looked to aspiration. Another clear line emerged with Adam Clarke (1760–1832) and especially William Arthur (1819–1901), whose *Tongue of Fire* (1856) was a formative writing. This tradition was popularly seen in James Caughey, who claimed to 'sanctify' thousands in towns like Rochdale to the consternation of the Wesleyan leaders. Not to be ignored is the rather different style of the American Phoebe Palmer (1807–1874), propounding and preaching a view of 'total consecration', laying one's whole life 'on the altar'. For Palmer the act of consecration and the reception of the blessing of the entire sanctification were linked as cause and effect. Outside Methodism we can follow Palmer's influence on the Church of the Nazarene, the Pilgrim Holiness Church and the Salvation Army and the rise of Pentecostalism.

In Wesleyanism this style was expressed in Bolton and Rochdale by Thomas Champness (1832–1905), whose work led to the establishment of Cliff College in Derbyshire for the training of evangelists. Thomas Cook (1859–1912) was appointed Principal in 1903. Cook asserted that 'regeneration is the beginning of purification... Entire sanctification is the finishing of that work... it is an eradication, the removal of all roots of bitterness, the seeds of sin's disease... we grasp by faith the sin-consuming power which sweeps the heart clean at a stroke... Believing now, we are pardoned now, believing now, we are cleansed from sin all sin now'. It is interesting that Cook makes no mention of the means of grace so vital to Wesley. Later, Samuel Chadwick (1860–1932) equated the 'baptism of the spirit' with sanctification, a matter now disputed by Methodist charismatics and New Testament scholars. The more 'Wesleyan' position can be found in Newton Flew and W.E. Sangster's *The Path to Perfection*.

When Methodist union took place in 1932, the much discussed *Deed of Union* took a very irenic line. It needs to be set out for both Methodists and Anglicans to note Methodism's place in the Catholic Church of Christ.

> *The Methodist Church claims and cherishes its place in the Holy Catholic church, which is the Body of Christ. It rejoices in the inheritance of the Apostolic Faith, and loyally accepts the fundamental principles of the historic creeds and of the Protestant Reformation. It ever remembers that in the Providence of God, Methodism was raised up to spread Scriptural holiness through the land by the proclamation of the evangelical faith and declares its unfaltering resolve to be true to its divinely appointed mission. The doctrines of the Evangelical Faith, which Methodism has held from the beginning, and still holds, are based upon the divine revelation recorded in the Holy Scriptures. The Methodist Church acknowledges this revelation as the supreme rule of faith and practice. These evangelical doctrines, to which the preachers of the Methodist church, both minister and laymen are pledged, are contained in Wesley's* Notes on

> the New Testament and the first four volumes of his Sermons. The Notes on the New Testament and the Forty-four Sermons are not intended to impose any formal or speculative theology on Methodist Preachers, but to set up standards of preaching and belief which should secure loyalty to the fundamental truths of the Gospel of redemption, and ensure the continual witness of the church, to the realities of the Christian experience of salvation.³⁰

That statement was acceptable to biblical scholars such as Professor A.S. Peake (Primitive Methodist), to whom 'the divine revelation revealed in the Holy Scriptures' was vitally important, avoiding fundamentalism, though he had argued for the omission of the *Notes of the New Testament* as the work of an 'outmoded exegete'. Part of it was based on the Pietist J.A Bengel, who gives the date of the Second Coming as 1836! Calvinists and Arminians, too, would argue as to what are the fundamental principles of the Protestant Reformation. There seems a deliberate lack of precision.³¹

Later statements such as the *Nature of the Christian Church* (1937),³² deeply influenced by Newton Flew of Wesley House, Cambridge, and the *Message and Mission of Methodism* (1946) took again a very inclusive view of the matter. The first statement said that 'particular stress has always been laid on three features of the original message:

> 1. *The doctrine of Assurance or the witness of the Spirit that is the personal certainty of the forgiveness of sins and restored sonship;*
> 2. *The need for believers to press on towards holiness or perfect love, a goal that is attainable in this earthly life;*
> 3. *The Practice of Christian Fellowship.*

The later statement was very similar. Conversion and assurance were stressed. On perfection difficulties we have noted are stressed, especially the definition of sin, but of particular value are:

> *The central emphasis upon sanctity or perfect love confronts us with our true destiny 'to present every man [sic] perfect in Christ Jesus'...*

Secondly, the doctrine of perfect love affirms that no limits can be set to the sovereign love of God. In the third place, the life of perfect love is a divine gift not a human achievement. Fourthly, the quest of perfect love co-exists with a sense of personal unworthiness. Finally, the quest of perfect love is the secret of growth and stability in the Christian community.

A further statement on the Toronto Blessing (1996) is worth noting, even if that particular phenomenon, like many revivalist manifestations, was short-lived. We can compare 'the Blessing' with events in Wesley's time, such as the great 'revival' at Cambuslang in Scotland in 1742 and Wesley's stress on the subsequent need for all the 'means of grace' to prevent it being 'a rope of sand'.

What of today?

Attempts to put Wesley's theology into modern terms occurred throughout the twentieth century, with a positive rebirth of 'Wesleyan' thought, especially in the USA. A popular summary of Arminian Methodism came from the founder of the Wesley Guild, William Fitzgerald, in 1903, which he called 'the four-Alls of Methodism' with a fifth added by George Eayrs and taken up by W.E. Sangster:

1. *All need to be saved*
2. *All can be saved*
3. *All can know they are saved*
4. *All can be saved to the uttermost*
5. *All must witness to their salvation*[33]

The danger here is that this seems now very individualistic, with no mention of the church, the sacraments or, indeed, the wider world.

More recently the American scholar Albert Outler[34] took up the Reformation scholar Richard Hooker's scheme of *Bible, tradition* and *reason*, adding *experience*, stating that this is Wesley's legacy to us. Outler adds:

> *He (Wesley) proceeded to develop a theological fusion of faith and good works, Scripture and tradition, revelation and reason, God's sovereignty and human freedom, universal redemption and conditional election, Christian liberty and an ordered piety, the assurance of pardon and the risk of 'falling from grace', original sin and Christian perfection...*

... with always God's initiative and human response. Geoffrey Wainwright, perhaps Methodism's leading contemporary theologian, states the challenge of Wesley superbly:

> *Wesley's vision, program and praxis were marked by the following six principal features. First, he looked to the Scriptures as the primary and abiding testimony to the redemptive work of God in Christ. Second, to the ministry of evangelism the Gospel was to be preached to every creature and needed only to be accepted in faith. Third, he valued with respect to the Christian tradition and doctrine of the church a generous orthodoxy, wherein theological opinions might vary so long as they were consistent with the apostolic tradition. Fourth, he expected sanctification to show itself in the moral earnestness and loving deeds of the believers. Fifth, he manifested and encouraged a social concern that was directed towards the neediest of neighbours. Sixth, he found in The Lord's Supper a sacramental sign of the fellowship graciously bestowed by the Triune God and the responsive sacrifice of praise and thanksgiving on the part of those who will glorify God and enjoy him for ever. These are the features which must be strengthened in contemporary Methodism if we are to maintain our historic identity, speak with a significant voice on the ecumenical scene, and keep on a recognisable Christian track as the paths divide.*[35]

I would want to add several more points to a discussion of Methodist emphases.

1. The idea of the *Connexion* is vital to Methodism. Ministers (now officially called presbyters) are received into 'Full Connexion' and ordained at the annual Conference *not* locally. A connexional way

seeks to avoid a party-line approach and also allows the strong to help the weak.

2. The evangelical Arminian tradition that's God's grace is for all, and indeed in all – prevenient grace – should enable Methodism to combine what Wainwright called a 'generous orthodoxy' with a concern for the inclusive nature of the church. Methodism can avoid a wooden Biblicism, the dead hand of tradition and too much reliance on intellect or emotion, and thus take part in inter-faith dialogue in a constructive manner and explore sexual diversity in a positive style.

3. Methodism at its best has secured a balance between responsive and free worship.

4. The belief in 'priesthood of all believers' does not mean that anyone can do anything, but that each has a role in Spirit-given tasks, the privilege of offering service, sacrifice and prayer.

What contribution can Methodism make now to the life of church and nation, which should be a major concern of the Anglican-Methodist Covenant? I suggest eight ways:

1. Making contributions to new styles of ecumenism.

2. Preserving a distinctive style of worship and preaching. This is the 'both... and' style of our tradition and quite fresh styles. The role of local preachers ensures (or should!) an inclusiveness here.

3. Taking a broad view of the use of Christian resources. We do not work independently of other churches. Common witness and service needs a shared emphasis.

4. Developing theological education at all levels of church life. Colleges and Resource Centres are not just to train presbyters and deacons but the whole laity – and *all* theological views need to be represented.

5. Telling the nation the truth about itself by word and deed. We have not the political 'clout' of the time around 1900 when Hugh

Price Hughes in London could preach genuine holiness *and* political action, but the contribution of lay Methodists in politics local and national, education and the Health Service is still very great, not to speak of bodies like Action for Children, MHA, etc. An informed commentary on political affairs is needed.

6. Committing itself energetically to mission including what are now called 'fresh expressions' – was not Wesley's system and later Primitive Methodism a fresh expression of the churches linking with peoples' need for a religion of the heart, as well as the mind?

7. Explaining and defending the Christian faith. Apologetic must be done at every level.

8. The maintenance of groups which can nurture faith. The 'class meeting' was the heart of early Methodism – otherwise so much else would have been, as Wesley often put it: 'A rope of sand'.

Dare one still say when we think again (in new ways) of Calvinism and Arminianism that 'the Wesleyan reconstruction of the Christian ethic of life is an original and unique synthesis of the Protestant ethic of grace with the catholic ethic of holiness'? [36]

Notes

1   McGonigle, H. (2001), *Sufficient Grace: John Wesley's Evangelical Arminianism*, London.
2   'Letter to Thomas Church' in Telford, J. (ed) (1960), *Letters of John Wesley*, London: Epworth Press, Vol. II p268.
3   MacCulloch, D. (2003), *Reformation: Europe's House Divided 1490–1700*, London: Allen Lane, p iii.
4   Calvin, J. (1951 translation), *Institutes*, London: SCM, Vol.2 pp902ff; cf Wainwright, G. (1987), *On Calvin and Wesley*, Melbourne; Sell, A. (1982), *The Great Debate: Calvinism, Arminianism and Salvation*, H.E. Walter. I have used my article 'John Calvin' in *Worship and Preaching*, June 1980, cf McGrath, A. (1993), *A Life of John Calvin*, Oxford: Blackwell.
5   Whale, J.S. (1955) ,*The Protestant Transition*, Cambridge: CUP, chaps 8-11 and especially pp140ff.
6   Cf. Schaff, P. (1877), *The Creeds of Christendom*, III. pp550–80; Sell (1982), pp13ff..
7   Bett, H. (1937), *The Spirit of Methodism*, London: Epworth Press, p153.
8   Cf. Sell (1982), p13; Bettenson, H. (ed) (1967), *Documents of the Christian Church*, Oxford: OUP, p268.

9 Baillie, D.M. (1958), *Out of Nazareth*, St Andrew Press, p11.
10 Nuttall, G.F. et al (1967), *The Puritan Spirit*, London: Epworth Press, p67; Turner, H.E.W. (1964), *The Articles of the Church of England*, London: Mowbray, especially Ch. 2 by J.I. Packer.
11 Bebbington, D.W. (1989), *Evangelicalism in Modern Britain*, London: Unwin, Hyman, pp2ff.
12 I am drawing on my *Conflict and Reconciliation: Studies in Methodism and Ecumenism in England 1740–1982* (1985), London: Epworth Press, Chs 4 and 6 and John Wesley (2002), *The Evangelical Revival and the Rise of Methodism in England*, Peterborough: Epworth Press, Chs 1-4.
13 *Letters IV* (Telford Edition) To John Newton 14th May 1765, p298; cf Jackson, T. (ed) *John Wesley, Works* Vol. VIII, Second Conference 1745.
14 Rupp, G. (1952), *Principalities and Powers*, London: Epworth Press, Ch. 5.
15 Orcibal, J. (1965), 'The Theological Originality of John Wesley and Continental Spirituality' in Davies, R.E. et al (eds), *A History of the Methodist Church in Great Britain*, London: Epworth Press, Vol. 1 p81ff.
16 Outler, A. (1964), *John Wesley*, Oxford: OUP, pp9–10.
17 O'Collins, G. (1987), *The Second Journey*, Paulist Press, pp21ff.
18 Niebuhr, H.R. (1943), *The Nature and Destiny of Man*, Nisbet, Vol. 2, pp180ff.
19 Morgan, D.L. (1988), *The Great Awakening in Wales*, London: Epworth Press.
20 Brown-Lawson, A. (1994), *John Wesley and the Anglican Evangelicals of the Eighteenth Century*, Pentland Press. Cf Valentine, S.R. (1997), *John Bennet and the Origins of Methodism and the Evangelical Revival in England*, Scarecrow Press.
21 Schlenther, B.S. (1997), *Queen of the Methodists: The Countess of Huntingdon and the Crisis of Faith and Society*, Durham University Press, especially pp111–116.
22 Fletcher, John (1837), *On Reconciliation: Checks to Antinomianism*, New York, Vol. 2, pp333-4; cf Streiff, P. (2001), *Reluctant Saint? A Theological Biography of Fletcher of Madeley*, Peterborough: Epworth Press.
23 Wakefield, G. (1990), *John Wesley*, Methodist Publishing House, p27.
24 Horne, M. (1809), *An Investigation of the Definition of Justifying Faith*, London: Longmans, pp1-4, 12, 14.
25 Runyon, T. (1998), *The New Creation: John Wesley's Theology Today*, Abingdon Press.
26 Eddy, G.T. (2003), *Dr Taylor of Norwich*, Peterborough: Epworth Press; Jackson, T. (ed) (1856), *John Wesley Works*, Vol. IX pp182–444.
27 Eddy (2003), p16.
28 Forsyth, P.T. (1957), *God the Holy Father*, IP especially pages 102–117.
29 *Letters* (ed Telford), p238 dated 15 September 1790.
30 *The Constitutional Practice and Discipline of the Methodist Church* 5th edition 1969 MPH pp3, 288.
31 Wilkinson, J.T. (1971), *Arthur Samuel Peake*, London: Epworth Press, p167.
32 (1984) *Statement of the Methodist Church on Faith and Order 1933–1983*, Methodist Publishing House, pp5f, 37.
33 (1951) *Proceedings of the Eighth Ecumenical Conference*, London: Epworth Press, p73. cf Watson, P.S. (1951), *The Message of the Wesley's*, London: Epworth Press.
34 Outler (1964), p viii.
35 Wainwright G. (1995). *Methodists in Dialog*, Abingdon Press, pp283-4.
36 Cell, G.C. (1935), *The Rediscovery of John Wesley*, New York: Holt, p347. Also see *Called to Love and Praise*, Peterborough: Methodist Publishing House, 1999.

Newman's model of the Church: A helpful paradigm for ecumenical ecclesiology?

Wendy Allen

Nearly ten years ago, I made my first foray into ecumenical thought by studying the Roman Catholic-Methodist dialogue, ably assisted by David Carter, who explores the current place the dialogue has reached in his contribution to this volume. I was also generously supplied with resources by the then participant in Catholic-Methodist dialogue John Newton. I suggested then that John Henry Cardinal Newman's ideas about the papacy, infallibility and conscience might help to bridge the gaps between Methodist and Roman Catholic understanding of the place of authority in the Church. This may seem surprising, given that Newman left the Anglican Church for Rome; that is hardly an ecumenical gesture. However, Newman valued each stage of his Christian journey, and his experience in two communities means that he is well placed to bridge any difficulties in terminology. Newman's model of the Church focuses on the dynamic interaction between the diverse roles of Prophet, Priest and King and offers, I believe, a constructive and challenging 'organically ordered'[1] model of the Church. This model might help and challenge the self-understanding and reflection of different ecclesial communities, including Roman Catholicism. In this paper I will outline the diverse roots of his model, describe and interpret the model, and finally make suggestions for how I see the model making a helpful difference to ecumenical understanding by holding diverse ecclesiologies together.

Of course, any paper that talks about an 'ecumenical ecclesiology' is already on difficult ground. As Karkkainen observed, 'Christians and Churches introduce into the ecumenical movement their own specific understanding of the church and the kind of unity they find theologically and ecclesiastically correct. Ecclesiology determines one's view of ecumenism.'[2] The most common model offered as being mutually acceptable is *koinonia* or communion ecclesiology. This understands the dynamic between unity and diversity in the Church as being rooted in the unity and diversity within the Trinity.[3]

In 1953, Leslie Newbiggin explained the difference between three ecclesiological streams in terms of a trinity of preaching, sacraments and power or miracles. Lutherans he suggested give priority to faith arising through preaching; Catholics favour the sacramental; while Pentecostals emphasise actions in the power of the Holy Spirit.[4] All three were equally important, suggested Newbiggin, and recognising and reconciling these different emphases in different ecclesial communities was at the heart of his ecumenical endeavour. Newman's model of the Church as prophet (developing and reflecting on theology), priest (connecting with a suffering world in devotional and sacramental ways) and king (order and authority bringing the world into conformity with Kingdom values) resonates with Newbiggin's idea. I believe that it offers a detailed and robust model of how different priorities shape and have shaped the Church as a whole through the ages, and how the three impulses should be held together in dynamic tension rather than leading to conflict and separation.[5]

Why Newman wrote his model

It was the mature Newman who wrote the new Preface to *The Via Media of the Anglican Church* (1877) in which he describes his model.[6] In 1837, while still an Anglican, Newman had written the original version of the *Via Media* and set out two arguments against the Roman Catholic Church: first, that the Roman Catholic Church fell down on the note of 'antiquity', since it had 'added' to the faith; second, that the Roman Catholic Church also departed from the 'Note of Sanctity':[7] she was unfaithful to her own principles – in abuses of authority, and in the differences between official teaching and both popular devotion and moral behaviour. By 1877, Newman considered that he had already fully addressed and contradicted the first argument in *The*

Essay on Development (1845).⁸ In the new Preface, Newman tackled this outstanding issue of sanctity head on by arguing that such departures were inevitable, and a mark of the inherent tension at the centre of ecclesiology between the three offices of Christ: the imperfections of the Church arise from her nature.⁹ Newman sought to explain the troubled history of the Catholic Church, making some sense of her weaknesses and unfaithfulness to her own principles. This is because of the 'action or interaction, or the chronic collisions or contrasts, or the temporary suspense or delay, of her administration, in her three several departments of duty'.¹⁰ He also expressed confidence and faith in her fundamental soundness and the ability to self-correct arising from the dynamic tensions at work within the threefold office.

Newman's particular disquiet with Catholicism in his own time was that he felt that a devotional and political orthodoxy was stifling the vital creative theological work of the Church.¹¹ Newman had personal reasons for wanting to defend theological expression; he had felt the heavy hand of Propaganda,¹² being suspected of heterodoxy since the *Rambler* controversy in 1859. However, although his Preface offers a challenge to over-centralisation and bureaucratisation of the Church, it cannot be used to champion what Newman still saw as an inappropriate stress on personal freedom and self-determination. The model insists on the corporate nature of the exercise of each of the three offices.

The diverse roots of the model

When offering a tool for ecumenical reflection it seems important to show that it is one based on scripture and tradition. Newman built his model on a scripturally-based exposition of the triple office of Christ, which he discovered initially in the writings of the 'Calvinist'¹³ writer Scott. Newman originally follows exactly Scott's application of Christ as 'Prophet', 'Priest' and 'King' to the individual believer's experience.¹⁴ When he later revisits this ground in his sermon 'The Three Offices of Christ' (1840), Newman extends Scott's image to highlight the role of the ordained minister as one who take Christ's place, and who 'suffers', 'teaches' and 'rules'. Newman also indicates that all Christians 'in some sense bear all three offices', though he sees this as most keenly focused in the roles of 'confessor and monk', 'doctor and teacher' and 'bishop and pastor'.[15]

By 1877, in his Preface, Newman differs still more from Scott in explicitly applying the three offices of 'Prophet', 'Priest' and 'King', not exclusively to the ordained as representing Christ, nor to the Pope alone as the Vicar of Christ, but to the whole Church, the Body of Christ, who participate in Christ through baptism. Newman roots his understanding of participation in the roles of Christ in the presence of the Holy Spirit indwelling the Church and the individual Christian. This Spirit enables the Christian to reflect 'the Saviour of the world' not only 'in all His perfections,' but also in 'all His offices' and 'all His works'.[16]

Newman reseeded and developed his idea of the triple office using 'Apostolical'[17] and Patristic writers. He would have found plenty there to add depth to the idea.[18] Augustine (d.430) is explicit: 'As we are called Christians because of our mystical chrism, our unction, so we are all priests in being the members of one Priest.'[19] A further reference is found in Eusebius's *Ecclesiastical History*. Eusebius begins with the theme of Christ as 'Prophet', 'Priest' and 'King', surpassing the Old Testament figures who pointed to him. He continues, '[Christ] has filled the whole world with Christians, that truly revered and sacred title of His; and he has committed to his followers no longer types or symbols, but the very virtues themselves'. Eusebius sees individual Christians as being gifted as 'Prophet', 'Priest' and 'King', and the Church as a whole as the new 'nation' honoured with the name of Christ.[20]

Newman, influenced by his early mentor Butler, also developed the idea throughout his preaching and writing works using the patristic technique of taking characters as an analogy between human experience and divine truths.[21] Moses, Jacob and David; Jeremiah, Joshua and Elijah; Peter, John and Mary and Benedict, Dominic and Ignatius are all used to illustrate what he understands by 'Prophet', 'Priest' and 'King'. His New Testament triad shows that he understands St John, with the characteristic of 'endurance' and 'suffering' leading to extraordinary visions, as the type of the 'Priest'. St Peter is the 'King':

the one who acts and rules. The Virgin Mary is given to us not, as we might expect, as an example of creative acceptance, nor of patient suffering, but of the prophetic 'use of Reason in investigating the doctrines of Faith'.

> ... *first believing without reasoning, next from love and reverence, reasoning after believing. And thus she symbolizes to us, not only the faith of the unlearned, but of the doctors of the Church also, who have to investigate, and weigh, and define, as well as to profess the Gospel; to draw the line between truth and heresy; to anticipate or remedy the various aberrations of wrong reason; to combat pride and recklessness with their own arms; and thus to triumph over the sophist and the innovator.*[22]

In several places in his preaching, Newman explores the ideal of a perfected tension between divergent impulses. One such example is in a sermon 'Keeping Fast and Festival' (1838),[23] in which he suggests that in Christ, transformed humanity holds together the active, the emotional and the contemplative. Similarly, when Newman associates Benedict with birth of poetry (*poesis*), Dominic with the birth of science (*scientia*) and Ignatius with the rise of the practical sense (*prudentia*),[24] he did not see the three characteristics as a progression, one replacing another, but as complementary impulses.[25]

Newman's model expounded

Newman explains that the three offices have different characteristics – a strength and a weakness. The 'Prophet' has truth as its guiding principle and reason as its tool. The chief danger for theology is the inclination of the intellect to 'rationalism'; to make reason an end in itself, and to become too self-dependent, forgetting 'revelation' and 'tradition'.[26] The 'Priest' is concerned with devotion to God and edification of the worshipping community. Since devotion involves the emotional nature, it has an inherent predisposition to 'superstition' or 'enthusiasm'. The office of 'King' has to do with polity or government, its guiding principle is expedience (*prudentia*).[27] Since rule or government has the tools of coercion or force available to it, there is an inbuilt tendency to 'ambition' and 'tyranny'. The internal tension between each strength and its associated weakness makes it very difficult to perform each individual office well. Although, in the historical life of the Church, one or other aspect has tended to dominate, pulling the Church towards the extremes, Newman suggests positively that these tensions within each office can be moderated or regulated by creative interaction between them.

Each office has a 'scope', 'direction' and 'interest'. But each also has to take account of 'the claims of the other two'. The forces at work are 'independent', 'divergent' and 'conflicting' and the course of any one aspect will be 'deflected from the line' it would have taken by the action of the others.[28] Newman is not principally looking for a compromise between two (or even three) extremes, but a mutual tension arising from the proper exercise of each of the three offices. If all act equally the model is held in perfect tension. For example, the Prophet's guiding principle of truth is a vital factor in regulating the Priest's tendency to superstition.

Newman reasons that the discrepancy between theory and practice in the way the Church acts principally arises because of 'ambition, craft and cruelty'[29] in the political aspect, and also, he adds, because of 'superstition' and 'wayward popular taste'[30] in the religious aspect. These elements are 'far more congenial... to the human mind, are far more liable to excess and corruption, and are ever struggling to liberate themselves from those restraints which are in truth necessary for their well-being.'[31] Theology, on the other hand, is in search of the pure truth, and formulates the principles. Consequently, 'religion [is n]ever in greater danger than when... the Schools of theology have been broken up and ceased to be', since theology is 'the fundamental and regulating principle of the whole Church system.'[32]

Newman's assertion that theology is the 'regulating principle' needs careful interpretation. It appears at first glance that he is giving precedence to one office over the other two, to theological schools as opposed to the exercise of 'King' by Pope and Curia. However, this is to misunderstand what he means and to look for a too-easy resolution of the inherent tensions. It is true that, in keeping with his second aim, Newman was concerned about the abuse of authority and the suppression of appropriate theological enquiry.[33] However, we cannot use Newman's model simplistically as a tool to defend the theologian against any suppression of freedom of speech and to stress the prerogative of the 'prophetical office', or theologian, to tell the 'kingly office' how it should exercise authority. Newman was equally concerned to grant the rights of the 'kingly office' to keep theologians in check and regulate heretical speculation, and the 'priestly office' to temper both of them with concern for pastoral need.[34]

So what does Newman mean when he writes, 'Theology is the fundamental and regulating principle of the whole Church system?'[35] The dictionary offers two meanings of the word 'regulating'. The most common meaning is given as 'supervise by means of rules and regulations'. A secondary meaning is to control the speed of a machine. The related word 'regulator' is a valve controlling fluid flow, such as the supply of steam to a steam engine.[36] Given how much space Newman gives in the Preface to demonstrating occasions when theology must give way to the other two offices,[37] he clearly does not mean that theology 'rules' or 'supervises' them, so his meaning must be closer to the second use of the term. Theology in this sense is like a safety valve: a discipline which on the one hand prevents the build up of too much pressure, perhaps by explaining or questioning what is happening,[38] and on the other prevents a loss of pressure which would lead to the engine ceasing to function, perhaps by disturbing complacency and challenging idleness.

A further example of the word 'regulate' also occurs in Newman's correspondence. 'Forms of power,' he writes, 'all require a drag or regulator'[39] to stop them becoming tyrannies.[40] The 'regulator' in this sense either slows down or stops the movement in a particular direction, or keeps the movement straying from the intended course and veering off in the wrong direction. Such a use of the word does not imply control in the sense of 'supervise' or 'direct', but rather the application of guidance or restraint.[41]

One last example of Newman's use of the words 'regulating principle' should be noted. I think that the concept of virtue that Aristotle defines in *Nicomachean Ethics*,[42] sheds significant light on the idea of the 'regulating principle' that Newman is working with.[43] Virtue is a mean according to Aristotle, but this does not mean some kind of mediocrity, nor can it be determined by a mathematical formula.[44] The 'regulating principle' in this sense is the 'practical wisdom' or phronesis that allows a person to make the best choice in the circumstances. Theology as the 'regulating principle', interpreted in this light, would be the wisdom required to decide correctly the virtuous middle course between alternate vices in the life of the Church. In terms of the note of unity, say, the virtuous mean lies somewhere between insisting on rigid conformity to a central norm which in turn stifles life, and a totally permissive diversity which can lead to fragmentation and disunity. Thus, theology could be understood as the skill of discerning the mean, not in the sense of finding a compromise, but of holding the two extremes in tension and restraining excess.

The interaction between 'authority' and 'private judgement' is like 'a never-ending duel' which is 'necessary for the life of religion'. The process is like the 'advancing and retreating' of the 'ebb and flow of the tide.' Newman continues by invoking the image of Christendom as a school, gathering all kinds of people under one roof, with different intellects and passions demanding attention. He contrasts this school with a hospital or prison, saying that Christian people are gathered together not to be 'sent to bed', or to be 'buried alive', but presumably to grow and to learn. When Newman looks for a way to enlarge the description he abandons the picture of the school in favour of the factory, describing the 'melting, refining and moulding' in an 'incessant noisy process' of the life of 'Catholic Christendom'.[45] The image of the tidal forces, and a factory such as a steel-works (hot, noisy, dirty and dangerous, rather than the ordered and sterile environment of something like a computer assembly line), are very powerful and anything but dull![46]

In the new *Preface*, Newman does not present a rigid statement of how the dialectical interplay of the three offices might work. Instead, he describes a series of instances in which he applies the model retrospectively to illustrate the interactions.[47] There is no failsafe rule to determine which office should 'win' in which case, nor even a prediction of what the result of the 'balance' of forces will be, but rather an account of what did happen in his time, and why. As he puts it himself, 'I am not obliged to maintain that all ecclesiastical measures and permissions have ever been praiseworthy and safe precedents'.[48] However, from his narrative it is possible to gain an insight into the forces involved in similar problems. This can bring a new perspective which might reduce the emotional intensity of some arguments. Understanding what factors are at work in any debate, and beginning to discern the motivations behind different positions, can help to facilitate an appropriate solution by, for example, asking the question as to what the perspective of another office might be in the situation concerned. Newman's instances of the working out of the model suggest that the outcome in a given case might well not be a compromise which takes some account of all interests, but rather a conscious decision to allow the concerns of one office to dominate.

To apply the model to the Church it is necessary to be conscious of the passing of time. At any one moment the model can be used to explain how the dominance or needs of one or two aspects has led to the other one or two giving way.[49] Whether in any given instance the dominance of one aspect is a problem or not is open to dispute.[50] The principle contained in the Preface is that the correct balance between the offices works out over time, even if only in 'the long, the very long run'.[51]

Holding diverse ecclesiology together

The most important thing about any 'model' of the Church, Avery Dulles argues in his seminal work, is that it must reflect the understanding of the Church as a mystery. Ecclesiology cannot be an exact science, Dulles suggests, but like our knowledge of God is rather apophatic or a *theologia negativa*. That is it is easier and more accurate to say what the Church is not. However, this does not mean that we can say nothing, since there are 'positive tools' available in the 'images', 'symbols', 'models', and 'paradigms' that are used biblically to describe the Church, and from which ecclesiology can be gleaned.[52]

As Dulles describes each of his five models, he begins to compare them one with another, and summarises this comparison by suggesting some criteria for analysis.[53] His concern with ecumenical dialogue, which motivated his study, features strongly. He asks three questions: what are the bonds, the beneficiaries and the benefits proposed by the model? He further suggests seven criteria: is it scriptural; is it traditional; does it lead to virtue; does it fit with experience; is it fruitful within and without? In proposing an additional model of the Church, Newman's 'Prophet, Priest and King', it is important to measure it against these criteria, to see whether there is any area in which the proposed model has a weakness.

There are some obvious similarities between 'Prophet, Priest and King' and the institutional model. Both models emphasise that the Church is visible, and given by Christ, stress the importance of continuity with the Church of the past and the place of obedience to those in authority. As in the 'institutional model', for Newman the bonds of the Church are linked to right profession and obedience and unity arises from the submission of the individual will to the corporate conscience. However, Newman places more emphasis on baptism as the start of a journey than in the institutional model. It is the sacrament with which Christian growth in the discernment of the truth and the struggle for right behaviour begins. The role of the Holy Spirit in binding people to Christ and the Church is also emphasised by Newman. Although Newman is clear that the main benefit of belonging to the Church is divinisation, he also sees that responsible growth in the exercise of the three offices will be of benefit to society as a whole, through intercession, education, family life and business.

A further contra-indication that suggests Newman's 'Prophet, Priest and King' model, although pre-Vatican II, cannot simply be categorised as "Institutional" in Dulles's terms is that since Newman is clear that participation in the offices of Christ arises from baptism, it must therefore belong to all Christians; to the laity as much as to the hierarchy. 'Authority' or oversight is exercised in all three offices by the episcopate, but Newman sets clear limits on the exercise of authority, and the *sensus fidelium* of the whole Church is vital in all three areas. Newman's model pre-supposes a full and active participation and a proper autonomy for each Christian in fully developing a healthy intellect (Prophet), a virtuous and active lifestyle (King) and a mature devotional life (Priest). Integration is necessary for 'health' both of the individual and the Church as a whole and the dynamic balances the 'spiritual', 'rational' and 'practical' aspects of human experience.

'Rule', for Newman, is much broader than organising the Church, and extends to the whole of life, particularly as lived by laity in the world. A vibrant, widely participative, and developmental theological office plays an important part in a healthy dynamic, not simply backing up the institution, or bolstering a conservative principle. Newman's understanding of the office of the 'Prophet' suggests something other than the rigid sterility in theology that Dulles associates with the institutional model. The simile of a school (the teaching and the taught) that Dulles suggests is appropriate for the institutional model, was, as we saw, rejected by Newman as an inadequate metaphor, in favour of the factory.[54]

Dulles contends that the roots of the 'Institutional' model in Scripture are meagre, though proponents of the idea might disagree. However, Newman's model is firmly rooted in scriptural metaphors, as we saw earlier when discussing his sources and his use of characters to illustrate the offices. Dulles also asks whether the model fosters Christian virtues. The strong stress on corporate identity of Newman's model does require obedience, humility and patience just as the institutional model does. However, Newman's stress on sanctification and growth throughout life towards a 'healthy' exercise of the individual offices, and his understanding that the proper integration of the three that Christ demonstrated is the goal for holiness, leaves no room for settling for passive obedience as the main virtue of the laity.

Next, Dulles asks, does the model resonate with the experience of Christians? The explanation of the tensions between the offices that Newman describes, I suggest, not only offers a way to understand the history of the Church, but also current unease and difficulties. An examination of human life in terms of a balanced development between the 'spiritual', 'rational' and 'practical' also fits with the experience of living. However, talking about the model to various groups suggests that the terms 'Prophet', 'Priest' and 'King' can cause some difficulties in understanding.

A 'Prophet' is the term most readily accepted, although it tends to be associated with 'protest' and opposition to authority, neither of which, as we have seen, are Newman's intention. However, to substitute the word 'Theologian' tends to remove the office in some minds to a professional group, studying in the academy, divorced from Church life, and sceptical about the traditional content of the faith.

'Priest' perhaps causes the least difficulty. People are generally quick to see that this does not mean 'clergy', which is a testimony to the Protestant stress on the priesthood of all believers and the later influence of the teaching of Vatican II and the liturgical movement. However, in practice this latter emphasis can, I believe, not only tend to diminish the understanding of the proper role of the ordained minister, but also encourages some laity to think that by becoming increasingly involved in the leadership of liturgical life of the Church, they have done all that they need to do. Consequently, they are comfortable with a superficial intellectual understanding of the faith (Prophet), and neglect action and service to transform the world (King). Still, I can think of no better term.

'King' remains the most difficult term to use for contemporary ears. For some it is a term that is hopelessly patriarchal and associated firmly with the abuse of power. Newman's use of the term is mediated by his use of King David rather than King Solomon as his archetype, and including the provision of goods, charity and service alongside conquering the enemy. The substitution of the term 'rule' helps in many ways, because it allows for ready application to self-rule, which is an important part of what Newman understands by 'King', and still incorporates the understanding of the need for submission of personal autonomy to some sort of government to prevent anarchy. 'Shepherd' has been a popular substitution for 'King', which tries to emphasise caring and service, and the ruler as laying down their life for others, and is associated with King David as well as Christ. However, in Newman's preaching, King David the 'Shepherd' was a type of all three offices and the element of suffering is more correctly associated with the priestly role.

In Newman's model, the mediation or balance of each term is arrived at by taking into account the impulse of the other two offices, rather than trying to alter the terms themselves. The original terms are 'personal' rather than abstract; this removes 'rule' from consideration.

Further, all three terms are associated with anointing in the Christian tradition, which is an important link for understanding the participation in Christ which is at the heart of the model. I conclude that there are no better terms, though some care is needed in introducing and explaining them. The richness of biblical images used by Newman in his preaching can help here.

My experience also suggests that the model is a helpful one ecumenically. Most Christian groups can see that 'worship', 'belief' and 'order' are part of their ecclesiology, however loosely framed, and that there is an interaction between them, and are able to discuss the differences in how these three areas are worked out in the different ecclesial communities.

Having shown how Newman's model comes out well against Dulles's criteria, and differs markedly from the 'institutional' model, what weaknesses are there? As I have hinted in my discussion of the term 'Priest' above, the participation of laity in the three offices is an 'ideal' which is not easy to achieve. Church life easily degenerates into two classes: the teaching/taught, sanctifying/sanctified, and ruling/obeying of the institutional model. It is easier for the baptised to settle for 'receiving grace' from the clergy, to allow the 'Prophet' to be exercised by the official teaching of the Magisterium, with or without help or challenge from the professional theologians, and for 'rule' in terms of transforming the world to be left to someone else. The 'institutional' model requires a lot less effort from everyone.

In terms of the 'health' of the Church, understanding the tension between the offices is not necessarily the answer to resolving it. The path of least resistance or expedience can be to allow the domination of one or other office. Newman is not entirely sanguine that there will be a resolution of the tension this side of eternity, although the presence of the Holy Spirit offers help and strength in the struggle and assurance of a final wholeness.

'Prophet, Priest and King' starts from a sacramental foundation in the participation of all the baptised in the offices of Christ. However, the 'sacramental' model is also part of Newman's understanding of the office of 'Priest', which includes the healing and sanctifying of the participants and 'realising' Christ as he is encountered in prayer, meditation and the sacraments. Dulles identifies a potential weakness of the 'sacramental' model, being a tendency to be preoccupied with good liturgy and aesthetics. In Newman's model, however, liturgy is within the 'Priest' and the impulses of 'Prophet' and 'King' help to balance 'other-worldliness' and devotional excess.

Newman's model, like the sacramental model, holds together the human and divine, the institutional and the mystical elements of the Church as he explains the sin that occurs and yet offers hope for transformation. Newman's inclusion of an authoritative exercise of each of the offices, infallibly exercised as far as the authoritative teaching of doctrine is concerned, upholds the institutional. However, the pneumatological or mystical element is also maintained in the understanding of the corporate discernment of truth (*phronema*).

The resonance with Dulles's 'Herald' model arises in the office of 'Prophet'. The Church in this model centres on the proclamation of revealed truth and calls the world to respond to it. This is the work of Newman's 'Prophet'. The limitations of the 'Herald' model, for example its lack of incarnational focus, is balanced in the tri-polar model by the 'Priest' focussing on sacramental realisation of Christ and the 'King' seeking to incarnate an anticipation of the kingdom of God in the world through fair and just rule.

The 'Servant' model integrates into 'Prophet, Priest and King' primarily under the office of 'King' exercised by the laity living out the truth of the gospel in their home, social and political lives, and so helping to gradually conform the world to the kingdom. The 'Prophet' too has a part to play here in preaching faithfully, and witnessing to, Christian values and offering 'views' of how the gospel can best be incarnated at any given time or place. The 'Priest' is also involved as the Church prays for those suffer and offers healing and hope through her sacramental ministry and intercession. As Dulles suggests, it is possible to begin with 'Prophet, Priest and King' and incorporate the best elements of the other ecclesiological types.

The unique element of Newman's model, the dynamic tri-polar tension between the three offices, leads to exactly the kind of flexible blending together of the ecclesiological impulses of the five models that Dulles views as essential for a good combined model. I therefore suggest that 'Prophet, Priest and King' is a really good candidate to be the kind of 'supermodel' that Dulles is looking for, not in the sense of being all that can be said about the Church, but in the sense that it 'combines the virtues of each of the five without suffering their limitations'.[55]

In conclusion

Newman's model of the Church as 'Prophet', 'Priest' and 'King' offers to the Christian a helpful tool in understanding the dynamic of the Church, both as encountered today, and as reflected in her history. Newman's originality consists in seeing the three offices not simply as powers exercised by the hierarchy, nor even as extended in a different and complementary way to the laity, but as mutually correcting and balancing each other. The tri-polar model encompasses the complexity of the mutual interaction between the three aspects, with each office having a moderating or regulating influence on the other two.

For the model to be useful beyond being a phenomenological analysis of the history of the Church it is necessary to view it in the context of the providence of God, and the indwelling of the Holy Spirit in the Church. The model itself is no guarantee of Christian perfection. In fact, it assumes that the Church fails on occasions in following Christ, and there are times when the pull of one office to its extreme has dominated and will dominate the others in an unhelpful way. His dynamic is both a tool for understanding the difficulties of Christian history and the many faces of the contemporary Church, and a hope that the strengthening of whichever office is weakest will help to rebalance her on the journey towards wholeness. This makes Newman's model distinctive and of immense importance to the Church's self-understanding and to ecumenical progress. Although at any given moment one or other of the three offices may dominate and skew the balance, over time there is hope that the three impulses will balance out, and the Church will move ever onwards towards the perfection of interaction between the offices that Christ alone demonstrates.

The model helps to explain the occasionally hesitant and meandering progress towards the understanding of the truth that occurs in the development of doctrine. In ecumenical dialogue there is ongoing debate about the balance between episcopate and papacy, the particular and the universal church. Newman's model will not allow ecclesiology to be reduced to a debate about authority.[56] The devotional life, the intellectual life and the practical action of the Church, and the dynamic between them are for Newman, as Coulson rightly states, 'logically prior to the application of [her] authority'.[57] Newman understands that effective *episcope* is exercised only when the overseer really knows his people, and 'consults' them, so that the relationship between pastor and people has a mutuality that can be described as '*in conspiratio*', or breathing together. The devotional, theological and practical impulses of the whole Church should each have something to contribute to any debate, and to the decisions that arise.[58]

Issues that separate Christians, maybe different attitudes to personal morality and sexuality, maybe matters of structure and discipline such as who is eligible for ordination, can become less divisive if viewed as part of the 'incessant noisy process'[59] of development. Although the model cannot be used to foretell the outcome of a particular discussion, in retrospect it shows the factors and influences that have been at work. In the midst of controversy, it can help by identifying which factors are at work, or which emphasis is being neglected in a discussion. The challenge for the Christian in any particular age is to be historically conscious and to understand that the particular questions that arise in their own generation are part of this long process. What may look like an obvious or overdue solution, from the perspective of one particular group within the Church at any given place and time, may not be implemented by the Church for a hundred years. With hindsight such a delay may show the change was unnecessary, or unimportant, or that now a more opportune time has arrived or a better solution has been found (or that the frustrated group was right!). Newman was very conscious of this historical perspective, although he was inclined to generalisation, and he was sustained through the controversies of his own day both by his strong sense of continuity with the departed saints, and of the reality of eternity. However, such patience is difficult to achieve.

While we wait, perhaps Newman's model can help us to keep our perspective and work together more fully without acrimony within, as well as between, our various communities. Newman's model is a challenge to an over-centralised and too authoritarian model of the Church, and also to models with little sense of apostolicity, catholicity or *episcope* and all shades in between. As each Christian community explores and seeks to incarnate the idea of Church as 'Prophet, Priest and King' more fully, I believe Newman's model could improve our self-understanding, further our dialogue, and ultimately help bring Christians together in the unity we seek.

Notes

1 Gréa, David (2007), 'Newman's Understanding of the Church' in Lefebvre and Mason (eds), *John Henry Newman: Doctor of the Church*, Oxford: Family Publications, p127.

2 Karkkainen, Veli-Matti (2002), *An Introduction to Ecumenism*, Illinois: IVP Academic, p81.

3 Several writers have sought to explain the different factors at work in matters of religion by using a 'tri-polar or "triangular" model of the things that people do and undergo'. Lash names Kant, Hegel, Fries, Schleiermacher and James, and we might add Möhler. This triangular dynamic, Lash suggests, goes back at least as far as the 'mediaeval transcendentals' of 'truth, goodness and beauty', but can also be detected in Augustine's earlier use of 'memory, understanding and will'. Further, he argues, following Walter Kasper, that such triangles are fundamentally rooted in the doctrine of the Trinity, even when this link is not acknowledged. Lash, N. (1988), *Easter in Ordinary: Reflections on Human Experience and the Knowledge of God*, London: SCM Press, p131.

4 Newbiggin, Lesslie (1953), *The Household of God*, London: SCM Press.

5 Newman explicitly links the three offices of Christ to the Trinity: 'And it will be observed, moreover, that in these offices He also represents to us the Holy Trinity; for in His own proper character He is a priest, and as to His kingdom He has it from the Father, and as to His prophetical office He exercises it by the Spirit. The Father is the King, the Son the Priest, and the Holy Ghost the Prophet.' *Sermons on Subjects of the Day*, V, p55. [All references to Newman works are to the standard edition, which is now available online at http://www.newmanreader.org].

6 This ninety-page Preface has rightly been called the pinnacle of Newman's theology of the Church. Ker, Ian (1970), *John Henry Newman*, Oxford: OUP, p701.

7 *Apologia*, p248.

8 Letter to Emily Bowles, 15/10/1874, Dessain, C.S. and Gornall, T. (eds) (1975), *Letters and Diaries*, Oxford: Clarendon Press, Vol. XXVII, p140.

9 In his earlier correspondence, Newman indicated that he was not disturbed by failings in the Church. He argues that catholicity, by its very nature, involves a threat to holiness: 'Doubtless the face of the Visible Church is very disappointing to an earnest mind, nay, in a certain sense, a scandal. I assert, rather than grant, this grave and remarkable fact.' Letter to Lady

Chatterton, 10/06/1863, in Dessain and Gornall (1975); Dessain, C.S. (ed) (1970), *Letters and Diaries*, Edinburgh: Nelson, Vol. XX, p465.

10 Preface to *The Via Media of the Anglican Church*, Vol. I, p xliii.

11 Thomas Rausch describes contemporary papal or magisterial fundamentalism as a tendency to 'imagine the pope as the source, after God, from which all power and authority flow and as the chief decision maker for contemporary questions. Such people still perceive the Church monarchically. Disputed questions are answered simply by citing what the pope has said.' Rausch, T. (2003), *Catholicism in the Third Millennium*, Collegeville MT: Liturgical Press, pp52–53.

12 The Congregation for the Propagation of the Faith. This department of the Holy See was responsible for all Catholic activity in 'mission' territories, which, until the re-establishment of the hierarchy in October 1850, included England.

13 Newman describes Scott as of the 'school of Calvin' in the *Apologia*, pp107–109. He also uses the term 'Puritan' to describe this stream of Anglican thought, but further adds that it is 'essentially Calvinistic'. *The Via Media of the Anglican Church*, Vol. I, pp18-19.

14 Scott follows the Christology of Calvin, who established this pattern in the *Institutes of the Christian Religion*. Francois Turrettini is a further example of a Reformed scholar following Calvin. See McGrath, Alister (1995), *The Christian Theology Reader*, Oxford: Blackwell, pp153-154.

15 *Sermons on Subjects of the Day*, Sermon V, p56.

16 *Parochial and Plain Sermons*, Sermon 19, Vol. II, p173.

17 Again, this is Newman's term (*V.M.* I, pp17-20). In the same section he also uses 'Anglo-Catholic' for the same group, and lists Andrewes, Laud, Hammond, Butler and Wilson as its protagonists. (See also *Apologia*, p169.)

18 In his sermon on Holy Chrism, Cyril states 'Ye were anointed with ointment, having been made partakers and fellows of Christ'. He goes on to add that the Old Testament figures were priests and kings, but that 'to them these things happened in a figure, but to you not in a figure, but in truth.' *Cat. Myst.* III, paragraph 2 and 5. *Library of the Fathers of the Holy Catholic Church anterior to the division of the east and west: translated by members of the English Church* (1838) London: Rivingtons, Vol. II, p268. It is interesting that, in the series of the texts of the Fathers edited by the leaders of the Oxford movement, Newman wrote the introduction to this volume of Cyril (d.386). Tertullian (d.225) hints at a similar understanding in *De. Bapt.* 7. *Library of the Fathers* (1842), London: Rivingtons, Tertullian Vol. I, p264, and Gregory Nazianzen (d.389) agrees: *Oration XL on Holy Baptism*, section IV in Wace and Schaff (eds) (1894), *A Select Library of Nicene and Post-Nicene Fathers of the Christian Church*, Oxford, Vol. 7, p360.

19 *Civ. Dei.* xx.x (1945 edn), London: J.M. Dent & Sons, Vol. II, p286.

20 Identified by Coulson, John (1970), *Newman and the Common Tradition*, Oxford: Clarendon Press, p168. Weidner, in his 'Introduction' to *The Via Media of the Anglican Church* (1990), Oxford: Clarendon Press, p liii, notices that Newman's source Pearson makes an explicit reference to the Eusebius text. Eusebius, *The Ecclesiastical History*, 1.3.7-20, p12ff. Eusebius 1.4.2, p14.

21 Newman reasons that 'since specimens of a typical correspondence between the history of the Old and of the New Testament are given to us in Scripture… We are intended dutifully to avail ourselves in our expositions of Scripture of the clue which Scripture itself has put into our hands.' In 'Elisha, a Type of Christ and His Followers' (1836), *Sermons on Subjects of the Day*, Sermon XIII, p167ff.

22 *University Sermons*, Sermon XV, p313–314. My emphases.

23 *Parochial and Plain Sermons*, Vol. IV, Sermon 23.

24 These monastic persons and the dominant characteristic of their orders resonate with the three offices of the model: the 'Priest' (the devotional life of the Church) with Benedict and *poesis*, the 'Prophet', or theologian, with Dominic and *scientia*, and the 'King' (rule) with Ignatius and *prudentia*.

25 '[The Catholic Church] did not lose Benedict by finding Dominic; and she has still both Benedict and Dominic at home, though she has become the mother of Ignatius. Imagination, Science and Prudence, all are good, and she has them all. Things incompatible in nature coexist in her; her prose is poetical on the one hand, and philosophical on the other.' Newman, 'The Mission of St Benedict', in *Historical Sketches* Vol. II, p369. Newman sees integrity (or fullness) in education, as in life in general, as something that depends on the interaction between persons: 'We need the (superadded) gift of other persons in order to be persons of integrity ourselves.' Buckley, James (2002), 'The Fullness of God: Catholics and Religious Exclusiveness' in *New Blackfriars*, Vol. 83, No972, p132.

26 Preface to *V.M.* I, pxli.

27 I do not think he is using this term pejoratively, but rather in the sense of 'determined by practical considerations', like the Aristotelian term *prudentia*.

28 Preface to *V.M.* I, pp xli–xlii. (The navigator of a sailing vessel plotting a course has to take account of the influence of wind and tide, as well as the leeway of the vessel when deciding the bearing on which to steer.).

29 Preface to *V.M.* I, p xlvi.

30 Preface to *V.M.* I, pl xxv.

31 Preface to *V.M.* I, p xlviii.

32 Preface to *V.M.* I, p xlvii.

33 *The Idea of a University* and the 'Letter to the Duke of Norfolk' both articulate this concern. Coulson rightly argues that Newman felt 'Romanism was inevitable' if there was a 'failure of the theological office to regulate the excesses of the kingly office.' Coulson (1970), p181.

34 'Theology cannot always have its own way; it is too hard, too intellectual, too exact to be always equitable, or to be always compassionate; and it sometimes has a conflict or overthrow, or has to consent to a truce or a compromise, in consequence of the rival force of religious sentiment or ecclesiastical interests.' Preface to *V.M.* I, p xlix.

35 Preface to *V.M.* I, p xlvii.

36 *New Oxford Dictionary of English*, p1564.

37 In fact the balance of Newman's Preface is in this direction. After making his proposition that theology is the regulating principle in section 7 of Part II, he then devotes sections 8 to 34 to illustrations of occasions when the sacerdotal or regal office take precedence. Richard Bergeron notes that the structure of part II of the Preface is an example of Newman's "cumulative probabilities". Paragraphs 3–7 are the core explanation of the idea. The rest, 8–35, are illustrative of the tensions. Newman demonstrates the truth of his theory by giving examples of how it works. It is not the formal logic of the idea which demonstrates its veracity, Bergeron suggests, but the capacity to find examples. Bergeron, Richard (1971), *Les Abus de L'Église D'après Newman: Étude de la Préface à la troisième édition de La Via Media*, Tournai: Desclée & Cie, p38.

38 Laws once made have to be interpreted and applied. What is meant in a given case will be decided not by the makers of the law, but by those who apply it. Similarly, Newman argues that, even after the definition of papal infallibility in 1870, it 'falls back to the Bishops and the Church to determine quite as much as before,' whether a given statement is infallible. Practical and pastoral application of papal or curial pronouncements will ultimately

determine what they mean, and in this process, the theological discussions of the '*Schola Theologorum*' will play their part. *Certain Difficulties felt by Anglicans in Catholic Teaching*, Vol. II, p176.

39   Letter to Lord Blachford, 28/12/1885, in Dessain, C.S. and Gornall, T. (eds) (1977), *Letters and Diaries*, Oxford: Clarendon Press, Vol. XXXI, p106.

40   One meaning of Newman's synonym 'drag' is an 'iron shoe that can be applied as a brake to a wheel or wagon'. Another is a 'drag-anchor' which keeps the bows of a ship pointing into the waves and helps to lessen leeway, thus preventing the wind or tide from dashing a vessel onto a shoreline, rocks or other obstacle. *New Oxford Dictionary of English*, p558.

41   'It is individuals, and not the Holy See, who have taken the initiative, and given the lead to <the> Catholic mind[s], in theological inquiry. Indeed, it is one of the reproaches urged against the Church of Rome, that it has originated nothing, and has only served as a sort of remora or break in the development of doctrine.' However, in keeping with his idea of the offices acting together, he goes on to add, 'And it is an objection[,] which I <really> embrace as a truth; for such I conceive to be the main purpose of its extraordinary gift.' *Apologia*, p355.

42   *Nicomachean Ethics* (1963 edn), London: OUP, 1106 b 36, p39.

43   The concept of *phronesis* or practical wisdom is essential to Newman's understanding of both intellectual and moral health and *phronesis* is the 'regulating principle' of the 'virtues of justice, self-command, magnanimity, generosity, gentleness and all others'. *Grammar of Assent*, p356.

44   Virtue stands in opposition to two vices: one is a deficiency or lack of the virtue, the other is the virtue taken to excess. Practical wisdom determines where the good is between the two vices in any given situation. For example, when faced with a test of bravery, discerning where courage lies in relation to foolhardiness and cowardice. Copleston, Frederick (1947), *A History of Philosophy Volume I: Greece and Rome*, London: Burns Oates & Washbourne, p337.

45   *Apologia*, p344.

46   Newman reasons that 'Authority and Reason need each other precisely because each is actually sustained by conflict with the other.' Ker, Ian (2009) 'The Church as Communion' in Ker, Ian and Merrigan, Terrence (eds), *The Cambridge Companion to John Henry Newman*, Cambridge: CUP, p142.

47   Bergeron notes that the structure of part II of the Preface is an example of Newman's 'cumulative probabilities'. Newman demonstrates the truth of his tri-polar theory by giving examples of how it works. It is not the formal logic of the idea which demonstrates its veracity, Bergeron suggests, but the capacity to find examples. Bergeron (1971) , p38.

48   Preface to *V.M.* I, p lxvi.

49   One example of a lack of interaction that Newman regards as unhelpful can be seen in his interpretation of the birth of Methodism, which he offers as a reproach to an incorrect suppression of the devotional and charismatic impulse by the regal office. 'Methodism has carried off many a man who was sincerely attached to the Established Church, merely because that Church will admit nothing but what it considers "rational" and "sensible" in religion'. *Historical Sketches II*, p165.

50   Newman's illustrations in the Preface of how the regal office has 'rightly' dominated are perplexing to modern eyes. It is important to remember Newman's context and his second aim of countering Ultramontanism. I also suggest that occasionally he was using irony.

51   Preface to *V.M.* I, pxlii. As Dulles suggests, 'Church History is not a rectilinear movement but is marked by frequent detours, compromises and adjustments'. Dulles, Avery (1985), *The Catholicity of the Church*, Oxford: OUP, p122.

52 Dulles, Avery (1974, 1987 Rev. Edn), *Models of the Church*, Dublin: Gill and Macmillan, p18.
53 Most criteria for analysing the models presuppose or imply a choice of values, Dulles acknowledges. Commitment to one model tends to involve establishing criteria that make other models less good, or to involve a circular argument. For example, he suggests, those who favour the 'Institutional' model decry a lack of conceptual clarity and regard for authority in other models. Those who prefer the 'Servant' model denounce the others as too introspective and church-centred. Dulles's analysis is most favourable to his preferred model of the Church as 'Sacrament', and least favourable to the 'Institutional' model. 'I may have been somewhat too severe on the institutional model,' Dulles adds in the additional chapter in the second edition. Dulles (1987), p205.
54 *Apologia*, p344.
55 Dulles (1987), p195.
56 Part of the difficulty lies in the interpretation of the role of 'Magisterium'. Edward Miller argues that Newman challenges any idea of the Magisterium as 'elderly relatives in a family who possess knowledge' that the youngsters don't have. 'The process of discernment,' he argues, 'does not take the bishops to some sequestered locations that are blocked off to all others.' Newman challenges a view of the Holy Spirit that tends to privatise divine influence. 'To be spirit-filled, according to Newman, is to be with others – other laity (meaning all the baptised) across place, time and cultures. This is the *sensus fidelium*. Our grasp of the truth must be personal and ecclesial: both my faith and our faith, both what the Spirit says to me and what the Spirit has been saying to us for so very long.' Miller, Edward (2007), 'The Sense of the Faithful' in Lefebvre and Mason (eds), *John Henry Newman Doctor of the Church*, p161.
57 Coulson (1970), p168.
58 However, the dynamic of 'Prophet, Priest and King' model at work can, I suggest, be discerned in the speeches *during* Vatican II about the Decree on Ecumenism. Congar, Yves, Küng, Hans and O'Hanlon, Daniel (eds) (1964), *Council Speeches of Vatican II*, London: Sheed and Ward, pp130ff, 134ff, and 137ff.
59 *Apologia*, p344.

Convergence in Catholicity and Communion

David Carter

Throughout his ministry, John Newton has made a richly holistic contribution to the Ecumenical Movement. As a church leader, he joined the already well known and ecumenically significant partnership of Archbishop Worlock and Bishop David Sheppard when he became Chairman of the Liverpool District in 1986. Soon afterwards he became Free Church moderator for Merseyside. As a theologian, he served on the seventh quinquennium of the Methodist Roman Catholic International Commission which reported in 2001. As a strong advocate of spiritual ecumenism, he continued the long Methodist tradition of learning from and benefitting from the spiritual riches of other Christian traditions, a practice which dates back to that of Wesley himself. In his delightful little book, *Heart Speaks to Heart*, he commended such learning to his fellow Methodists and to others in a manner that showed his ability as communicator and scholar.[1]

John has a particular interest in and concern for Methodist–Roman Catholic relationships. The longest chapter in *Heart Speaks to Heart* is entitled 'Methodism and Catholicism'. It is followed by a chapter on the Ecumenical Society of the Blessed Virgin Mary in which John played a much-appreciated role, showing his willingness to be engaged in a pioneering area of dialogue which had previously been almost entirely eschewed on the grounds that it would be too difficult and controversial.

It is in gratitude to John both for his wide-ranging contribution to the Ecumenical Movement and for his personal encouragement over many years that this essay is written. The aim of this essay is not to tell the entire history of the Catholic–Methodist relationship and dialogue. This has already been done by two excellent scholars, David Butler and David Chapman.[2] Rather, it is to examine certain features that, as it were, lie deep within the theological and spiritual DNA of the two traditions and to examine how they have enhanced particular features of the relationship and dialogue.

For a long time, these commonalities went almost entirely unrecognised. Prior to the revolution in ecumenical relationships unleashed by the Second Vatican Council, Roman Catholics and Methodists lived out their Christian lives in almost complete isolation from each other. Where contact did occur, it was often marked by suspicion, even outright hostility, frequently backed by misconceptions about the life and teaching of the other tradition.[3] It was sometimes assumed that the traditions were polar opposites, an opinion expressed in somewhat triumphalistic Wesleyan terms, as recently as 1937, by Henry Bett. He talked of the 'absolute antithesis between Catholicism and Methodism', of the issue being 'between the authority of tradition and the authority of experience' and between an emphasis upon the Church as institution and an emphasis upon personal experience in religion.[4] That Bett, a distinguished contemporary Methodist scholar, could write in such terms, was tribute, in part to the degree of mutual ignorance then existing, but also a recognition of the way in which, at that date, a degree of hardening of opposition to contrasting theologies and ecclesiologies had long led to a lopsidedness within both traditions and to the effective obscuring of elements which belonged to the common fullness of both traditions. Thus, on the Methodist side, there had been, ever since the death of the Wesleys, an attenuation of the more 'catholic' and sacramental elements within the Wesleyan heritage. There had also developed, partly under the influence of the wider evangelical movement, a greater individualism than had characterised the originally more corporate and ecclesial stress of the early Methodist movement. On the Roman Catholic side, there had been a tendency ever since the Council of Trent to reduce ecclesiology to hierarchiology. There was also an accompanying tendency to overlook the elements of truth within the thinking of the reformers, which a later generation would see as authentically catholic, in favour of an apologetic position that was almost uniformly hostile to everything the reformers had stood for.[5]

By the time that Bett wrote in 1937, there were the first signs of a change within both traditions. The Methodist Sacramental Fellowship was beginning, albeit under a cloud of some suspicion, its search for a restoration of a more authentically Wesleyan sacramental emphasis within Methodism. From the Roman Catholic side, men like Yves Congar and Henri de Lubac were beginning to engage in *ressourcement*, a well-researched re-reception of the roots of the Roman Catholic tradition in Scripture and in the writings of the early fathers. Within both churches, albeit on an unofficial and frequently discountenanced fashion within the Roman Catholic Church, a few people were beginning to lay the foundations for an important renewal of both traditions that would, in due course, aid their rapprochement. The process was aided by the entry of both churches into the Ecumenical Movement, Methodism being involved in it from its beginnings, the Roman Catholic Church only officially embracing it at the Second Vatican Council, albeit then with a zeal that put it right at the heart of the burgeoning process of bilateral ecumenical dialogues.

The re-reception of the ancient creedal concept of catholicity and the development of the now central ecclesiological concept of Church as communion were to play a key role in the process of convergence between the Methodist and Roman Catholic traditions. Both concepts can be held to have firm roots in the New Testament and the church of the first three centuries, although the term catholicity first appears as such only in sub-apostolic times, first being used by Ignatius of Antioch.[6] It is these concepts and their influence that I now intend to examine.

The concept of catholicity relates to the rounded wholeness of the Christian tradition. It is the concept that ultimately validates that of unity in diversity, of a church which can flourish in and draw from the strengths of all the human cultures in which it becomes grounded. Catholicity is about unity in the essentials of the faith and legitimate multiplicity in the way in which these essentials are formulated doctrinally, expressed liturgically and lived out in differing styles of mission and service. Catholicity, as St Cyril of Jerusalem affirmed, is about the way in which the Church, through the generous endowment and provision of the Son and the Spirit, is able to meet every human need and enable humanity to progress towards maturity in Christ. It is about the fullness and plenitude of divine grace, poured out to meet every human need in terms of response to the gracious invitation to be involved as the adoptive sisters and brothers of Christ in the service of the great plan of the Father for the reconciliation of all things (Eph 1:9-10).

Common to both traditions is this stress on the nature of the God who calls all people to share in his loving plan. According to the most recent official ecclesiological statement of British Methodism 'The Church is catholic because there is one universal God, who has declared his love for all creation in Jesus Christ'.[7] Common also to them is a stress on the dynamic nature of catholicity, which is seen as ever expanding as the Church, under the guidance of the Spirit, continues its pilgrimage towards the promised Kingdom. From the Methodist side, we may cite the opening paragraph of the British Methodist ecclesiological statement of 1937.

> *The Church of Christ is the home of the Holy Spirit, and is therefore a family with a unique and developing life. It is a life of a distinctive quality, a life which under the guidance of the Spirit should be richer as time goes on, with fresh manifestations as new nations and races are added to the Church, and a new apprehension of divine truth is given.*[8]

From the Roman Catholic side, we may mention the reorientation of the concept of catholicity that took place in the early and middle years of the twentieth century as, under the influence of such theologians as Yves Congar, the Roman Catholic Church moved from an exclusivist and institutional ecclesiology, based upon the concept of the Church as a perfect society, towards an ecclesiology based on the concept of communion, stressing the priority of the interior life of the Church, based on its participation in the trinitarian mystery. In a manner reminiscent of the Methodist statement just cited, Congar and others stressed catholicity as involving both the taking up of human diversity into the life of the Church and its purification under the influence of the Gospel.[9] At the same time, they stressed that very real elements of catholic truth were to be found outside of the Roman Catholic Church, elements that could and should find their place within the life of the Roman Catholic Church. Such thinking was subsequently enshrined in the teaching of the Decree on Ecumenism of the Second Vatican Council.[10]

The concept of catholicity was important in the thought of the Wesleys and in early Methodism. John Wesley, in his famous Christian Library, designed for the education of the first Methodist preachers, included spiritual writings from both Protestant and Catholic spiritual traditions, commending them to the Methodist people. William Shrewsbury, a minister of the post-Wesley generation, talked of the way in which the Methodists were the debtors of all, Caroline Anglicans and Puritans, Moravians and continental pietists alike.[11] Methodist catholicity did not stop at the level of reading and intellectual debt, but also expressed itself in practical support and prayer for the missions of other churches.[12] Methodists were, of course, no more fully consistent with their tradition than are other Christians and this no doubt explains the famous Conference call of 1820 in which the Methodists were reminded of their heritage and exhorted to 'ever remember the kind and catholic spirit of primitive Methodism' and, in their bearing towards 'all denominations of Christians holding the Head', 'to be the friends of all and the enemies of none'.

Later Methodist fathers stressed the importance of catholicity. Alfred Barrett argued that the greatness of Christian truth was such that no one denomination could hope to compass it all unaided by the witness of others.[13] John Scott Lidgett talked of the theology of all separated churches as being marked by provincial accents which needed complementing.[14] It is interesting to note the increasing convergence of the Catholic and Methodist understandings of catholicity even within the pre-Vatican II period when contacts were still extremely limited and formal theological dialogue had not yet begun. Both churches were becoming increasingly aware of the need to share in the gifts that had been given to others. The two positions were, naturally, differently nuanced in view of their differing ecclesial claims.

The Roman Catholic Church continued to claim that it alone possessed the institutional fullness with which Christ had endowed his Church, the necessary coping stone being the petrine ministry. It was, however, now able to admit that there were valuable elements of the overall Christian heritage which had been better preserved within other traditions but which now needed to be reintegrated within the Catholic wholeness of the Church.[15] It was able to admit that its own catholicity had been wounded by reason of the schisms that had cut it off from such authentic elements as had been preserved elsewhere.[16] John Paul II further developed this understanding in his encyclical 'Ut Unum Sint' when he talked of the rich embellishment of the tradition which had taken place despite the objective sin of schism.[17] He also subsequently taught his fellow Catholics that they must recognise new styles of Christian devotion and service wherever they were to be found, thus witnessing to a Catholic acceptance that the Spirit of God was indeed creatively at work in other Christian traditions.[18]

Methodism 'claims and cherishes its place within the Holy Catholic Church, which is the Body of Christ' and recognises, as a necessary consequence, its call to work for the unity of the one Body but without any prejudice to the claims of other trinitarian churches also to be recognised as equal parts of the Body[19]. It recognises its need to learn from the spiritual riches and traditions of the rest of the Universal Church.

Both churches thus converge in practice in their positive desire to see their catholicity enhanced by the gifts of others. It is not without significance that the third session of the international Roman Catholic dialogue centred upon the doctrine of the Holy Spirit and registered a very high degree of consensus. It was accepted that the differing traditional emphases and forms of expression in the pneumatology of the two communions were 'complementary and mutually enriching, rather than divisive and a cause of dissension'.[20]

This particular session of the dialogue also registered approval of the Methodist emphasis upon the significance of religious experience, thus rendering the dichotomy registered by Henry Bett over forty years earlier redundant. It recorded that the members of both communions could find inspiration in Wesley's heart-warming experience. It paid tribute to the rediscovery at Vatican II of the stress on Christian experience, 'understood afresh as intimacy with Christ in prayer and as liberating presence in persons and communities'. It forecast that an exploration of the similarities between Wesleyan and Roman Catholic spirituality would play a key role in future reconciliation. 'A reclamation of our complex heritage by both sides would benefit our respective communities'. It affirmed the crucial importance of 'heart religion' and the work of the Holy Spirit both as 'the prime artisan of Christian experience and in prevenient grace', this last a strong Wesleyan emphasis.[21]

This early work, in a field relatively rarely treated in formal dialogue, pointed the way forward to the creativity of the sixth and eighth quinquennia of the dialogue.[22] In the former, the report, *The Word of Life*, stressed the three fold nature of faith as *fides quae*, the content of belief, as *fides qua*, the fiduciary element and *faith as fruitful* in terms of that constant development of new forms and styles of Christian discipleship, spirituality and community living which has been at the heart of both traditions with their joint cherishing of both the *instituted* means of grace and the *providential*.[23] The later report, *The Grace Given You in Christ*, represented an important challenge to both churches in terms of the further enrichment of their mutual catholicity. They were told that their relationship had now reached a point at which it was 'time now to return to the concrete reality of one another, to look one another in the eye, and with love and esteem to acknowledge what we see to be truly of Christ and of the Gospel, and thereby *of the Church*, in one another'.[24] Significantly, this section of the report was entitled *Deepening and Extending our Recognition of One Another* and it revealed a complex relationship in which the two communions were called both to challenge themselves as to what they should be seeking to receive from each other and challenging the other as to what they might consider receiving as a gift within their developing mutual search for a greater catholicity and wholeness.

Some of the important challenges there recorded are currently being taken up in the ninth quinquennium of the dialogue, centring upon the sacramentality of the Church. In the meantime, it is instructive to note that the British Roman Catholic–Methodist dialogue has already set an important precedent in its conversations of the early 1990s concerning the role of and devotion to the mother of Christ. These resulted in the publication of a pamphlet, *Mary Sign of Grace, Faith and Holiness*, an admission by the Methodists that they could profitably explore the role of Mary as model disciple and elder sister within the community of faith and an acceptance of the truths to which the marian dogmas of 1854 and 1950 were intended to point, viz the availability of grace for a special vocation and the eschatological destiny awaiting the entire people of God.[25]

In the context of the significantly creative first Durham Conference on Receptive Ecumenism in January 2006, Bishop Michael Putney gave moving testimony to the way in which his own practice had been enriched through his learning about the life and mission of the Wesleys.[26] It is clear that the common search for a fuller catholicity has led the two communions to a closer relationship. Finally, one may say that their converging understanding of catholicity holds out a way of reconciling their respective ecclesiological claims. Both churches claim to belong to the one holy catholic Church as established by Christ, but with the key difference that the Roman Catholic Church claims that it alone has preserved the vital focusing ministry of the Bishop of Rome, a claim that is at its assertion at Vatican II that unity subsists in it. Methodism, by contrast, simply claims to be a *part* of that one holy, catholic and apostolic Church.

Within the dialogue to date, important statements have been made pointing to the possibility of future agreement on this point. As early as the third quinquennium, it was accepted that 'the papal authority was no less than any other a manifestation of the spirit of love in the Church' and that it had been established for the building up of the Church.[27] It was, however, accepted that Methodists were unlikely in the foreseeable future to feel comfortable with many of the claims of the papacy. In the succeeding report, an important advance was registered when it was stated that 'Methodists accept that whatever is properly required for the unity of the whole of Christ's church must by that very fact be God's will for his church. A universal primacy might well serve as focus of and ministry for the unity of the whole church'.[28] Since then, a few Methodist scholars have considered the claims of the petrine ministry, both from the point of view of a possible biblical basis for it and in terms of its compatibility with Methodist tradition and structures, a point on which more will be said in the context of the joint understanding of Church as Communion.[29] Methodists have also declared themselves open to the reception of the sign of the episcopal succession, something that alongside an agreed reception of the petrine ministry would be essential to full communion between the two traditions.[30] An important step forward was made when the Methodists declared in 2006 that 'in the light of the present crisis of authority in the Christian Church, Methodists may come to value a petrine ministry at the service of unity. In particular, with proper safeguards, Methodists may be prepared to receive a petrine ministry exercised collegially within the college of bishops as a final decision making authority in the Church, at least insofar as essential maters of faith are concerned'.[31]

Two important contributions from individual Catholic theologians may further help towards reconciliation. In 1970, the late Cardinal Willebrands put forward his concept of the existence of multiple authentic styles or *typoi* of being church, each characterised by a particular style of discipline or canon law, a characteristic style of theologising and particular forms of liturgical life and spirituality.[32] Clearly, both communions can claim to have such styles. Yves Congar has reinforced Willebrands's case with his stress on diversity as a necessary internal facet of true unity and in his teaching that the Church is bound to realise ever more fully its catholicity.[33] This, it should be noted, tunes in with more recent ecumenical thinking about diversity as not only legitimate but positively enriching.

One problem for all churches possessing the episcopal succession is that of recognising the full catholicity and apostolicity of churches which lack it. Methodism, by contrast, has always stressed that recognition of the work of the Spirit in churches arising by initiative independent of the work of the apostles or their episcopal successors is, in fact, an apostolic duty.[34] One could argue that this received a limited degree of reception in the thought of the late John Paul II, exemplified in his dictum that 'preparing ourselves for unity means... knowing how to recognise the action of the Holy Spirit, opening ourselves to fresh aspects of Christian commitment'.[35]

According to Jean-Marie Tillard, it is part of the duty of the Roman Church, in virtue of its double apostolicity including that of Paul as well as Peter, to attest the unforeseeable work of God.[36] According to Congar, the Roman Catholic Church is 'not closed to the idea of a space being open for the unforeseeable intervention and activity of the Spirit beyond current ecclesiastical structures'.[37] One wonders how, in the light of the assertions of these two prominent ecclesiologists and ecumenists, the Catholic Church might reassess the Methodist Revival, possibly coming to accept the traditional Wesleyan assertion that it represented not just a revival of apostolic teaching but also of authentic primitive church life.[38]

If the developments suggested over the last few paragraphs can take place and bear fruit, then we will see a genuine exchange of gifts and an enhancement of the catholicity of both churches as envisaged in the Decree on Ecumenism and carried out in a manner that respects the historic claims of the two churches, both the Catholic claim to embody the fullness of the institutional and sacramental structures essential to unity and the Methodist claim to have been raised up to spread scriptural holiness and to embody a true *typos* of Christian life and witness. The future will not be one of capitulation or submission on either side, but of that mutual going forward together into a fuller catholicity as envisaged by the English Catholic bishops in their response to the *Called To Be One Process* of CTE. The dynamic understanding of catholicity, so acutely stressed in the thought of Congar as dual loyalty to the Tradition *and to its future development*, will have played a vital role in the search for unity.[39]

The understanding of Church as communion, so prominent in ecumenical thought since Vatican II also lies deep within the spiritual and theological heritage of both communions. Modern ecumenically aware biblical scholars have shown how fundamental the concept of *koinonia* is to the Church as described in the New Testament. The late twentieth century revival of trinitarian theology has also played a vital role in pushing the concept to the fore in ecclesiology throughout Christendom and not just within the Roman Catholic Church and Methodism.

The contemporary revival of communion ecclesiology has roots both in the Methodist revival and in the tradition of Roman Catholic ecclesiology that began with Joseph Adam Möhler in the early nineteenth century. In both cases, the primary interest was in the lived experience of the Church of the first three centuries, in particular in the unity engendered within the early communities by the love of the Spirit. Charles Wesley sang this experience in his hymns, Möhler theologised it lyrically in his famous *Unity in the Church or the Principle of Catholicism*.[40] Both insisted on the primacy of the work of the Spirit in ecclesiology, regarding the developing ecclesial structures as expressions of the love and unanimity wrought by the Spirit and only secondarily as disciplinary, an insight to which Möhler gave graphic expression in his opinion that in the first three centuries the bishop was practically invisible within his local church only later having to develop a more disciplinarian style.[41] It was out of the common sense of unity and global interdependence of all the faithful that both the Methodist Connexional Principle and the Catholic emphasis on the collegial responsibility all the bishops subsequently developed.

Later developments in both traditions followed the common insight. Wesley was a great innovator in forms of ecclesial life and discipline, but he regarded his innovations as usually having some parallel in the life of the Church of the first three centuries even if, as he admitted, this was only later discerned.[42] W.F. Slater in his Fernley lecture of 1885 stressed the apostolicity of the life of the early Methodists.[43] In recent times, Ted Campbell has reviewed Wesley's debt to the practice of the Early Church and his admiration for its purity of life.[44] Above all, the Methodist people have continued to sing the perennially popular *Hymns for the Society* of Charles Wesley with their stress upon the unity given by the Spirit. These, and indeed other Charles Wesley hymns, stress the unity, love and joy of the people of God in pilgrimage, aware of their oneness across the ages and continents and, supremely of their unity with the Church above. We may instance just a few verses that illustrate the richness of this sung ecclesiology.

The hymn 'All praise to our redeeming Lord' covers most of the themes, stressing the mutual building up of each other within the societies and their peace, joy and harmony. Particularly interesting is verse three:

> *The gift which he on one bestows,*
> *We all delight to prove:*
> *The grace through every vessel flows,*
> *In purest streams of love.*[45]

With its implication of the mutual recognition of differing charisms within the context of a common experience of the love of Christ and of the community. This finds a parallel in Möhler's stress that 'the principle of the Church is this, that a man cannot live a Christian life without the influence which is exerted on him by the community of the faithful, inspired by the Holy Ghost'. Möhler emphasised within his ecclesiology the gentle leading of the Spirit rather than any direction of Christ. 'If we say merely that the Church is a so called construction, we leave the impression that Christ had, so to speak, *ordered* his disciples *together* without arousing in them an inner need that brought and held them together.[46]

In both Wesley and Möhler one finds an implicit stress on the centrality of the *sensus fidelium*. Möhler states that the community kept up as long as possible the habit of referring the solution of any problem to the whole of the community.[47] Wesley, in an interesting comment on the community sharing of goods recorded in Acts 2, states 'How came they to act thus, seeing that we do not read of any positive command to do this? I answer, there needed no outward command: The command was written upon their hearts. It naturally and necessarily resulted from the degree of love that they enjoyed. Observe! They were of one heart, and of one soul'.[48]

Within the Roman Catholic tradition, Möhler was followed by Newman and both by Congar with his emphasis upon the importance of the lived life of the Church as both prior to theological reflection and dogmatic formulation and also a proper subject for subsequent theological reflection.[49] The trinitarian basis of ecclesiology was the subject of theological reflection at Vatican II and subsequently with some close parallels in contemporary Methodism. We may instance a key quotation from each tradition. 'The Church is one because of her source: the highest exemplar and source of this mystery is the unity, in the Trinity of persons, of one God, the Father and the Son in the Holy Spirit...' to which Susan Wood adds the comment 'Ecclesial communion is modelled on the communion or perichoresis of the Father, Son and Spirit in their trinitarian relationship.'[50] From Methodism, we may cite, 'In whatever way we think of the Trinity, we cannot have an adequate ecclesiology without a proper trinitarian doctrine, since the Church is called to mirror, at a finite level, the reality which God is in eternity.'[51]

The significance of communion ecclesiology has been affirmed in the international dialogue, particularly in its fourth and eighth reports.[52] There was strong affirmation of the common understanding of the total interdependence of all local churches as enshrined in the Methodist Connexional Principle. The Church is by nature a 'connectional society', a 'vital web of interactive relationships'. Both Methodists and Catholics have an essentially 'connectional understanding of Christ's call to discipleship, holiness and mission, always as God's gift and rooted in our sharing in the invisible koinonia that is the life of the Holy Trinity... The dynamic of connection and communion belongs not only to local disciples gathered together in community, but also to the worldwide community of those local communities gathered together as one Church.'[53]

When the report *Called To Love and Praise* was discussed in the British Roman Catholic–Methodist Committee in 2000, the Roman Catholic members pointed out that work still needed to be done on the question of the nature and role of ordained ministries within the communion of the Church. Here there are still some differences. While both churches agree that the ordained ministry is part of God's provision for the Church and that its nature and function are essentially pastoral, there are continuing differences over the extent to which the orders of ministry are regarded as laid down by Christ or as being variable at the discretion of the Church according to historical circumstances. For Roman Catholics, the threefold ministry of bishop, priest and deacon is regarded as normative for all time, as is the Petrine ministry as a universally focusing ministry. Methodists regard the form of the ministry as legitimately variable, even though they have, in some conferences, a threefold order of bishop, elder and deacon. There are differences too as to the extent to which presbyters and, even more, layfolk should be associated with bishops in the highest courts of the Church.[54]

It has long seemed to me that the solution of such difficulties requires a deeper examination of the relationship between trinitarian theology and the understanding of human nature as created in the image of God alongside the understanding of redeemed human nature as recreated in Christ. Traditional Catholic theology has emphasised the governing role of the bishop as parallel to the role of the Father. 'Follow the bishop', says St Ignatius of Antioch, 'as Christ followed the Father'. A close examination of the relationship of the Father and the Son as presented in John's Gospel shows us that the relationship is more complex than suggested by Ignatius' quotation that presents only one side as it were of the relationship. Certainly, Christ asserts that he came to do not his own will but the will of the Father who sent him. However, Christ also witnesses to the fact of his equality with the Father as the Father's gift to him from before all time. 'Just as the Father has life in himself, so he has granted to the Son to have life in himself' (John 5:26). Jesus points to the complete trust that the Father resides in him in giving him full jurisdiction (John 5:22). The relationship of the Father and the Son is one of complete mutual love in which the Father holds nothing back from the Son, even though in the fullest love and adoration the Son continues to do exactly as the Father wills.

The relationship that Jesus establishes with the disciples is of precisely the same nature. His prior statement 'For the Father loves the Son and shows him all that he is doing' is paralleled by the later 'I have called you friends because I have disclosed to you everything that I have heard from my Father' (John 15:15). The first and all later disciples enter into the relationship of adoptive sonship in which 'our regeneration answers to the eternally Begotten, our adoption to the eternally Beloved'[55].

This being the case, the relationship of Christians with each other within the Body of Christ calls for relationships of trust, confidence and mutual respect that faithfully parallel those of the Father and the Son. The case for this is further reinforced by the biblical teaching that human beings are made in the image of God with the implicit capacity for creative and responsible relationship with him and with each other. Equal dignity does not, however, imply equality in vocation, charism or particular ministry. It does, however, imply that those with special charisms and ministries respect those for whom they exercise their gifts and ministries which are intended for the building up of the body and the equipping of the saints (Ephesians 4: 12-13), enabling the spiritual growth and maturity of all the faithful.

Within a true appreciation of the communion nature of the Church, all ministry, ordained or otherwise, needs to be seen as ministry *in* and *for* the Church rather than *over* it, as particularly understood in post-Tridentine Roman Catholicism, or ministry *under* it, as a hired agency, as understood in some of the groups that split from Wesleyan Methodism in the early nineteenth century.[56] It is an understanding of ministry that requires on the part of ministers and faithful alike a particular discipline and ascesis. As William Shrewsbury wrote, amidst the conflicts over the role of the ministry within the Wesleyan Connexion of his time, the greatest evil that could befall any church was a lack of confidence between ministers and people; conversely, the 'greatest good to be desired... is generous and unlimited confidence, disposing to habitual co-operation in every plan'.[57]

Strong as was the belief of Shrewsbury and the other classical Wesleyan ecclesiologists of his time in the nature and prerogatives of the pastoral office, they never denied the importance of co-operation with the laity and especially of the need to affirm and support the ministries of local preachers and class leaders. The classical Wesleyans saw ministers as 'ruling servants and serving rulers' within the Church, as exercising focal ministries of oversight and connexion, enabling the finest circulation of love and insight throughout the Connexion.[58] Möhler emphasises the mutual spiritual indwelling of bishop, clergy and people:

> *The apostles did not send their epistles to the bishops of the congregations but to the congregations directly... the bishop was considered part of the whole congregation... he was not raised above the others, since he was understood as one with the congregation, and it was not considered aside from him nor he aside from it.*[59]

From the Methodist side, Gregory emphasises the frank but harmonious discussion amongst all the faithful at the council recorded in Acts 15 in which there was 'the freest circulation through every part of the system, a process that was neither democratic nor authoritarian but carried out trusting in the Holy Spirit.[60]

Modern Roman Catholic ecclesiology has recovered some of this emphasis. Tillard stresses that bishops have a duty to articulate the concerns of their local churches and to safeguard their traditions, a duty for which they are responsible to their people.[61] Pope John Paul II has set an example in seeking to recognise and receive the riches inherent both in other Christian traditions and within the developing life of the Catholic Church itself. The whole Church, as Nicholas Lash has suggested, is a learning community in which there is reception both from above through the teaching of the pope, bishops and theologians, but also from below through the reception of the practical experience of the faithful and their reflection on the *sensus fidei*.

Within the international dialogue, these points are increasingly being taken up. It has to be stressed, however, that, in the last resort, an act of profound reception and conversion is called for in both communions. The Roman Catholic Church must move towards a much greater association of the laity with the decision making bodies of the Church even at the highest level, a point that has already been made within that Church by those calling for reform.[62] Within Methodism, there must be a much greater awareness of the need to receive from other traditions and, in particular, from the Roman Catholic Church. It must be understood within both churches that the role of the whole People of God is as it was on the day of Pentecost:

> ... to devote themselves to the learning, to the experimental realisation and to the assiduous practice of those truths which it was the principle work of the apostles to teach.[63]

In doing this they will discover a symphonic harmony, as it were, between the leadership of ministers, as both tradition bearers and facilitators of the transmission of new insights, and the active role of all Christians as witnesses lending credibility to the Gospel in their manner both of service within the world and in the rich attractiveness of their own community life. Within the context of the experimental realisation of apostolic truth lived out by the faithful in ways both traditional and innovatory, the two communions will find the true convergence in the Spirit of their contrasting traditions. Bett's dichotomy, mentioned at the beginning of this chapter, will have been transcended in a way unimagined by most of his contemporaries.

Much remains to be done in terms of dialogue and achieved in terms of the vital reception process. However, there can be no doubt that by living in legitimate and enriching catholic diversity and true communion, based on that generous mutual confidence of ordained ministers and lay faithful, the Roman Catholic and Methodist people could set a fruitful example to the rest of Christendom and, beyond that, to our fractured world which finds it so difficult to attain that true justice and peace which can alone be the fruit of true human communion engendered by the Spirit of God. That, however, must be the subject of a further enquiry.

Notes

1 Newton, John(1994), *Heart Speaks to Heart*, Darton, Longman and Todd.

2 Butler, D. (1995), *Methodists and Papists*; Chapman, D. (2004), *In Search of the Catholic Spirit: Methodists and Roman Catholics in Dialogue*...

3 A key feature of the international dialogue has been the way in which this unpromising history has been faced and admitted. See, for example, the summary of Catholic–Methodist relationships in the most recent report of the international Commission, *The Grace Given You in Christ: Catholics and Methodists Reflect Further on the Church* (2006), Lake Junaluska, paras 20-33.

4 Bett, H. (1937) *The Spirit of Methodism*, London: Epworth Press, pp144-5.

5   Yves Congar sometimes described the extremes of post-Tridentine ecclesiology as hierarchiology. See the excellent study of his thought by Fameree, J. and Routhier, G. (2008), *Yves Congar*, Paris, p183.
6   In his *Epistle to the Smyrnaeans*, 8.2.
7   *Called To Love and Praise*, para 2.4.4 , cited in *Statements of the Methodist Church on Faith and Order*, Vol. 2 (1984-2000), 2000, part 1, p20.
8   'Nature of the Christian Church' (1937), cited in *Statements of the Methodist Church on Faith and Order 1933-1983* (1984), Peterborough, p7.
9   Fameree and Routhier (2008), pp62, 65, 190.
10 Decree on Ecumenism, para 4.
11 Shrewsbury, W.J. (1840), *An Essay on the Scriptural Character of the Wesleyan Methodist Economy*.
12 Gregory, B. (1888), *A Handbook of Scriptural Church Principles*, pt 1, p25 describes the setting up within early Methodism of a monthly prayer meeting for the missions of *other* churches, Gregory commenting that 'true catholicity is the very essence of Wesleyan Methodism'.
13 Barrett, A. (1849), *Pastoral Addresses*, London, p371.
14 Lidgett, J.S. (1927), *God, Christ and the Church*, p231.
15 A point first stated by Paul Couturier with his emphasis on the cosmic scope of the Orthodox understanding of redemption and his praise for the biblical scholarship, study and piety of Protestants.
16 *Decree on Ecumenism*, para 4.
17 *Ut Unum Sint*, para 85.
18 Ibid, paras 15, 28. See also *The Wisdom of John Paul II*, CTS, 1995, p103.
19 Quotation from the Deed of Union of the British Methodist Church.
20 *The Honolulu Report*, para 7, cited in Meyer, H. and Vischer, L. (eds) (1984), *Growth in Agreement: Reports and Agreed Statements of Ecumenical Conversations on a World Level*, New York/Geneva, p368.
21 *The Honolulu Report*, paras 23-32, Meyer and Vischer (1984), pp373-6.
22 The report of the sixth quinquennium, *The Word of Life: A Statement on Revelation and Faith* is cited in Gros, J., Meyer, H. and Rusch, W. (eds) (2000), *Growth in Agreement II: Reports and Agreements of Ecumenical Conversations at a World Level, 1982-1998*, New York/Geneva, pp618-646.
23 The term is, of course, a Wesleyan one but one which I believe can be received within the Roman Catholic tradition since the term 'instituted means' refers to the cardinal importance of those means of grace directly attested in Scripture, such as the sacraments and the reading and hearing of the word, read and preached, and the term 'prudential' means to later developments in spirituality which are consistent with the gospel, albeit not directly derived from Scripture. The latter do not *have* to be used by the believer though Wesley always counselled his people to use 'all' the means available.
24 *Grace*, para 97.
25 The pamphlet was written by Fr (now Bishop) Michael Evans and published jointly by MPH and CTS in 1995. It should be noted that though the Methodists concerned accepted the truths noted as underlying the marian dogmas they recorded the continuing difficulties that they would have with their requirement as such on account of the lack of a clear biblical basis for them per se. It may also be noted, in this particular context, that the topic was one dear to Dr Newton's heart and one on which he has made contributions, particularly through addresses at conferences of the ESBVM, as noted above.

26 'Receptive Learning Through Roman Catholic-Methodist Dialogue' in Murray, P. (2006), *Receptive Ecumenism and the Call to Catholic Learning: Exploring a Way for Contemporary Ecumenism*, Oxford, pp122-133.

27 *Honolulu Report* in Meyer and Vischer (1984), para 35.

28 *Towards a Statement on the Church*, para 58. Report of the fourth quiquennium of the dialogue, cited in Gros, Meyer and Rusch (2000), p593.

29 I have myself explored some of the issues in an article in *One in Christ*, 'A Methodist Response to Ut Unum Sint', 1997, pp125-137. I have also drawn attention to Benjamin Gregory's stress on the itinerant superintendency of Peter in the Palestinian churches as witnessed to in Luke 9.32. See Gregory, B. *Holy Catholic Church*, London, 1873, p43. Most recently, I note Bishop Walter Klaiber's opinion that there is indeed a petrine ministry recorded in the New Testament albeit not one that, in his opinion, corresponds closely to the recent and current exercise of the ministry of the Bishop of Rome. For this, see Geoffrey Wainwright's Marquette lecture of 2000, *Is the Reformation Over? Catholics and Protestants at the Turn of the Millennia*, Marquette UP, 2000, p36.

30 British Methodism has several times declared itself willing to receive episcopacy in the pursuit of wider unity. In its response to the Baptism, Eucharist, Ministry Process of the World Council of Churches, it stated 'we await the moment for the recovery of the sign of the episcopal succession'. See Thurian, M. (ed), *Churches Respond to BEM*, vol 2, p215.

31 *Grace*, para 113.

32 An account of his sermon was given in *The Tablet*, January 1970.

33 Fameree and Routhier, op cit, p69.

34 Gregory, B. (1873), *Holy Catholic Church*, p50 , commenting on the visit of Peter and John, as recorded in Acts 8, to the churches founded after the first dispersion of the disciples from persecution in Jerusalem, 'what the apostles did with the results of sponataneous evangelistic action was to lose not time in recognising and *connecting* it' [my italics].

35 Cited in *The Wisdom of John Paul II*, CTS, 2001, p105.

36 Tillard, J-M.(1995), *L'Eglise Locale*, Paris, p540.

37 My translation from Congar as cited in Fameree and Routhier (2008), p66.

38 Rigg, J. (1897), *A Comparative View of Church Organisations, Primitive and Protestant*, London, p207.

39 In his *Christians in Dialogue* (ET), 1964, p349.

40 Möhler (1825), *Unity in the Church or the Principle of Catholicism*. ET by Erb, Peter C. (1996), Washington DC.

41 Ibid, pp217-221.

42 See for example his *A Plain Account of the People Called Methodists*, 1748.

43 *Methodism in the Light of the Early Church*, London, 1885.

44 Campbell, Ted (1991), *A. John Wesley and Christian Antiquity*, Nashville. This admiration is also reflected in many of Charles' hymns.

45 *Hymns and Psalms* (1983), no. 753.

46 Möhler (1825), p209.

47 Ibid, p63.

48 From the sermon 'On the Mystery of Iniquity', cited in Jennings, T. (1990), *Good News to the Poor*, Nashville, p112.

49 Fameree and Routhier (2008), pp176-9.

50 Catechism of the Catholic Church, para 813, cited in Wood, S. (2009), 'What Makes the Church One? A Roman Catholic Perspective', *Ecumenical Trends*, May 2009, p9.
51 *Called To Love and Praise* (Methodist Conference Statement on the Church, 1999), para 2.1.9, cited in *Statements and Reports of the Methodist Church on Faith and Order 1984-2000* (2000), Peterborough, p10.
52 Already referred to above. *Towards a Statement on the Church*, para 1; *Grace*, paras 60-66, 82-3.
53 *Grace*, paras 60-61.
54 A question particularly raised in the seventh quinquennium of the dialogue, *Speaking the Truth in Love*, 2001, paras 77-80.
55 Pope, W.B. (1880), *Compendium of Christian Theology*, London, vol 3, p4. Pope was the last of the great Wesleyan systematic theologians.
56 For example the Protestant Methodists, as described by John Kent in his *Jabez Bunting, the last Wesleyan*, London, 1955, p47.
57 Shrewsbury (1840), p54.
58 Gregory (1873), pp103, 54ff.
59 Möhler (1825), p226.
60 Gregory (1873), pp54, 58.
61 Tillard (1995), pp222, 326.
62 See, for example the Belgian symposium, Bihin, G. and van Vlaenderen, P. (1998), *Gouverner l'Eglise autrement: Pour une Eglise-Communion*, Brussels.
63 Gregory (1873), p76, commenting on *proskaterountes* in Acts 2:27.

Mary – Mother of all God's children

Norman Wallwork

Mary: Mother of Jesus Christ the Son of God

Pope Benedict, in his days as Cardinal Ratzinger, was not the first, nor is he likely to be the last, to emphasise the absolute necessity of the church's understanding of and devotion to Mary needing to be totally bound to its Christology; and always in an honoured but relative and subordinate mode. The permanent titles and the eternal vocation of Mary are derived from and are wholly dependent upon the permanent titles and eternal vocation of her Son.

This is reflected in a popular fashion in the hymn of Justin Mulcahy – alias Paul Cross – containing parallel but dependent imagery for Christ and Mary:

> *Mary the Dawn, but Christ the Perfect Day;*
> *Mary the Root, but Christ the Mystic Vine;*
> *Mary the Chalice, Christ the Saving Blood!*
> *Mary, the Mirror, Christ the Vision Blest!*

As is well known, within the New Testament, and into the Fathers, the language of Christology becomes ever richer and fuller. All Christology in the New Testament is, of course, retrospective, as we contemplate with the earliest Christian writers and apologists what is meant first by the *names* Jesus and Emmanuel, then by the early *titles* Rabbi and Master, leading on to Son of Man, Messiah, Lord, Son of God and Logos.

The rich Christology of the Fourth Gospel is everywhere matched by that of Paul, who both worships and proclaims Jesus as the Christ, the risen One, whose name is above every name, whether on earth or in heaven[1] and the One in whom the whole fullness of deity dwells bodily.[2] Finally we see the Christ in whom St John the Divine beholds the First and the Last, the Alpha and the Omega, and the Lamb slain before the foundation of the world,[3] and of course the Christology of the New Testament is not simply about the nature and the titles of Christ, but about the depth and universality of his saving work. For the New Testament writers Christ is not only the one who commands the wind and the waves, heals the sick and raises the dead, but the Saviour who by his blood takes away the sin of the world, who by his death inaugurates a kingdom and who by his resurrection is the sign and first-fruits of the life of the world to come. The Christology of the New Testament grows and blooms afresh in the writings of the Fathers.

Indeed it is within the burgeoning and foundational Christology of the first Christian writers, when the full implications of the true nature of Christ are tested, rehearsed, celebrated, debated and consolidated, that a similar and parallel process of reflection, revelation and consolidation attaches itself to the church's understanding of and devotion to Mary.

It is quite impossible to maintain that while there was a dynamic movement within the New Testament concerning the evolution of Christology, there was no fairly early movement in the church's understanding of and devotion to Mary. All four gospels have a primitive, rich and developing Christology and out of these Christologies Luke and John in particular formed a rich foundation for the church's view of Mary.

For Luke Mary is 'favoured by God', 'full of grace', 'handmaid of the Lord', 'virgin mother', 'overshadowed by the Spirit', and 'blessed among women'. She is the one who 'ponders all things in her heart.' She is a prophetic voice in the Magnificat, she is a representative in the Temple of the poor of Israel, she is the recipient of the piercing sword and she is with the twelve at the descent of the Spirit on the Day of Pentecost. Here is the beginning of the church's rich understanding of and devotion to Mary from the seventies of the first century.

Only slightly later, in the Fourth Gospel, does Mary first carry the enigmatic title 'Mother of Jesus'. Then she has a decisive role in the first of the signs of Jesus at Cana, when he first reveals his glory.

Then, ultimately, in the Fourth Gospel, at the foot of the Cross, at the hour of Christ's glory, Mary becomes the mother of all loved disciples of the Lord.

The interdependence of Christology and the church's understanding of and devotion to Mary is continued outside the New Testament tradition with Justin Martyr (*c.*165) and Irenaeus (*c.*202), who in response to Paul's designation of Christ as the second Adam conclude that Mary had a vocation as the Second Eve. Mary is part of God's grand reversal plan to restore God's children to paradise – a theme elaborated by Tertullian at the end of the second century, celebrated by Ephrem the Syrian in the middle of the fourth century and continued by his near contemporaries Gregory of Nyssa and Ambrose of Milan.

Dating from the mid-fourth century is the earliest known invocation of Mary in which either an individual or a private family of Christians sought the patronage and protection of one whom they addressed, in the surviving scrap of Greek papyrus, as *Theotokos*, Mother of God:

> *Beneath the shelter of your tender compassion*
> *We flee for refuge, Mother of God!*
> *Do not overlook my supplications in adversity,*
> *But deliver us out of danger;*
> *For you alone are chaste and blessed.*[4]

Mary's title in this prayer, 'Mother of God', appeared first in the Provincial Council of Alexandria (318–320) and moved through the First Council of Constantinople in 381, to be proclaimed at the Council of Ephesus in 431. The fathers of that Council, in opposition to Nestorius and in order to proclaim Christ as a single, undivided person who is God and man at once, declared, 'the Holy Virgin is *Theotokos* – for she *brought forth* according to the flesh the Word of God made flesh'.

This definition was intended, in the words of John Henry Newman, 'to protect the doctrine of the incarnation, and to preserve the faith of catholics from a specious humanitarianism'.[5] What is sometimes overlooked is that Mary's title *Theotokos* and prayers for her protection were being hammered out in the same generations that were attempting to finalise the canon of scripture, craft the great creeds of the church and arrive at a satisfactory understanding of the great mystery of the Trinity.

Mary: Mother of All Christians

It is comparatively easy to comprehend that Mary is the mother of all Orthodox and Catholic Christians. Indeed it is not difficult to see Mary as the adopted mother of those Reformation Christians whose tradition has undergone some form of Catholic revival and renewal. There are other Christians, outside the mainstream of Catholic and Orthodox life, who through travel, pilgrimages and retreats have, by ecumenical osmosis, come to value, know, love and enjoy the company of the Virgin Mother of God. But *if* Mary is – by God's grace and choice – Mother of God and Mother of the Church – head and members – is she not *de facto* the mother of all the baptised, the mother of all believers – Catholic, Orthodox, Protestant, Evangelical and Pentecostal? Is Mary not indeed the mother of all who are in Christ?

We cannot surely take the view that Mary is only the mother of those in communion with Constantinople and Rome – and those Catholic-minded Christians of the Reformation traditions who like going to Walsingham or Lourdes! All who are 'in Christ' are bound eternally to the Lord's Mother whether they know it or not. A mother does not cease to be a mother even if she goes unacknowledged by some of the members of the family.

So I think it could be helpful, at this point, to use the language of *estrangement*. Many Christians of the Reformation traditions are *estranged* from the Mother of God. The reasons for this estrangement from Mary may be due mostly to inheritance and tradition. As my mother used to say to my father, in the days when grandparents didn't usually have a phone, 'Frank, it's time for you to write your annual Christmas letter to your mother'.

Saint Theresa of Lisieux was one of those who didn't lay all the blame for neglect of Mary at the Protestant door. She said that if she had been a priest she would like to have preached but a single sermon on the Blessed Virgin:

> *I should have set forth a point of view about the life of the Blessed Virgin which is now so little heeded... One should not say of her either things that are improbable or of which we are not assured... the Blessed Virgin is more Mother than Queen... We should strive to make her loved. Who knows if some souls may not go so far as to feel a certain estrangement from a creature who is represented as being so far above them.*

Estrangement of some of Mary's children from a living and dynamic relation with the Mother of God may well be due to the extravagance of some of her other children.

When the indifference of most Reformation Christians to the Mother of God is challenged they often point to an extravagance of Catholic or Orthodox devotion to Mary which they neither understand nor find attractive. But there are deeper reasons. Most Reformation Christians would claim that prayer involving Mary and the saints is not present in Scripture and that it is not safe to build a substantial part of the Church's life and devotion around post-apostolic traditions which really only began to blossom in the fifth and sixth centuries.

Hence, part of the way to reduce the *estrangement* involving Reformation Christians and the Mother of God is to open a very serious conversation about the notion and indeed the doctrine of *development* – a process much loved of course by Newman. Are there key doctrines and devotions already embraced within the tradition of Reformation Christians which they might acknowledge are embryonic and not fully developed in scripture?

A full blown doctrine of the Trinity would be a case in point. No serious teacher or writer among Reformation Christians would trace the fullness of Trinitarian development without citing the early and later Church Fathers – both Eastern and Western – who wrestled with and took forward the doctrine and mystery of the Trinity until it had broken free of the classic heresies that sought to distort its fullness.

All international ecumenical consultations about Mary have involved the interplay of scripture and tradition. Only blessings have followed these national and international consultations, where the place of Mary in salvation history and in the life of the church has been explored in dialogue between Catholic, Orthodox and Reformation Christians. The great strength of the international dialogues on Mary is that the official representatives from among the Reformation Christians have included not only Catholic-minded scholars, with an existing devotion to the Mother of God, but those who were agnostic about Marian dogmas and devotion at the beginning of their journey.

The great blessing of the national and international gatherings of the Ecumenical Society of the Virgin Mary is that there has been a huge amount of exploration of Marian issues – doctrinal, devotional and liturgical – and the blessings of residence and pilgrimages together. We have not swept our differences under the carpet. We have attended one another's Eucharistic liturgies without breaking our own disciplines. We have created a common office of prayer and we have generally learnt to blend courtesy and honesty. But the journey is not over and it may not be getting any easier.

Among the children who love Mary very dearly there is more than one sort of Anglican – even more than one sort of Catholic Anglican. Is there a place for them all at the table of ecumenical dialogue and formal Eucharist? Is there a serious way of ending the estrangement between Mary and most Reformation Christians?

The cynic would say 'yes'. It requires that most of the Reformation Christians shut up shop and become either Catholic or Orthodox, for only within the rich theology, liturgy and devotion of the two ancient Christian traditions of the East and the West can all real estrangement from Mary be healed.

I would hold out to Reformation Christians a slightly different olive branch. Just as Archbishop Geoffrey Fisher once invited the English Free Churches to take episcopacy into their system, I would invite Reformation Christians who have not already begun to do so – Anglican, Lutheran, Methodist, Reformed, Evangelical and Pentecostal – to begin take Mary into their system.

As I hinted earlier, I believe the way to a fully developed appreciation of Mary in doctrine and devotion is through a full and healthy life of doctrine and devotion towards the Trinity. We can only come to a full Trinitarian faith via a doctrine of development. Trinitarian doctrine and devotion among Reformation Christians is based on a Biblical *and Patristic* understanding of the Trinity. Without the doctrine of development – without a deep honesty about the interplay of scripture and tradition – Reformation Christians cannot truly understand themselves.

Indeed, without a healthy doctrine and devotion towards the Trinity, many Reformation Christians have a tendency to go all out for Jesus or for the Spirit. The full Christ fades; the Father is diminished; and Mary, the one who brings forth God, becomes no more than the lady stooping over the manger. Eric Mascall was timely and discerning in his reminder that the Holy Spirit made Mary a mother not in the cradle at Bethlehem but in her womb at Nazareth.[6]

Mary: Mother of all other Faiths

When the Prince of Wales hinted that he would like the title he might one day inherit to be changed from *Defender of the Faith* to *Defender of Faiths* it met with a mixed reception. Of course there was a double irony here, since the title was first given by the Papacy to a Catholic king defending the Catholic sacraments against a Protestant Reformer. The faith defended between the era of the first Queen Elizabeth and the second has been a Christian faith both Catholic and Reformed.

If we return to the interdependence of Christology and a fullness of doctrine and devotion concerning Our Lady, then whatever we say about the relationship between Christ *and adherents of other world faiths* has a bearing on the role of Mary as *mother* of those of all great world faiths.

The Catechism of the Catholic Church teaches that when the Church delves into her own mystery as the people of God in the New Covenant, she discovers her link with the Jewish people and sees their faith as a response to God's revelation.[7] The Catholic Church also sees God's plan of salvation as including, 'in the first place among those who acknowledge the Creator, the Muslims who adore the one merciful God'.[8] The Catechism goes on to teach that the Catholic Church recognises in other religions the goodness and truth which God has given because he enlightens all people so that they may have life.[9] The Prologue to the Fourth Gospel speaks of Christ, the eternal Word, as the true light which enlightens everyone. When the Johannine Christ is lifted up from the earth in crucifixion his glory and grace will, at the last, draw everyone and all things to him. The light of the incarnate Word who enlightens all is conceived in this world and born into it through the Blessed Virgin Mary who, as Mother of her God and Saviour, is then, henceforth and forever, bound to her son's saving work.

The eternal Christ, the true light, is already within the worship and culture of other world faiths. Christ the true Light is present with God's children of other faiths in the eternal company of Mary, his Mother. Mary, who is the Mother – acknowledged or unacknowledged – of all Christians, is similarly the Mother – acknowledged or unacknowledged – of those of all faiths. She is eternally present with all who have received the light of God within their own faith and culture.

In 1986 the late David Flusser, erstwhile professor of Comparative Religion at the Hebrew University of Jerusalem, wrote as a Jew about Mary and Israel. Professor Flusser saw in Mary:

> *an aspect of the uninterrupted way of suffering of Mary's own people, the Jews... Mary is as much a symbol of her own people, the Jews, as she is a symbol of the church, one who was never defeated by her pain... Mary is the Jewish mother of Christ.*[10]

The professor sees the suffering of Rachel weeping for her children in the wake of Herod's slaughter of the innocents of Bethlehem as a pain symbolic of the suffering of Mary in relation to her son. The professor also reminds us that when John XXIII viewed a film on Auschwitz he said at the scene of the murdered Jews, '*Hoc est corpus Christi*'. (This is the Body of Christ.)

The cross of Jesus, says the professor, belongs both to Christology and to Jewish martyrdom and through this a mostly unperceived dimension accrues to the sorrowful Mary. Mary is a suffering Jewish mother. The Christian tradition of the descent of the Spirit on Mary at Pentecost is, he says, an elevated destiny for a Jewish mother.

The professor thinks that after the intense suffering of the Holocaust, Mary of Sorrows could heal many wounds. He sees in Mary the exaltation of one who can exalt all women and thinks that the remembrance of her purity can in some way remove the defilement of modern humanity.

It is wholly logical to take the view that Mary's longing and prayer is to bring the children of the Christian gospel and children of Israel into the same family of relationships. 'I am more than ever certain that a great place belongs to [Jesus] in Israel's history of faith' wrote Martin Buber.

Because Islam partially grew out of some of Muhammad's contacts with various strands of Byzantine, Eutychian and Nestorian Christianity, it is not surprising that Mary, as the mother of 'Jesus the Prophet', has a place within the pages of the Qur'an and within Islamic teaching. Mary is important in the Qur'an because she is the mother of Jesus. For the Qur'an Mary is one 'who guarded her chastity and so (God) breathed into her some of (his) spirit and made her and her son signs to the world' and Mary, as in the gospels, is celebrated as one who submitted to God's will. In Islamic teaching and legend Mary and Jesus are the only children of Adam who are not touched by a demon at their birth. Indeed, Jesus is touched at his birth by Gabriel's wing.

Professor Geoffrey Parrinder thought that some of the Islamic confusion about Mary and Jesus in relation to the Trinity was bound up with the brand of Nestorianism with which infant Islam came into contact.[11] There are some clear parallels between the infancy of Mary in the Qur'an and the Book of James in the Apocrypha. It is generally, though not universally, accepted that the Qur'an proclaims the conception of Jesus without a human father, and many Muslims defend the virgin birth in the face of Christian sceptics.

There is an ancient story that when the prophet Muhammad entered Mecca he gave orders for the idols of the Ka'ba and its paintings to be destroyed. He placed his hands on the picture of Jesus and Mary and gave the instruction, 'Wash out all except what is beneath my hands.'[12] In a number of countries where Muslims and Christians live side by side, followers of Islam, particularly women called Maryam, resort freely to Christian shrines of Our Lady: in North Africa, Palestine, Syria and India.[13] In September 1994 William Dalrymple attended Vespers in the ancient Syrian Convent of Seidnaya and found to his astonishment that the congregation prostrating itself before the icon of Our Lady of Seidnaya consisted almost entirely of Muslim men.[14] Is the Islamic Jesus, the Son of Mary, a Muslim prophet who submits to the One God? The inter-faith scholar Dr Martin Forward takes the view that this is for Muslims to determine, not for Christians. Perhaps Christians need to trust the present vocation and reconciling work of Mary within the life of contemporary Islam without worrying overmuch how she is doing it.

Within Vedantic Buddhism, Jesus has been accepted as one expression among many of appearances of the divine among humans. By some Buddhists, Jesus has been accepted as a lower order teacher. The Jain beliefs that deeply influenced Gandhi drew him inexorably to Jesus.[15]

In the continuing grace of prayerful listening within each world faith, in the presence of the others, in that *larger ecumenism* Mary takes her place in the great circle and surely plays her part as she leads all good people to knowledge of her Son – the eternal Christ found deep within the inter-faith depths that we have only begun to explore.

Mary: Mother of all the Oppressed

A fundamental aspect of the vocation of Mary, Mother of God, clearly set forth by Saint Luke, is that of her standing in the Hebrew prophetic tradition and announcing what the arrival of the holy child, the Son of God, will mean for those who perpetrate injustice and those who are the victims of it. The offering that Mary and Joseph made – of two young pigeons or turtle-doves – at the presentation of Jesus in the Temple was the offering of those identified with the poor.

In Mary's *Magnificat* – which most Biblical commentators and scholars have now returned to believing is of Our Lady's own composition[16] – the Mother of God not only rejoices in God's choice of her own lowliness, but notes five of the great kingdom marks of God's salvation breaking into history through the birth: now vouchsafed to the mother of the Lord. God has now 'scattered the proud in the thoughts of their own hearts, he has brought down the powerful, he has lifted up the lowly, he has filled the hungry and he has sent the rich away empty'.[17]

We cannot enter into Mary's personal joy in the first part of the *Magnificat* unless we embrace the fact that in the second part of her song Mary became and remains the champion of God's poor. In the conceiving and bringing forth into the world of the Word made flesh, Mother and Son together, through the grace of the Cross, betroth themselves to humanity for ever – for richer for poorer – in sickness and in health.

One fulfilment of Our Lady's commitment to the poor is that the stories and devotions surrounding her apparitions are generally among the poorer communities of the world. In addition, many of the base communities in South America are looking to Mary in their ongoing life and struggles. As they integrate theology, faith and practice, priests, religious and congregations see Mary as the symbol of a hope that nourishes them in their poverty.

Indeed, there has been a noticeable shift from a concentration on the 'Mother of Heaven' to one who is the people's companion on their way. Mary is now much more readily invoked as 'Mother of the Oppressed', 'Our Lady of Latin America' and 'Mother of the Forgotten'.[18]

Leonardo Boff, in writing of Mary as *prophetic woman of liberation* says:

> *A prophetic, liberating image of Mary is the only legitimate conclusion theology can come to against the backdrop of our situation of captivity and oppression. We in Latin America read a divine revelation written in [gospel] times with today's eyes, eyes full of questions, expectations and interests springing from our own present reality. The Magnificat of Mary sprang from a network of relationships very much like our own... Mary becomes our contempo-*

rary... *Mary has one ear completely open to God, and the other open completely to the cries of the poor... Mary raises her voice and speaks out... she praises God and intercedes for the people... she praises God's mercy, and begs his liberation of the lowly and the starving...*[19]

In the prayer which Dom Helder Camara addressed to *Our Lady of Liberation* he prayed:

O Mary, Mother of Christ and of the Church...
you took no complacency in your blessedness,
but concentrated your thoughts on the whole human race.
Yes, you thought of everyone,
but you made your forthright option for the poor...
... what is it in you that no one dares to call a revolutionary,
or regard you with suspicion?
Lend us your voice!
Sing with us!
Beg your Son to accomplish in us, in all their fullness,
his Father's plans.[20]

From Father Tissa Balasuriya, in his book on *Mary and Human Liberation*, which of course met with the wrath of Joseph Ratzinger and the Congregation for the Doctrine of the Faith, and resulted in excommunication for its author, there came the following longing and plea:

Mary has to be liberated from traditional speculation which has made her a woman who is not female, a woman who does not know what it is to be human, who does not go through the birth pangs of bringing forth Jesus, who does not know sin, who does not feel the trials of human existence. Mary in heaven may be sad that for so long Christians did not appreciate why Jesus had to suffer and give his life in the social conditions of his time.[21]

As we proclaim Mary as Mother of the Oppressed, it is important not simply to single out the poor, the persecuted, the hungry, the broken and the forgotten, but to raise the issue of gender. None of the Abrahamic religions have a consistent and altogether worthy record with regard to their own women, nor to justice and equality for women in their surrounding culture.

Reflecting the dignity that Jesus clearly gave to women, Saint Luke, in his gospel and in the Acts of the Apostles, brings a number of women to the fore in his presentation of the life and teaching of Jesus, and as he tells of the guidance of the Holy Spirit within the young church in action. The place of Mary in the first two chapters of Saint Luke is part of the pre-eminence that Luke gives to women in the prologue to the public ministry of Jesus.

It cannot be other than the permanent vocation of Mary to long for the true dignity of all women within the family, within the structures of society, within the councils of communities, within the professions of healing, learning, commerce and communication. It is at the heart of Mary's vocation to establish, raise and celebrate the dignity of women within all world faiths. It is most certainly within the vocation of Mary to raise to appropriate dignity all women within the life of the church. 'Let them be content to be faithful wives, loving mothers, devout nuns, good catechists and first rate caterers' is not where Our Lady is coming from.

Of course Our Lady sees the profound complementary nature and gifts of men and women who are created in God's image. However, let us be well assured that as Mary the Mother of God forever raises the dignity of women, within all communities, and within the life of the church, it would be very foolish to try and pin on her a rosette for or against the ordination of women to the priesthood. Our rosette would simply fall off her. If we said to Our Lady: "Holy Mother, are you an absolutist taking the view that women can never be priested or do you think it is a matter that will eventually be decided by the church universal saying yes?" I think we would be nonplussed by Our Lady's enigmatic smile and her profound silence!

As Lavinia Byrne wrote in her book, of which unsold copies were subsequently ordered by her superiors to be destroyed:

> *When the Most high overshadowed Mary, she did more than conceive Jesus: she assumed the power and dignity given to all who*

are obedient to the will of God. By removing this understanding from our theology, we displace Mary – and all women with her. In their place, we put a deeply secular model, based on biological determinism of a most primitive sort. The destiny of women proclaimed by the incarnation of Jesus in the flesh of Mary is a destiny which uses the natural order but is not constrained by it.... If biology were destiny, Mary would be no more than the mother of Jesus in the flesh. But instead she is more than that; her identity in the symbolic ordering of all things means that she can stand before and with God.... Mary has a distinctive place in the dispensation of grace because of her relationship with God.[22]

Mary: Mother of all the Earth

In 1984 Donald Allchin published an Anglican anthology and meditation on Mary 'The Joy of All Creation'. In the Epilogue to the anthology Father Allchin points out, as have others before him, how often Our Lady is associated with a particular place. We may think of Our Lady of Guadaloup, Our Lady of Czestochowa, Our Lady of Medjugorje, Our Lady of Knock and Our Lady of Walsingham. Father Allchin then reminds us:

> *[Mary] it is who, by her vocation to be the place of God, by her fulfilment of that vocation, reveals her true destiny of all places, indeed of all humankind and all creation, which shares in that high calling to become the place of God's habitation. This again is why she is called the joy of all creation, because the whole creation finds its possibility of fulfilment in her.... In her this world revealed its true quality, as the good earth, the land of promise, the place where God's blessing descends in its fullness.*[23]

Another contemporary writer who has compelled us to take seriously the question of the Virgin Mary's relationship to God's fundamental work of creation is Sarah Boss. As she considers the Mother of God and the cosmos she probes the cosmic significance of Christ's conception.

> *The world's redemption in Christ is in fact its re-creation. The Spirit who breathed creation into existence breathes into creation afresh in the person of Mary. Mary's own flesh and blood are transformed into the divine microcosm that is her son. At the conception of Christ, the Word made flesh; Mary shares an identity with the depths of God before the dawn of time. Through her bringing forth of Christ, Mary is mysteriously present in all things and as well as to the re-creation of all things in Christ. Mary is present in the foundation of all physical things.*[24]

Sarah Boss reminds us of this strand of theology within the prayers of St Anselm:

> *All nature is created by God and God is born of Mary.*
> *God created all things, and Mary gave birth to God....*
> *God who made all things made himself of Mary,*
> *and thus he re-fashioned everything he had made....*
> *God is the Father of all created things,*
> *and Mary is the mother of all re-created things.*
> *God is the Father of all that is established,*
> *and Mary is the mother of all that is re-established.*[25]

God in Christ has *re-fashioned* everything he has made through Mary. God in Christ has *re-created* all that he has made through Mary. God in Christ through Mary has *re-established* all that he has made. This new work of God in Christ achieved through Mary, of re-fashioning, re-creating and re-establishing all things is at the very heart of Mary's prayer and work in relation to the needs of our present earth and the plight of our planet and its peoples.

As Mary said 'Yes' to God so that this new work of re-creation could begin through Christ, the Word made flesh, so that work continues. The revolution of re-establishment involves not just those who inhabit the earth, but the earth itself. The holiness and renewal of our physical environment is at the very heart of the co-operation between Mary and God the Father, brought to fruition in Christ, Son of God and Son of Mary, through the Holy Spirit. The damage that we are doing to the gift of creation is part of the tragedy on which

Mary gazed at Calvary. The justice at the heart of the *Magnificat* is justice for the environment of God's people as well as the people themselves. There can be no justice for God's people – the people of the *Magnificat* – in isolation from their environment.

Notes

1 Philippians 2.9.
2 Colossians 2.9.
3 Revelation 13.8.
4 McHugh, J. (1981), *The Earliest Known Invocation of the Mother of God*, ESBVM Paper, p3.
5 Newman, J.H. *An Essay on the Development of Christian Doctrine*, Notre Dame Press, p426.
6 Mascall E. (ed) (1949), *The Mother of God: A Symposium*, Dacre Press, p39.
7 Chapman, Geoffrey (1994), *Catechism of the Catholic Church*, Article 9: Para. 3, p839 [hereafter *Catechism*].
8 *Catechism* Article 9: Para. 3, p841.
9 *Catechism* Article 9: Para. 3, p843.
10 Flusser, D. (2005), 'Mary and Israel' in Pelican, J., Flusser, D. and Lang, J. (eds), *Mary: Images of the Mother of Jesus in Jewish and Christian Perspective*, Fortress Press, p3.
11 Parrinder, G. (1965, 1995), *Jesus in the Qur'an*, Oxford: Oneworld, p63.
12 Creswell, K.A.C. (1958), *A Short Account of Early Muslim Architecture*, London, p2.
13 Attwater, D. (1957), *A Dictionary of Mary*, Longmans, Green and Co., p131.
14 Dalrymple, W. (1997), *From the Holy Mountain*, Harper Collins, pp186–189.
15 Forward, M. (1998), *Jesus: A Short Biography*, Oxford: Oneworld, p144.
16 McHugh, J. (1975), *The Mother of Jesus in the New Testament*, Darton, Longman & Todd, pp73, 445.
17 Luke 1.51-53.
18 Gebara, I. and Maria, Clara (1989), *Mary, Mother of God, Mother of the Poor*, Bingemer: Burns & Oates, p163.
19 Boff, Leonardo (1979), *The Maternal Face of God*, Collins, pp188-192.
20 Ibid. pp202–203.
21 Balasuriya, T. (1997), *Mary and Human Liberation*, Mowbray, p77.
22 Byrne, L. (1994), *Woman at the Altar*, Mowbray, pp118-119.
23 Allchin, A.M. (1984), *The Joy of All Creation*, DLT, pp204-205.
24 Boss, S. (2003), *Mary*, Continuum, p4.
25 Ibid. p117.

Rescue, Release and Redemption: Mary and Exodus traditions in the Gospel of Matthew and their relevance for today

Sandy Williams

During his years in Liverpool, and especially through his personal friendship with Archbishop Derek Warlock, John Newton became increasingly interested in the significance of Mary, both theologically and devotionally. In any large port and maritime, cosmopolitan city such as Liverpool, people from all over the world gather and John came face to face with those who, like Mary, found themselves in a foreign land.

> *Now after they (the wise men from the East) had left, an angel of the Lord appeared to Joseph in a dream and said, "Get up, take the child and his mother, and flee to Egypt, and remain there until I tell you, for Herod is about to search for the child to destroy him." Then Joseph got up, took the child and his mother by night, and went to Egypt, and remained there until the death of Herod. This was to fulfil what had been spoken by the Lord through the prophet, "Out of Egypt I have called my son."*
> (Matthew 2.13-15)

The portrayal of Mary in the Lukan birth narratives has been the subject of much scholarly work and devotional practice, whereas, in contrast, little has been written about the picture of Mary in the first gospel. Although the Matthaean text seems to say less about Mary, what it says, and the context in which it says it, may have particular relevance to today's world.

Consider an incident that happened early in 2009:

> *It is 4am in Bristol and a mother and a small child are woken from sleep by a loud knocking on the front door. The mother struggles downstairs in her nightclothes and is confronted by men who have arrived to take her and her baby to Yarl's Wood Detention Centre. They do not allow her to dress or go to the toilet, even though she pleads to be allowed to visit the bathroom. In the Black Maria they give her a plastic bag and she has to relieve herself in front of her small daughter. This mother and child have fled to Britain from Congo and now face deportation and almost certain death.*

Current books on homiletics have encouraged the use of story telling and a great deal has been written about narrative preaching and about the 'big story' – or metanarrative – of the Bible. This paper will argue that the story of Mary in Matthew's gospel resonates with the Exodus narrative and therefore with the stories of today's 'Exodus people', especially those who, like the woman in the story above, are powerless and at the mercy of dictators and political systems. There are many people like her who are also displaced people who flee from the horror of genocide in today's world.

The Matthaean narrative invites readers to enter into the biblical story imaginatively as they encounter not only the Herods of today and their henchmen, but also Mary, the bearer of the one who is 'Emmanuel', God with them. Such an encounter, it is argued, invites a response that is 'devotional' and therefore leads to 'true worship'. Such worship breaks down prejudice and confronts those who seek to damage or destroy others in order to protect themselves and their own power-bases. To read scripture in this way is 'a risky business'.

The Exodus as the Biblical Metanarrative

The underlying premise of this paper is that the story of the Exodus provides the significant, biblical metanarrative that shapes, and continues to shape, the identity of Christian people and their relationship with God. Post-modernism rejects the view that the Bible has a metanarrative, a 'big story' or an overarching world-view.

Different scholars have suggested a variety of possible biblical metanarratives and, although this paper argues from the perspective of the Exodus, it is evident that the Exodus is not the only contender in the search for *the* biblical metanarrative. It would be possible, for example, to speak of the Bible in terms of God's self-revelation to the world and to the incarnation as its culmination and therefore 'the central interpretive principle' of the Bible.[1] Although this paper will argue that it is the Exodus story that provides *the* biblical world-view, it is important to recognise that the relevance of the argument does not stand or fall on this premise. It is possible to accept that the Exodus provides one interpretive approach and provides a 'metanarrative framework', that is, one possible world-view from which to read biblical texts.[2]

This paper argues, however, that it is the Exodus story that provides a basis for the biblical worldview in both the Old and New Testaments and becomes the *'founding and pivotal event'*[3] for Christian people today who, like Jews and Christians throughout history, recognise that they, too, are part of the Exodus story, enter into this same narrative of liberation and redemption and become partners in the divine enterprise that is nothing less than the transformation of creation! The Exodus story of rescue, release and redemption challenges individuals, communities, institutions and nations as people seek to live in peace with each other, and with the planet, in relationships characterised by the loving kindness of the God encountered in the Exodus narrative of which we are a part.

The Exodus as the defining story for the people of God

The Exodus story tells of God's rescue of dispossessed and oppressed people. These disparate folk from Aramaic tribes grew in numbers and became a threat to Pharoah, who gave the order that male babies should be drowned at birth (Exodus 1.22).[4] The story, therefore, begins with genocide and the untold misery of countless mothers. It is also the story of 'the great escape' as God, through Moses, rescues his people and enables them to cross the sea – and it is salutary to remember that in scripture the sea often stands for the waters of chaos; all that threatens to overwhelm and destroy people[5] – and to survive in the wilderness until they arrive at the mountain of God. Only at Sinai, with the giving of the law, do the people from various tribes become united in their new identity, the people of God, as the covenant is sealed and a nation is born.

The covenant relationship remains at the heart of the nation's identity. Those who belong to 'the people of God' are those who, in response to the God who promises to remain faithful, commit themselves to keep his law and live righteously (i.e. in right relationship with God and with each other, and indeed with all creation).

For both Old and New Testament writers, Abraham is 'the Father of the Nation'. He epitomised the covenant relationship before the law was given because he trusted in God's promises and obeyed God's command to leave his home and travel to a new land.[6] (The significance of Abraham in Matthew's portrayal of Mary will be explored later in this discussion.)

It is not surprising, therefore, that throughout the history of Israel, the Exodus became the defining story. In the Old Testament the Exodus story not only reminded people of their identity, but also helped them to put their trust in God in times of trouble and turbulence, especially when neighbouringnations threatened national security (e.g. Micah 6.4, Amos 2.10 and 3.1-2, Hosea 11.1 and 13.4).

During the time of the Exile, following the Babylonian invasions of 598 and 597 BCE, it was the retelling of the Exodus traditions[7] that gave a divided nation hope that the exiles would return, and also enabled a new generation, born in a foreign land, to discover that this was their story and that they, too, were Israelites, God's holy people (Deut. 6.20-24a).

The Exodus story was retold in liturgy, for example in Psalm 81.8-10, in order to remind the people of their history; it is because God rescued them from slavery in Egypt that they continue to offer worship and bring the first fruits to God as an act of thanksgiving (Deut. 26.5-9).

Following the Christ event, Israel was redefined as, through the ministry of Paul, gentiles received the Spirit and were accepted into the *ecclesia*, the Church of Christ, along with Jews who had also acknowledged Jesus as Lord and entered into a new covenant relationship through his death and resurrection. The New Testament writers continued to tell the story of the Exodus to enable Christians from both Jewish and Gentile backgrounds to make this their own story.[8]

Mary and Exodus Traditions in Matthew 1-2

Two methodological tools will be used to enable the study of Mary as portrayed in Matthew 1-2. First, typology will be used to explore the Matthaean portrayal of the main characters: Mary, Joseph and Herod; that is, how they are modelled on Old Testament figures who played their part in the Exodus story.[9] Secondly, since reader-response theories argue that the reader is an active participant in the creation of meaning of the text, this paper will explore how the story of the Matthaean Mary invites the reader to use imagination to engage with the Exodus theme and respond in the light of those allusions that resonate with today's world.[10] This reading of Matthew 1-2, therefore, assumes that 'meaning is a productive, creative process set in motion by the text but involving the imagination and perception of a reader'.[11]

The Exodus theme begins not with Mary, but with Joseph – and standing behind Joseph is the memory of another Joseph who – sold into slavery by his brothers – became the dreamer of dreams and the patriarch who both nourished and forgave those same brothers, giving them life when they had sought death for him.[12] This Joseph was the eldest son of Jacob and Rachel, to whom Jacob gave the 'coat of many colours' who, in the Genesis cycle, is portrayed as the archetypal wise man. Matthew's Joseph, his namesake, is also wise; he is the one who recognises that the baby Mary carries is God-given and indeed will be named Emmanuel, God with us (Matthew 2.23). His wisdom is evident in the designation 'just' or 'righteous' (*dikaios*) v.19. To be just was to observe the law and, in this case, the law that an engaged woman who, if found not to be a virgin, should be returned to her father's house and stoned to death by the men of the city in order to restore family honour.[13] If Joseph became betrothed to Mary he was risking dishonour and disgrace that would have affected both his own reputation and that of his family, yet he acts with the generosity of his predecessor as he too becomes a dreamer of dreams, accepts the word of the angel, obeys the divine command, takes Mary as his wife and names Mary's son Jesus because he will save his people from their sins (Matthew 1.18-21).[14] The first Joseph saved the brothers who sinned against him. Like him, Matthew's Joseph, to whom God speaks through an angel, is also portrayed as an archetypical wise man, the one who epitomises God's wisdom. Mary does not stand in need of forgiveness; nevertheless, Joseph's resolve to marry her, despite the shame that might ensue, echoes the divine generosity that offers forgiveness and calls people back into familial relationships.

The decision was Joseph's. Mary was in no position to make a choice and would have to accept whatever decision he made. What she thought or felt was immaterial.[15] At that time, in that culture, as in many cultures today, the honour of the man was paramount. Even if a woman were the victim of rape she would be thought of as the transgressor.

Mary is the recipient of God's generosity, chosen by God to further his salvific purposes. Like Joseph, Mary is identified with figures from Hebrew scripture. In the genealogy the line of male ancestry is interrupted by the inclusion of five women: Tamar (1.3), Rahab (1.5), Ruth (1.5), the wife of Uriah (1.6) and Mary (1.16). It is helpful to look briefly at the four women who precede mention of Mary, commencing with Tamar, whose story is told in Genesis 38. Judah's legitimate sons were born by his wife, the daughter of Shua,[16] yet the line of David comes through the illegitimate son of Tamar, who seduced him and conceived by trickery. The second woman listed is Rahab, the prostitute who saved the life of Joshua's spies (Joshua 2.1-21).[17] Next comes Ruth, who lay with Boaz (Ruth 3.14), and whom he married and finally 'the wife of Uriah', who is identified in 2 Samuel 11.2-5 as Bathsheba, who committed adultery with David and who, after David ensured Uriah's death in battle, became his queen and the mother of Solomon. It has been argued that the four women have been included because the irregularity of their sexual history prepares Matthew's readers for the inclusion of Mary and the circumstances of Mary's pregnancy.[18] It has also been argued that the four women are included to demonstrate that non-Israelites have played their part in the salvation history that has led to the birth of the Messiah and that their inclusion encourages other gentiles, such as the Magi (Matthew 2.1-11), to follow Jesus.[19,20] More interesting, for the purposes of this discussion, is the suggestion that the link between these four women and Mary is that they, like her, 'were all relatively powerless, marginalised and in need of help'.[21] Here is the link with the Exodus story:

> *These women in Matthew's list both unnerve us and give us hope. Their inclusion hints that danger lurks... and that Mary is going to find herself at great risk. At the same time it suggests what God is about to do.*[22]

In Luke's gospel Mary's 'yes' to God is 'writ large'. This is not part of the Matthaean portrayal of Mary who is moved, like a pawn in a game of chess, by other characters. It is Joseph who is the chess master and decides, in accordance with the divine guidance he receives in his dreams, what the moves will be. Mary's personal circumstances, combined with the dangerous political climate, leave her with little choice; she is not the one taking the initiative. For Mary, like those who were brought safely out of Egypt, and for countless powerless people throughout human history, the story of the Exodus is her own story. Many women today are the passive recipients of men's decisions, like those trafficked into the sex trade for Eastern Europe. Mary, therefore, seems to play a minor role in Matthew's gospel, but it is in her powerlessness that Mary becomes a representative figure for many people as she plays her part in the Exodus narrative.

Egypt for the enslaved Israelites was a place of enforced, hard labour. It was also the place where the firstborn were slaughtered by Pharaoh. Egypt in Matthew's gospel, conversely, becomes the place of safety for Mary and the family as they escape the hell of infanticide perpetuated by Herod. Mary and the mother of Moses are inextricably linked in the minds of the reader; the danger for both women was real and imminent as the lives of their firstborn sons were imperilled.

Herod is compared with Pharoah and, by implication, with all those leaders who will stop at nothing to protect their own power-base and prevent uprisings. This view leads to the assertion that Mary becomes a representative figure for all mothers whose children's lives are in danger; for all who find ways to thwart the will of tyrants; for all who flee from danger; for all those who, having escaped from danger, find themselves living in a foreign land.

Now think of Mary who, like Moses' mother of old, sought to protect her baby from being slaughtered by Herod's men. The journey she faced was more than 150 miles, both long and arduous, and would take all her strength. Mary and her family fled 'by night' (Matthew 2.14), a more dangerous time to travel but necessary because of the immediacy of the threat to the baby's life.[23] Like Joseph, and like Abraham, Mary trusts the divine messenger and is ready to face uncertainty and hardship in order to protect her son. Mary, therefore, becomes a representative figure for all mothers whose children's lives are in danger.

> *A voice was heard in Ramah,*
> *wailing and loud lamentation,*
> *Rachel weeping for her children;*
> *she refused to be consoled,*
> *because they are no more.*
> (Matthew 2.18)[24]

Here in Matthew's gospel Rachel, the mother of Joseph and Benjamin, stands for Israel. Matthew is citing Jeremiah 31.15[25] in which Rachel weeps for the Israelites being taken into captivity in Babylon. Yet her weeping expresses solidarity with all generations who suffer at the hands of cruel regimes.[26] Mary, like Rachel before her, knew what it was to weep for those whose children were killed. Here, the end of the story and the crucifixion are prefigured, although Mary is not mentioned in Matthew's crucifixion scene and instead she weeps at the start of the story. While Old Testament commentators debate the context of the quotation[27] McKeating comments:

> Famine, military conquest, and other disasters, brought about their refugee problems in ancient times as they do today. Genocidal war was as regrettably familiar then as now. A man of Benjamin, reflecting on Benjamin's violent history, could have identified occasions in almost any generation when Rachel had cause to weep for her children.[28]

Mary, like Rachel, knew what it was to be uprooted and make a home in a foreign land and Mary, like Rachel, is also the mother of the nation, a representative figure, as the new Israel is inaugurated through the Christ event.

The Visit of the Magi

The 'Magi from the East' are introduced in Matthew 2.2. The term 'Magi' is variously translated as 'astrologers', 'wise men' – and in popular tradition, 'kings'. 'Magi' was the word used to describe a caste of Persian priests who interpreted dreams[29] and, in Matthew, they are astrologers who use their knowledge of the stars to interpret events on earth. It is not surprising, therefore, that they were considered to be wise.[30] The theme of 'wisdom' runs through the Matthaean birth narrative. Joseph, like his predecessor, is the recipient of God's wisdom as he hears the angelic messages through the medium of dreams and also demonstrates this wisdom in his obedient response. To hear the divine word, in scripture, is to obey, and hearing and obeying God is the beginning of both true wisdom and true worship. The Magi, often designated wise men, come into the story seeking the child *'who has been born King of the Jews'* and they come *'to pay him homage'* (Matthew 2.2). (It is interesting to note that the only other place in Matthew's gospel where Jesus is given the title 'the King of the Jews' is in the passion narrative, where the words are insults invested with mockery (Matthew 27.11,29,37) and, as such, are the antithesis of true worship.[31]

The child posed a threat to Herod's power that he could not ignore. Herod and *'all Jerusalem with him'*, presumably all those whose interests lay in keeping him in power, were filled with fear, hence Herod's command to the Magi, *'Go and search diligently for the child; and when you have found him bring me word so that I may also go and pay him homage.'* (Matthew 2.3)

The first readers of the gospel would have been under no illusion that Herod lied when he spoke of paying homage to the child and, like readers today, would have made the connection between true and false worship. It was the Magi, so often described as wise men, who offered true homage to the baby which, according to Eastern custom, would have involved full prostration,[32] a physical expression of their acceptance of the royal sovereignty of the child. On their arrival they saw Jesus *'with Mary his mother'* (Matthew 2.11). That Mary is placed in apposition to the 'wise men' enables the reader to recognise that Mary is the one who, as mother, offers 'true homage', and therefore she too is portrayed as wise.

The Magi are not the only people who embark on a journey, whether physical or metaphorical, to worship the child. *The astrologers are symbols of a journey now being undertaken by the nations, the floods of Gentiles entering the church of Christ* (Matthew 38.19).'[33] True worship, therefore, acknowledges the sovereignty of God in Christ and is ready both to hear and obey the God whom the Magi encountered with Mary his mother. It is Mary, not Joseph, who, with the child, takes the central place in the story, as she does at the end of the genealogy (Matthew 1.16). [34,35] It is through Mary that this child comes into the world and in the narrative that follows mother and child are always referred to 'in the same breath' and are not separated (Matthew 2.11 c.f. 2.13,14,20, 21).[36]

The Slaughter of the Innocents, the Flight to Egypt and the Return

Both the Magi and Joseph continue to experience dreams that, on the one hand, help to build the narrative tension of impending danger, intensified by the necessity of starting their journey *'by night'* (Matthew

2.14), and, on the other hand, reinforce the connection between Joseph and the Magi as 'wise'. They receive God's message and have the wisdom to hear and obey. The Magi return home by another route (Matthew 2.12) and Joseph responds immediately by 'getting up' (Matthew 2.13) and fleeing with his family to Egypt. Egypt, in Exodus traditions, was the place where Moses was saved despite Pharoah ordering the midwives to slaughter all newborn Hebrew boys at birth (Exodus 2.16) or, as noted above, when the midwives thwarted his plan, to have them drowned in the Nile (Exodus 2.22).

Genocide has always been a shameful part of human existence and continues to blight the lives of individuals, communities and nations.[37,38] Whenever and wherever tyrants seek the destruction of those who stand in their way, brave women and men have been ready to put their own lives at risk on behalf of their victims. In the gospel narrative both John the Baptist and Jesus suffer and die at the hands of an occupying force.

Egypt was also the place from which Moses fled as an adult to escape Pharoah's wrath (Exodus 2.11-15) and to which he returned when 'those who sought his life had died' (Exodus 4.19), a phrase echoed in Matthew 2.20. Here is a reminder that neither Pharoah nor Herod acted alone; others were also prepared to condone murder for their own advantage.

These days it is not unusual to hear the Holy Family described as 'a refugee family'. Now, as then, many people flee from danger encountered in their own countries. The story of the mother and child with which this discussion was introduced is one such story. Yet these days there is, on the one hand, public outrage at the resources that are being spent on asylum seekers and refugees at the expense of the taxpayer, while, on the other hand, others speak out for those whose lives are in danger and who seem to be 'criminalised' by the present system. Admittedly, the waters are muddied by those who are seeking a better quality of life than they have in their own countries and whose lives are not obviously in danger, yet the rich/poor divide between wealthier and poorer countries cannot be denied and has contributed to the present situation. The journeys undertaken by many asylum seekers are beyond imagining.

The Exodus typology, in the first gospel, enables the reader to recognise that Jesus is part of the great biblical metanarrative of the Exodus that culminates in the quotation formula from Hosea, *'Out of Egypt I have called my Son'* (Hosea 11.1, Matthew 2.15). In Hosea, the quotation introduces a section in which God agonises about his relationship with his rebellious son: Israel/Ephraim. The allusion is to the wandering and disobedience of the wilderness years before the entry into the land of promise. To explore the nature of such typology effectively is not to press its inconsistencies; clearly the Matthaean passage is about Jesus and the passage from Hosea about the nation, but rather to allow the resonances of the past to inform present understanding.[39] Here, Mary and her child are also the recipients of God's promise and, on the death of Herod,[40] will be brought safely out of Egypt by God.[41] That the journey will eventually lead not to Bethlehem – Joseph is afraid of Archelaus – but Nazareth, in the gentile area of Galilee with its Graeco-Roman decapolis cities, is a reminder of the significance that Mary's child will have for all people.

Mary as a representative figure today

Matthew's gospel commences with a genealogy that goes back not, as in Luke, to Adam, but to Abraham, the father of the nation. Mary, therefore, is identified not with Eve but with Abraham, who obeyed God's call for him to leave his familiar land to journey to a foreign destination. For Matthew, Mary is identified with the new Israel, the nation of God's people – those who, like the Magi, recognise the identity of the child. Mary is also identified as the mother of the Church of Christ and, as such, is the representative figure for all God's people.

Mary's story is of a mother whose child's life is endangered, of a long and hard journey to a foreign land where she has to remain until it is safe to return. Even the return is not to Bethlehem but to Nazareth, a different region, where she has to pick up the threads of her life. There are many people today whose personal stories resonate with the story of Mary: those who have experienced the horror of genocide, those who are displaced people and refugees and those who have to make their home in a foreign land. Many who return to their own countries are unable to return to the same location or find that 'home' has changed out of all recognition.

In conclusion, Matthew's gospel portrays Mary as a representative figure who becomes the mother of the new Israel, the Church of Christ, just as Abraham was the father of the nation. Mary's story, as recounted in the prologue in Matthew's gospel, resonates with the great biblical metanarrative of the Exodus which becomes her own story and the story of the Church.

This paper began with the account of a mother and child being taken to Yarl's Wood Detention Centre by night. It was both night in a literal sense and also night in a metaphorical sense. Mary too travelled *'by night'* (2.14) and she travels with those today who are also 'Exodus people' and calls us to do the same.

It is time for the Matthaean Mary, who is often eclipsed by the Lukan Mary, to step out of the shadows and into the limelight; for it is Matthew's Mary, who, in her helplessness, becomes a representative of all those who suffer under cruel regimes today and she challenges God's people actively to oppose the might of all those who inflict suffering upon any, who like Mary and her child, are vulnerable, in danger, in need of nurture and a place to call home.

Notes

1   N. T. Wright suggests that a metanarrative should answer the questions 'Who are we?', 'Where are we?', 'What is wrong?' and 'What is the solution?' For further reading about biblical metanarrative see e.g. Wright, Christopher J.H. (2006), *The Mission of God: Unlocking the Bible's Grand Narrative*, Nottingham: IVP.

2   'For those of us who believed in the presence of a biblical metanarrative, the temptation is to think that we can exhaustively or definitively explain it, or to equate our systematic understanding of the metanarrative with the metanarrative itself. That's why it is perhaps best to think in terms of metanarrative frameworks.' www.postmodernpreaching.net/metanarrative.htm (accessed 24/2/2009).

3   Middleton, J. Richard and Walsh, Brian J. (1997), *Truth Is Stranger Than It Used To Be*, London: SPCK, p88. Chapter 5, pp88-107, offers a concise consideration of the Exodus as transforming metanarrative within the periods of Old and New Testaments and subsequently.

4   Hyatt, J. Phillip (1980), *Exodus: The New Century Bible Commentary*, Grand Rapids: Wm B. Eerdmans/London: Marshall, Morgan & Scott, p61: 'This is the third stratagem of the

Egyptian king, the first being forced labour, the second a command to the midwives to kill the males. This implies a more rigorous campaign to exterminate the Hebrews.'
5. Genesis 1.26. See especially Genesis 15.12-14 and note that the primeval history includes material that forms a prelude to the Exodus narratives; also cf. Galatians 3.6-28.
6. Genesis 12.1.
7. For example, Jeremiah 31.31-34, Ezekiel 20.1-44.
8. Cf. John 6.31f., Acts 7, Hebrews 3.16, 8.9, Jude 5.
9. Typological interpretation is the practice of reading certain persons (although this can also extend to objects and places) in the Hebrew Bible as 'symbols' or 'types' of persons in the New Testament.
10. Achtemeier, Paul (1999), *Inspiration and Authority*, Peabody MA: Hendrikson Publishers, p304 notes that reader response criticism also assumes that there will be common ground shared by the text and the reader, i.e. the symbolic world presupposed by the text, in this case the Exodus traditions, and shared emotional responses.
11. Achtemeier, *Inspiration and Authority*, p305, reiterating the words of Iser.
12. Genesis 50.15-21.
13. Harrington, David (1991), *The Gospel of Matthew*, Collegeville MT: The Liturgical Press, p34; Schnackenburg, Rudolf (2002), *The Gospel of Matthew*, Grand Rapids MI/Cambridge: Wm B. Eerdmans, p19.
14. Hagner, Donald (1993), *Matthew 1-13*, Dallas TX: Word Books, p34 considers that 'the resemblance between the two Josephs is not particularly convincing, nor is it important to Matthew,' although he acknowledges that 'both Josephs were concerned with dreams and kings, and for a time both lived in Egypt out of necessity.'
15. Dennis, Trevor (2007), *The Christmas Stories*, London: SPCK, p26.
16. The sons of the daughter of Shua are listed before those of Tamar in 1 Chronicles 2.3.
17. In the genealogy Rahab is said to be the mother of Boaz. This has been disputed by scholars who argue that Matthew is referring to Rahab of Jericho, e.g. Brown, R.E. (1982), 'Rachab in Mt.1.5', *Biblica Roma* 63, pp79-80.
18. This may, however, be to read back a present-day preoccupation with irregular sexual relationships into the biblical text – a position argued by e.g. Freed, E.D. (1987), 'The Women in Matthew's Genealogy' *JSNT* 29, pp3-19.
19. France, R.T. (2007) *The Gospel of Matthew*, Grand Rapids, Michigan, Cambridge: Wm B Eerdmans Publishing Co., p37.
20. It is generally accepted that Tamar and Rahab were Canaanites, Ruth a Moabite and Bathsheba a Hittite although Bauckham, R.J. (1995), 'Tamar's Ancestry and Rahab's Marriage: Two Problems in Matthean Genealogy' *NovT* 37, pp314-18 argues that she was not, strictly speaking, a gentile.
21. Schnackenburg (2002), p17 considers that the inclusion of the four women is to introduce an irregular element into the genealogy in order to prepare the reader for the extraordinary event that is about to take place through Mary.
22. Dennis (2007), p23.
23. France (2007), p7.
24. France (2007), p94 notes that this quotation from Jeremiah 31.15 functions as a commentary on the tradition of the slaughter of the innocents rather than its source. Its relevance is to develop further the Matthaean presentation of Jesus as the fulfillment of scripture..
25. Jeremiah 38.15 in the LXX.
26. Schnackenburg (2002), p26.

27 McKeating, Henry (1999), *The Book of Jeremiah*, Peterborough: Epworth Press, pp149-150 comments that opinion is divided about whether Jeremiah 31:15 refers to the exile of the Northern tribes in 722 BC or, as in 40.1, to Ramah as the staging post for people being taken into exile in Babylon in 586.
28 Ibid. p150.
29 Schnackenburg (2002), p42.
30 Although notice that Dennis (2007), p38 argues against the designation 'wise men'.
31 Hagner (1993), p27.
32 Schnackenburg (2002), p24.
33 Ibid. p24.
34 Hagner (1993), p30.
35 France (2007), p75 notes that in 2:13, 14, 20 and 21'the child and his mother' are the object of Joseph's actions. Also, note Nolland's view that the focus on Mary reflects the source of this material rather than reflecting the writer's concern to shine the spotlight on Mary: Nolland, John (2005), *The Gospel of Matthew*, Grand Rapids MI/Cambridge: Wm B. Eerdmans Pub. Co., p116.
36 Nolland (2005), p121.
37 www.ushmm.org/conscience/history (accessed 30/12/08). Genocide is defined in Article 2 of the *Convention on the Prevention and Punishment of the Crime of Genocide* (CPPCG) as 'any of the following acts committed with intent to destroy, in whole or in part, a national, ethnical, racial or religious group, as such: killing members of the group; causing serious bodily or mental harm to members of the group; deliberately inflicting on the group conditions of life, calculated to bring about its physical destruction in whole or in part; imposing measures intended to prevent births within the group; [and] forcibly transferring children of the group to another group.'
38 www.historyplace.com/worldhistory/genocide/index.html (accessed 30/12/08). In the twentieth century statistics showing deaths by genocide include: 'Armenians in Turkey: 1915–1918 – 1,500,000 deaths; Stalin's Forced Famine: 1915–1918 – 7,000,000 deaths: Rape of Nanking: 1937–1938 – 300,000 deaths; Nazi Holocaust: 1938–1945 – 6,000,000 deaths; Pol Pot in Cambodia: 1975–1979 – 200,000 deaths; Rwanda: 1994 – 800,000 deaths; Bosnia-Herzegovenia: 1992–1995 – 200,000 deaths.' In the twenty-first century genocide continues in places such as Darfur.
39 Hagner (1993), p36 argues that Matthew recognises the similarity that exists between two moments of redemptive history in which the earlier foreshadows or anticipates the latter. The fulfilment motif shows how God's son, Israel, and God's Son, Jesus, are both in Egypt of necessity and are both delivered by divine provision. Jesus, therefore, participates in Israel's sufferings and anticipates her liberation.
40 Herod died in 4BC.
41 France (2007), pp80-81.

Bibliography

Achtemeier, P. (1999), *Inspiration and Authority*, Massachusetts: Hendrikson Publishers.

Barton, J. (1997), *Making the Christian Bible*, London: Darton, Longman & Todd.

Bauckham, R.J. (1995), 'Tamar's Ancestry and Rahab's marriage: Two Problems in Matthean Genealogy', *NovT*, 313-29.

Brown, R.E. (1982) 'Rachab in Mt.1.5', *Biblica Roma*, 79-80.

Dennis, T. (2007), *The Christmas Stories*, London: SPCK.
France, R.T. (2007), *The Gospel of Matthew*, Grand Rapids MI/Cambridge: Wm B. Eerdmans..
Freed, E. D. (1987), 'The Women in Matthew's Genealogy', *JSNT* 29, 3–19.
Harrington, D. (1991), *The Gospel of Matthew*, Minnesota: The Liturgical Press.
Hyatt, J.P. (1980), *Exodus*, Grand Rapids MI: Wm B. Eerdmans/London: Marshall, Morgan & Scott.
McKeating, H. (1999), *The Book of Jeremiah*: Peterborough: Epworth Press.
Middleton, J. R. and Walsh, B. J. (1997), *Truth Is Stranger Than It Used To Be*, London: SPCK.
Nolland, J. (2005), *The Gospel of Matthew*, Grand Rapids MI/Cambridge, Wm B. Eerdmans..
Schnackenburg, R. (2002), *The Gospel of Matthew*, Grand Rapids MI/Cambridge: Wm B. Eerdmans.
Wright, C. J. H. (2006), *The Mission of God: Unlocking the Bible's Grand Narrative*, Nottingham: IVP.
All Biblical quotations are taken from the NRSV.

Web Sites

www.ushmm.org/conscience/history
www.historyplace.com/worldhistory/genocide/index.html
www.postmodernpreaching.net/metanarrative.htm

Whither the wider ecumenism?: A Methodist perspective

Martin Forward

When John Newton gave his presidential address to the Methodist Conference of 1981, he mentioned the growing importance of interfaith issues to church and society, and pointed to my own interest in dialogue. It was a characteristically gracious touch by a superb colleague. To have John as your superintendent minister was to be cherished and appreciated not only by him, but also by Rachel, Mark, Chris, David and Bill. My wife Udho and I are vastly in their debt.

John's interest in the wider ecumenism is all of a piece with his commitment to the narrower ecumenism of inter-Christian appreciation and cooperation. In an age when foolish Christians think it a virtue to have no knowledge of the churches' past, John is sustained by and embodies two of Methodism's guiding principles: its commitment to social holiness and to Arminian inclusivism. He is one of the holiest men I know, and a firm believer in Charles Wesley's conviction that God's 'undistinguishing regard was cast on Adam's fallen race'.

It is an odd fact that many Christians engaged in inter-faith dialogue have been Methodists. I remember attending a World Council of Churches' gathering and being met by an Episcopalian colleague's cheery greeting: 'Not another one!' He was referring not to my ethnicity or gender, but to my denominational affiliation. Those two guiding principles of inclusivism and the quest for holiness help explain why so many Methodists are interested in what God is up to outside the Christian family of faith. Our instinct is to suppose that she delights in all her children, especially when their faith leads them to do and be good.

This essay takes a swift look at four British Methodists who have contributed mightily to advancing relationships between Christians and people of other faiths: Geoffrey Parrinder; Kenneth Cracknell; Eric Lott; and Elizabeth Harris.[1] I am privileged to call them friends, and each of them has taught me a great deal about God's 'undistinguishing regard'.[2] So that this essay does not become a Methodist 'love-in', I shall also make a few comments about Ursula King, a Roman Catholic, another dear friend and supervisor of my doctoral thesis (which was about Geoffrey Parrinder's contribution to the study of religion; she herself had Geoffrey as her doctoral supervisor!) Each has made many and varied contributions to our knowledge about this world of many faiths, so it is not possible to touch on all their achievements. I shall simply draw attention to a few things (sometimes not the things they are best known for) they have emphasised as important in the pursuit of the wider ecumenism. I shall then make some suggestions about where aspects of their work could be taken by present and future scholars and practitioners of inter-faith dialogue.

Geoffrey Parrinder died in 2005, at the advanced age of 95.[3] As a young man on board ship for missionary service in French West Africa in 1933, he was greeted by the sight of Nazi flags in Porto Novo, Dahomey (now Benin). Geoffrey hated Nazi racial ideology and any kind of discrimination and bigotry. He enjoyed telling the story of Edwin Smith, the distinguished Primitive Methodist anthropologist and scholar a generation older than he. When Smith was dining one day in 1930 with the biographer Emil Ludwig, who used psychology to gain an understanding of Bismarck, Jesus and other notables, Ludwig asked him: 'How can the untutored African conceive God?' Smith replied that Africans were quite able to know God as a living power, but Ludwig, armed with Teutonic scholarly certainty but with no practical experience of Africa, would not believe him and retorted, 'Deity is a philosophical concept which savages are incapable of framing'.[4]

This kind of uninformed racial arrogance of the 1930s had its counterpart in theological *hauteur*. Hendrik Kraemer's influential book *The Christian Message in a non-Christian World*, written for the 1938 meeting of the International Missionary Conference in Tambaram, South India, applied an exclusivist Barthian interpretation to other faiths. This 'more Barthian than Barth' approach to religious diversity had a baleful influence for almost two generations on Protestant inter-faith dialogue, blinding churches and theologians to (among other things) the dark aspects of European colonisation and the long Christian history of anti-Semitism. Geoffrey's first published work, an article for *Expository Times* in 1939, took Kraemer's work to task. In a masterly piece of English understatement, he described its unwillingness to see any meaningful and sustained revelation of God outside Christ as an 'over-statement'. Although Geoffrey once drily told me that it was his wife Mary who was the family's real Methodist, this is belied by his courteously combative Arminianism, which looked to God more as an encourager of saints than as a pedantic schoolteacher drilling important information into recalcitrant pupils, and therefore approved a person's quality of life more than the correctness of her statements of belief.

Unlike Kraemer, Geoffrey had no problem in seeing God at work among other faiths. Indeed, his major contribution to the study of religion was to give Africans pride in their ancestral religions. He believed that, despite its variety, all sub-Saharan African religion demonstrated four characteristics: a Supreme God; chief divinities; the cult of clan ancestors; and the widespread use of charms and amulets. Whether you were a Yoruba in Nigeria or a Masai in Kenya or a Zulu in South Africa, this fourfold classification could make sense of your religious life. Geoffrey believed that African Traditional Religion (ATR; he was the first to use this term, in a book of that name published in 1954) was a religion worthy to be compared to Christianity, Islam and any other of the world's great faiths. He taught this religion at University College, Ibadan, Nigeria, where he worked from 1949 to 1958, and inspired a generation and more of African scholars and religious leaders, not all of whom were gracious enough to acknowledge their clear indebtedness to him and his views.

Nowadays this model seems excessively essentialist, even though it allowed for considerable diversity between different expressions of ATR. A stronger criticism is that it was forged somewhat on the template of a Christian understanding of what counts as a respectable religion. For instance, Geoffrey's response to the fact that Africans had no scripture was to depict art and other aesthetic endeavors as playing the role of scripture for ATR. By looking at a painting, or a carving or some other artistic product, African traditionalists could see God or the gods' will revealed to them. Nowadays, scholars of religion would more readily concede that religions, in order to be reputable, do not need the equivalent of a holy book. Still, for all its faults, Geoffrey's model of a highly-regarded African indigenous religion not only empowered Africans to study and appreciate their religious heritage, it also undermined European colonialist arrogance about untutored African savages and, sixty years later, its influence can still be detected in many contemporary formulations of primal faith.[5] So it ill becomes some churlish scholars, pygmies stamping petulantly on the shoulders of a giant, to sneer at Geoffrey's fourfold categorisation, dismissing it as some kind of colonisation of the African mind.[6]

Certainly, Geoffrey was no romantic about the future of indigenous religions. He was persuaded that African ancestral faith was giving way to either Christianity or Islam, though some of his writings presciently explore the beginnings of what some would now call new African religious movements, which fuse together elements of religions old and new into sometimes surprising forms, only tangentially related to mainstream forms of those two Abrahamic faiths. He was not persuaded by pluralist views that all religions were equally valid ways of salvation, but remained committed to the belief that Christian religion was the noblest of all expressions of faith, and used biblical ideas about the cosmic Christ to establish and justify his view. At bottom, Geoffrey was an outstandingly fine exemplar of what Kenneth Cracknell calls the obligation of missionaries and theologians to pursue 'justice, courtesy and love', treating 'otherness' with admiration and curiosity, rather than bringing to it disdain and views formed in advance of any true meeting. (In this, he was very unlike his Kraemer-inspired British missionary contemporaries, Lesslie Newbigin and Stephen Neill).

One of Kenneth's considerable achievements has been to give a hearing to many Christian missionary and theological pioneers who showed such positive appreciation.[7] Now retired in Vermont, Kenneth is from the generation after Geoffrey, and unlike him has been much used by the churches, especially as the first executive-secretary of the

British Council of Churches' Committee for Relations with People of Other Faiths and then teaching in the Cambridge Theological Federation, of which he became president. His razor-sharp mind takes on board an interest in biblical theology, church history, Judaism and many other good things (including trains. I well remember a wander around the York National Railway Museum with him, when I was entranced by his ability to move effortlessly from discussing the Great Commission to explaining the Great Western Main Line).

I remain most impressed by Kenneth's remarkable ability to ask the right question. Once, at a conference of lay people interested in inter-faith issues, he told me, at a moment's notice, that he was going to ask me to respond to his questions as an informed Muslim would. I thought I would make a pig's breakfast of things but instead found that, in response to his queries, all sorts of interesting stuff was coaxed out of me. But it was his triumph, not mine. Like the best sort of orchestral conductor drawing out of his instrumentalists sounds and sweet harmonies they thought themselves incapable of producing, he conjured forth from me rather a dazzling performance; so much so that some people could not believe that I was a Christian and not a Muslim! Not just in that but many other contexts, Kenneth retains the capacity to make you look at many things (*inter alia*: scripture, the church, your partner in dialogue, God's ways in the world) from perspectives that light them up with new possibilities of faith, hope and love.

Another of Kenneth's significant achievements was to help create and teach a course on 'Jewish and Christian Responses to the Holocaust' in Cambridge University's Faculty of Divinity. This course attracted many bright Christian students and helped them learn to be lovingly critical of the tradition that shaped them. Undiscerning people could assume that Kenneth's bonhomie implies that he is the sort of fellow for whom all religions are good except perhaps their own. But in fact Kenneth makes the perceptive person confront her or his tradition of faith lovingly and critically, aware of what it has done and can do for good and evil. That person is then better placed to have an equally balanced view of the faith-traditions of their dialogue partners. As one of Mr Wesley's travelling preachers should,

Kenneth inspires people (and enthuses them to encourage others) to choose from their faith what deals life and does good.

Kenneth is first and foremost not a scholar of world religions (though his knowledge of them is formidable), but a Christian theologian; more to the point, a Christian biblical theologian. His written works and oral presentations on the Bible are riveting. He makes his hearers think afresh about scripture, even when they cannot quite go with him where he wants to take them, which is the mark of an excellent teacher.[8] I am much indebted to Kenneth's exegetical skills. He lit up the Bible for me and made me want to try and do so for others. He has the historian's skill of making the past a strange, strange country, yet to encourage one to hope that one can learn from it, if one is patient and exploratory, and respectful of its foreignness. Too many Christian bible scholars and systematic theologians seem to have little understanding of history. So their work makes Jesus seem like a nineteenth or twentieth-century German idealistic philosopher who absent-mindedly wandered into first-century Palestine in order to offer a few anachronistic though noteworthy thoughts to groups of receptive peasants.

Or else they treat other faiths as tightly-boundaried systems of teaching and doctrines that can be assessed for their nearness or distance from a perceived body of more truthful Christian teaching and doctrines. Like his mentor, the Canadian Wilfred Cantwell Smith, Kenneth sees that religions are much more fluid systems than that. He recognises that they are second order categories. He has often been heard to remind Christians that the Book of Revelation sees no Temple in the City of God (Revelation 21.22). There will be no need of it, for we will see God face to face, and the Lamb. In other words, we should critically love our faith and our religion, and (just as critically) admire and honor the faith of others; but we should love God more.

My second meeting with Eric Lott was at Hyderabad airport,[9] where I arrived having just vomited down my shirt and trousers! He and Christine looked after me in their home until I moved over to stay for two years with Indian friends. Their love for India kindled my own. I had the most wonderful tour of Hindu temples of South

India with them. I was most comfortable exploring the congenially Abrahamic worlds of Indian Islamic diversity, but Eric made me look further to admire and learn something about the voluptuous profusions of Hindu faith. I came to marvel at the western Enlightenment obsession with naming and characterising things, which reduced their wild profusion to an essential core, and so often missed many important points. Incidentally, in later years, as I studied Geoffrey Parrinder's views about African Traditional Religion, I pondered whether, if Geoffrey had lived in Hyderabad, India, rather than Porto Novo, Dahomey, he would have persuaded us to acknowledge and value the profusion of Indian Traditional Religion, instead of the dubious monolith of Hinduism.

No doubt because he and Chris gave over thirty years of their lives to India, Eric has been much and unwisely underappreciated and overlooked in the wider academic world, but his books repay careful attention. Like my other 'gurus', he has contributed widely and significantly to many aspects of inter-faith dialogue. A number of us have learned important things from him not just about Hindu views of religious reality, but also about ecology, and the emergence of Dalit theology that empowers the former outcastes of Indian society. His capacity for attention to detail no doubt helps explain why he is as much a theoretician of religion as he is a Christian theologian of religious diversity (and a remarkable linguist as well). Geoffrey and Kenneth have mostly been content to assume the importance of a theological interpretation of the study of religion (in other words, to put it somewhat crassly, to take for granted the importance of God for religion), whereas Eric has been interested in the social scientists' obsession with theory and scientific inquiry.[10] His mentor, Ninian Smart, was also interested in such inquiry, but tended to shape it on a theological template. For all his deep faith-full convictions, Eric has been more cautious in doing so and, at his urging, I learned more about various theoretical approaches to the study of religion than otherwise I might have.

If Kenneth has trains to pass his 'spare' time, Eric has birds. He and Chris holiday in places where they can observe our feathered friends, and I sometimes think that Eric is more pleased by and proud of his photographs in (highly regarded) books about birds than he is about his own published works. One of my most treasured memories of him is of an ornithological slide-show he gave in Bangalore to a group of people interested not in theology or religion but in birds. His enthusiasm was unbounded and conveyed knowledge and insight about his subject-matter. For the duration, I too could catch the excitement. Their interest in birds is part of his and Chris's convictions about a proper care and respect for the environment. You should love what God has made! They helped me realise, somewhat later on my inter-faith journey than I should have, that religions can and should work together to change (or, indeed, preserve) the world for good. Differences matter but need not and should not get in the way of people of divers ways of faith doing good together, for others and for God's good earth.

It would be too much to say that I arrived in India thinking that I was bringing God with me. However, I had much to learn about God's universal care of his human and wider family and much work to do to begin reconciling my Christian faith with developing views about God. Eric helped me in that process. Both he and I have occasionally mused together about whether we have given up too much in order to arrive where we are. But it has not seemed like a choice so much as a necessity: 'Here I am. I can do no other'. In fact, Eric's tendency towards introspection and his times of depression have enabled him to write movingly and helpfully about how Indian views of deep Christian faith (views, moreover, that are also shaped by Hindu analyses of reality) can help and heal others.[11]

Elizabeth Harris loves Sri Lanka with a similar passion to Eric's love of India. I first met her there at a meeting of the World Council of Churches sub-unit on Dialogue. I returned a few months later with David Craig, then the Head of Religious Broadcasting for the BBC World Service, to make some radio programmes on religions in South Asia. Liz organized trips to various parts of the country for us, with interviews on the way. Her boundless energy was exhausting and exhilarating, and our programmes benefitted greatly from her contacts with Buddhist and Christians there. As religions go, Theravada Buddhism seems to me to be quite different from most forms of Christian faith. On the face of it, building meaningful bridges from one to the other, still less drawing inspiration from one to breathe new life into the other, would seem to be futile. But in religiously plural settings, significant encounters across faith boundaries happen: not least, people of faith fall in love with those of different faith and have to make sense of their partner's different religious allegiance, and contemplate how to introduce their children to religious belief and practice.

Of course, you do not have to take the step of matrimony or parenthood in order to engage significantly with issues of religious diversity; you just have to be curious. And if you are both curious and a good Methodist, as Liz is (she was the British Methodist Church's spokesperson on inter-faith matters for a decade before moving to teach at Liverpool Hope University), you will want to inquire what God has been up to in the wide world outside Christian faith. Her research introduced her to some crass Christian attitudes towards Buddhism during the British colonial period (and also to other views of 'justice, courtesy and love'),[12] but in her daily life she met and was befriended by inter-faith pioneers, such as Fr Aloysius Pieris. With their encouragement, she began to explore how Buddhist spirituality could inform her own. During Liz's sojourn in Sri Lanka, the country was torn apart by civil war, which developed her interest in peace issues, and what Buddhists and Christians were doing to reconcile national and community divisions.[13] And (as Jewish, Hindu, Christian and other peace-activists in South Africa during the twilight years of the apartheid era found), it proved natural to ask whether such actions could be devoid of joint prayer and other forms of worship. Then, to go a step further, it is equally natural to query whether Buddhist patterns of meditation can be integrated into a Christian spiritual discipline.

Liz thinks so. She strikes me as a conspicuously noteworthy exemplar of what Julius Lipner has called hyphenated-religious identity and John Berthrong has termed multiple religious participation. John has pointed out that, in China and other centers of East Asian faith, many people 'belong' to a number of religions (e.g. forms of Buddhism, Confucianism and Taoism) but that they are usually rooted in one faith, even if they engage more readily with other religions than many adherents of Judaism, Christianity and Islam would think appropriate or desirable. Deeply embedded as she is in her Methodist tradition of faith, Liz also strongly identifies with another, Buddhist way of belonging. In this, Liz may prove to be a pioneer for other Christians who would integrate other forms of spirituality thoughtfully and knowledgably into their own, rather than in a haphazard, self-centered way.

Ursula King is a Christian theologian, the leading authority on the life and ideas of Pierre Teilhard de Chardin, a significant voice in the burgeoning area of women and religion, an important contributor to theoretical approaches to the study of religion, and... Well, one could go on! This Roman Catholic scholar is as inclusive and as interested in issues of holiness as my Methodist subjects, illustrating that any denominational emphases are just that: emphases, not monopolies. She does show an instinctive Roman Catholic appreciation for God's presence in the wider world of nature as well as the narrower history of salvation; again, an emphasis not a monopoly.

At an international meeting of inter-faith worthies, Ursula pointed out to me that, although women were present and had contributed greatly to the conference debates and discussions, the photo of the religious leaders had only men in it. Her work in gender studies has been characteristically incisive, inclusive and generous. The liberation of women can also include the liberation of men from roles that disable them from fulfilling their potential, too. Her generosity in this area is worth underlining. Despite her renown, Ursula's career has had its share of setbacks because she is a woman. It is no surprise that this has frustrated and angered her, but it is a measure of her human qualities that it has not embittered her or affected her generosity of spirit.

However, I have learned most from Ursula about the importance of the mystical experience of God. Indeed, my most recent book[14] is rather shamelessly indebted to many conversations with her and to her surpassingly lovely book on Christian mystics.[15]

Mystics are important witnesses to God's capacity to speak to the poor and marginalised in a direct and unmediated way. Significantly, many have been women and even children. They do not all come from the upper strata of society. Crucially, these facts subvert ecclesiastical structures. Mystics may choose to accept the authority and the teaching of officially sanctioned leaders of their religion, usually men, but they may feel that they do not need to, since their own experience is often overwhelmingly more important to them. They are also inclined to see dogmas, religious law and the like, and even religion itself, as second-order categories, useful and even necessary to guide one to God, but as means to that end and not as ends in themselves. Paid employees of religious structures often privilege their own power and thereby miss the true point of religion. The great Muslim mystic, Jalāl ad-Dīn Rūmī (1207–73) described some officially-sanctioned Muslim scholars as 'curs baying at the moon'. (He was one himself, so the jibe was the more offensive). He told such people: 'you think the shadow is the substance'. Religion is not intended to empower some men but to give value to all humans and indeed all things: 'Jew, Muslim, shaman, Zoroastrian, stone, ground, mountain, river, each has a secret way of being with the mystery, unique and not to be judged'. All this is, of course, subversive to those who picture God as a testosterone-charged potentate and themselves as his sole or major representatives.

Ursula makes the important point that mystics go through stages in order to achieve and make sense of their encounter with the divine. A Methodist like me would put it this way: it takes hard work to reach what Charles Wesley calls 'thy love's ecstatic height, the glorious joy unspeakable, the beatific sight'. So much spirituality in our contemporary world is trivial and surface: people want an instant fix, and an egotistical one that is for them and them alone. But love, generously given by God, needs to be accepted with all one's heart and soul and mind and strength, and given to others with comparable risk and generosity.

More recently, Ursula has written an important book about, to quote its subtitle, our global quest for a spiritual life.[16] In it, she looks at various aspects of the spiritual life. She reflects, among many other things, on: whether spirituality can be entirely divorced from religion; issues of spirituality and gender; spirituality and children; spirituality's relationship to nature and science and to the arts. She makes plain that true spirituality is, at source, a mystical experience, and that it has wide-ranging implications for all aspects of personal and social life.

Geoffrey's insights into the world of religions took shape in West Africa, where he spent most of the years between 1933 and 1958. Eric and Ursula spent many years in India, and Liz a significant amount of time in Sri Lanka. It is, of course, perfectly possible to spend many years in someone else's country and learn nothing of importance. But to do so in the expectation of finding God alive, well and at work among other of his human children is an inestimable blessing for inter-faith people. Some writers on religious diversity fail to convince because they lack the insight and discernment that can arise from patient and hopeful reflection on 'otherness' that is all around you and in which context you are the 'other'.

As time passes, so issues that people address develop and even change. Religion was such an important issue for Geoffrey that he honored traditional African faith by interpreting it as a world religion in its own right, rather than a collection of local superstitions as many other westerners regarded it in the closing years of the imperial adventure in Africa. In Ursula's book on spirituality, she makes a strong case, against the assumptions of many contemporary people, that religion even now has things to say of value to inform and guide their spirituality. Something has changed in the last half century in our attitudes to religion!

Thankfully, Kenneth, Eric, Liz and Ursula are still labouring in the vineyard of religion and dialogue. Since Geoffrey was writing well into his nineties, if they follow his example they will have many more things to add to their already distinguished contributions. Still, it is worth asking: what aspects of the work of my five 'gurus' can be taken further by present and future scholars and practitioners of inter-faith dialogue?

I would like to mention three. First, religion matters. At present, religion is under assault. There are trivial attacks by new atheists, whose view of religion and science alike is as narrow as that of the fundamentalists whom they oppose and whom they take to represent the entirety of religion. They display in spades the arrogance of secularism, which assumes its own rightness and has little or no self-criticism: the genocides of the twentieth century were as much the work of secular figures as of religious leaders, but the new atheists and others who associate religion with violence seem to imagine that Stalin, Mao, Pol Pot and others were somehow not secular. There is also the drift from religion into self-serving spiritualities, which comfort but rarely seem to challenge their adherents.

One common current assertion by critics of religion is that morality does not depend upon religion. Things are not quite as simple as that contention implies, but my point here is that this affirmation unhelpfully draws attention away from the important matter at stake. The real issue is not about who is good or evil, but how to recognise and choose the good and be empowered to pursue it. People of faith have access to profound analyses of the human condition that make them aware of a person's capacity for immeasurable good and catastrophic evil, and offer healing. If secularism is to offer similar analyses, it will have to do better than, for example, Marx's inability to comprehend the real source of human motivation for good and evil, or Freud's foolish, unproven and unprovable fantasies about the origin of religion in the human mind.

If religion matters, then, of course, it is always in need of reform and updating. To do that requires religious people to accept the past for what it is: a resource to teach us what to do and be and what not to do and be. It is not to be romanticised or discarded, if we are to reclaim religions as vessels of faith and hope and love in our twenty-first century.[17] My five 'gurus' acknowledge that the purpose of religion is not as an end in itself but to point to the divine lover. Their defence of religion has not just been of some narrow Christian interpretation, but has acknowledged the work of God in the wider worlds of faith. For it is to God that true religion must point.

But is my last sentence true? A second area for future work is to do with methodological issues in the study of religion. There has been a great deal of debate in recent years about the meaning of religion. Some scholars, particularly those from the social sciences, regard religion as somehow not a respectable subject precisely because it is usually taken to be about God. These scholars wax particularly eloquently and indignantly about the hegemony of theological interpretations of religion. Religion is, they contend, really sociology or some other field of experimental inquiry.

Still, most religious people (which means most people) think that religion deals with transcendent reality, whether named as God or whatever. They recognise that religion needs to make a difference in society as well as in individual lives, hopefully for good, but are not usually persuaded that their religious actions are an end in themselves or done simply to bolster a social function rather than as a means to a higher, inspirational end. When social scientists are let loose on religion, they are often alarmingly reductionist and essentialist in their interpretations, and inclined to discount mystery and wonder in favor of dubiously-attested evidence. In fact, the social sciences' emphasis on independent variables functioning with static systems seems increasingly alien to the world as we know it, and somewhat out of date as an evidence-based, scientific field of inquiry.[18] It is time for the heirs of Wilfred Cantwell Smith to take a tilt or two at the folly of those who seem to think that religion can only be rescued as an academic discipline in the shadow of the social sciences. Useful as they are, these disciplines can be like India's banyan tree, an enormous and impressive phenomenon under which nothing can flourish.

Kenneth has pointed out that Wilfred Smith moved away from a Marxist interpretation of history when, returning from furlough to Pakistan, he stood amid the ruins of Britain's partition of India, when Hindus and Muslims turned on each other and on Sikhs, and people died in thousands upon thousands. Religion will not wither away. It is always with us, a powerful force for good and evil. So what sort of religion should we have? The third aspect of the work of my five gurus to be taken forward is to answer that question, and bring up to date our vision of social holiness and Arminian inclusivism. How do we make saints for the twenty-first century? As we live faithfully amid religious diversity, how we can give religion its true valuation, how are we to combine individual flourishing with the common good, how do we cause holiness to increase? Those who deal faithfully with these questions will honour and continue the work of my five gurus.

I am sure John would approve, since somewhere near the heart of religion for him has been holiness, enabled by a careful reading of the past so as to give empowerment for the present and hope for the future.

Notes

1. Pleasingly, given the point of this book, two of these four 'gurus', Kenneth and Eric, were students at Richmond College when John Newton was assistant tutor there. They remember him with much affection; how could it be otherwise?
2. Because they are my friends, and because this is not quite an academic article, I shall call them by their Christian names. And because of my dealings with them, I shall intrude myself into this essay rather more than I do in most of my other writings. I apologise to those readers who think the intrusion too much. Living as I do with a teenage daughter, my excuse would be that I so rarely have the opportunity of making anything (however inappropriately or tangentially) about me.
3. For a summary of Geoffrey's life and achievements, see Forward, M. (1998), *A Bag of Needments: Geoffrey Parrinder and The Study of Religion*, Bern: Peter Lang. Of Geoffrey's many books, an entertaining and anecdotal account of his own views can be found in Parrinder, G. (1987), *Encountering World Religions*, Edinburgh: T&T Clark.
4. For a remarkably fine account of Edwin Smith's life and importance, see Young, W.J. (2002), *The Quiet Wise Spirit: Edwin W. Smith (1876–1957) and Africa*, Peterborough: Epworth Press.
5. Oddly enough, a fairly recent attempt to offer paganism as a universal category of primal spiritual practice owes a great (and unacknowledged) debt to Geoffrey's work, just as most religionists are, for better and worse, abandoning such ambitious, macro-cosmic projects: York, M. (2005), *Pagan Theology*, New York: NYU Press.
6. A relatively early and alarmingly polemical critic of Geoffrey Parrinder's views, and similar ones, was the Ugandan poet and anthropologist Okot P'Bitek in his (1970), *African Religions in Western Scholarship*, Nairobi: East Africa Literature Bureau.
7. Cracknell, K. (1995), *Justice, Courtesy and Love: Theologians and Missionaries Encountering World Religions, 1846–1914*, London: Epworth Press.
8. A number of excellent observations about the Bible can be found in Cracknell, K. (1986), *Towards a New Relationship: Christians and People of Other Faith*, Peterborough: Epworth.
9. Our first meeting was at the Methodist Missionary Society, 25 Marylebone Road, London, surrounded by portraits of past worthies who had travelled for God and Jesus, east and south of Suez.
10. Lott, E. (1988), *Vision, Tradition, Interpretation: Theology, Religion, and the Study of Religion*, Berlin: Mouton de Gruyter.
11. Lott, E. (1998), *Healing Wings: Acts of Jesus for human wholeness*, Bangalore: Asian Trading Corp.
12. Harris E. (2004), *Theravada Buddhism and the British Encounter*, London: Routledge.
13. Harris, E. (2009), *What Can Buddhism Offer to a Violent World?*, Peterborough: Epworth Press.

14 Forward, M. (2008), *The Nature and the Name of Love: Religion for the Contemporary World*, Peterborough: Epworth Press.
15 King, U. (2001), *Christian Mystics: Their Lives and Legacies throughout the Ages*, New York: HiddenSpring. (The British edition is London: Routledge, 2004).
16 King, U. (2008), *The Search for Spirituality: Our Global Quest for a Spiritual Life*, New York: BlueBridge. (The British edition is Norwich: Canterbury Press, 2009).
17 An excellent resource for Christians about the use of their past is Dean, J. (2009), *Servitude and Freedom: Reading The Christian Tradition*, Peterborough: Epworth Press.
18 A formidable challenge to claims that the social sciences convey impartial and objective knowledge is mounted in Gaddis, J.L. (2004), *The Landscape of History: How Historians Map the Past*, Oxford: OUP, 2004.

PART THREE
Christianity and the Future

Two Women Facing Death: Julian of Norwich and Etty Hillesum

Melvyn Matthews

At first sight Julian of Norwich and Etty Hillesum would seem unusual, if not totally incompatible bedfellows. They appear to have very little in common. Julian was a devout pre-Reformation Christian while Etty was a post-Enlightenment secularised Jew. Julian was an anchoress, following a daily pattern of worship, while as far as we can see Etty had no pattern of worship and only towards the end of her diaries did she find herself forced to kneel. Julian would have been vowed to celibacy, but Etty was a modern woman who classed herself as 'among the better lovers'. Nor could their circumstances have been more different, for Julian lived alone in a mediaeval English country town, albeit one beginning to experience some economic revival, whereas Etty lived a busy, socially packed life with many friends in modern Amsterdam studying languages and literature. Moreover their outlook on religion was totally different. Julian questioned her received faith in the light of her experience, while Etty, as we shall see, questioned her experience in the light of her slowly emerging but totally unstructured faith.

On the other hand there are a number of important similarities between them. Both were single women – and it should be said, as we shall see later, that both their womanhood and their singleness were tremendously important factors for each of them. Both of them were literate and educated. Although Julian, as any mediaeval woman was forced to do, called herself *'a simple creature, unlettered'*, the evidence of the Showings is that she was familiar with a wide range of mediaeval theological writing. Both women deliberately kept diaries or wrote personal accounts which were important to them both, Julian even rewriting her account some years later to clarify and enlarge upon what she had said earlier. Both women were ill and knew that their illnesses were important to them as part of their respective spiritual journeys. Both of them faced death within themselves and within the society of which they were a part. In spite of, or perhaps because of this, both arrived at a position of some internal illumination so that then both of them could speak meaningfully and movingly of the centrality of faith, hope and charity in human life.

So, there are differences and similarities, the most important difference being that of faith and practice, while the crucial similarities concern the questions of womanhood and suffering. All of these are also enormously important issues for the modern mind – namely crossfaith understanding, the centrality or not of religious practice, the place of women and singleness in society and the role of the body in self-understanding. We also face death in our world in the most acute fashion. Indeed the fortunes of both women turned on the question of death. So while they may be different from each other they feel tremendously familiar to us now.

What sort of death did they face? Let us look first at the 'death' which Etty Hillesum faced in Holland during her lifetime. For her as a Jew, the most horrific feature of life was the sequence of events which comprised the outbreak of war, the invasion and occupation of Holland by Germany and the subsequent persecution and extermination of the Jews both in Holland and across Nazi-occupied Europe. This Holocaust was the 'death' that Etty Hillesum faced. I think we need to realise that the roots of the Holocaust lie very deep in European history, and that it has a religious dimension. The

Early Fathers of the church and the Reformation theologians were all deeply anti-semitic. They engaged in a teaching of contempt for the Jews as those who murdered Christ. John Chrysostom (344–407) says,

> *Brothel and theatre, the synagogue is also a cave of pirates and a lair of wild beasts.... Living for their belly, the Jews behave no better than hogs...*[1]

While Martin Luther (1483–1546) encouraged his congregations to

> *..set fire to their synagogues or schools and bury or cover with dirt whatever will not burn... this is to be done in honour of our Lord and of Christendom.*[2]

This was an instruction which came to fulfilment on *Kristallnacht* in 1939 when synagogues were burned throughout Germany.

The arrival of the Age of Enlightenment appeared to offer a way out of the religious bigotry of both Catholic and Protestant by affirming the centrality of human reason and the inevitability of progress, both of which would become central characteristics of what we now call modernism. But it has also been said that the arrival of the purely secular state simply meant that the old 'teaching of contempt' was freed from religious controls against violence, thus unleashing the power of that teaching in society. Others emphasised the rise of science, saying that this gave the state the capacity for efficient transport and the destruction of millions of people. Indeed the rise of the secular state was often, particularly in France, said to be the responsibility of the Jews. But whatever the causes – and they are complex – the Holocaust saw something like six million Jews being singled out, deported, used as slave labour and finally destroyed.

There were of course particular facets to the Holocaust in Holland. Holland had been neutral during the First World War and for a number of reasons resistance in Holland was slow to form and in many ways more 'spiritual' than, say, the resistance in France. There was a strike of municipal workers in Amsterdam and in 1943 eighty-five per cent of the student body refused to sign the oath of allegiance to the occupying power. But meanwhile Rotterdam had been practically destroyed by bombing, Queen Wilhelmina had fled to Britain and of the 140,000 Jews who were in the country in 1940 when the country was invaded 107,000 had been deported by 1945, while about 30,000 survived mainly by fleeing the country. Seventy-five per cent perished in the Nazi death camps. A few, like Anne Frank, went into hiding, but others, like Etty Hillesum, who rode her bicycle fearlessly though the streets of Amsterdam while Anne Frank was hiding in her attic, refused to flee. Etty Hillesum had found work with the Jewish Council, the body set up by the occupying power to deal with Jewish questions, but found that difficult and was transferred to 'The Department of Social Welfare for People in Transit' at her own request in 1942. This meant she worked in the transit camp at Westerbork where Jewish people awaited transfer to the death camps. She said she 'wished to share her people's fate'. So 'death' for Etty Hillesum was all around her. It was also within her, as she had some acute personal infirmities. Her family also contained a degree of suffering as her brother Mischa was very unstable. Then the love of her life, the psychochirologist Julius Spier, died of leukaemia. In spite of all this, or perhaps because of it, she wrote:

> *Suffering is not beneath human dignity. I mean: it is possible to suffer with dignity and without. Most of us in the West don't understand the art of suffering and experience a thousand fears instead. We cease to be alive, being full of fear, bitterness, hatred and despair. I wonder if there is much of a difference between being consumed here by a thousand fears or in Poland by a thousand lice and by hunger? We have to accept death as part of life, even the most horrible of deaths.*[3]
>
> *My heart is a floodgate for a never-ending tide of misery.*[4]

Meanwhile the England of the fourteenth century, the century in which Julian was born, was completely different but still contained within itself a 'death' of almost holocaust proportions. Ostensibly it was a time of enormous religious energy and vitality. This was the time of the building of great Gothic churches and cathedrals. In Wells the Chapter House was built, the Quire was extended and the Vicars' Close built to establish the Vicars Choral as a college. Similar developments were happening all over Europe. This was also the time when the English language developed as a language of great sonority and elegance, when Chaucer wrote his *Canterbury Tales* and, of course, Julian became the first to write a great theological work in the English language.

But it was also the most terrible century, full of death of the most horrible kind. The Plague arrived in England in August 1348, reached London in November and Norwich in January 1349. One third of the population of Norwich died, along with half of the clergy. Politically the country was putting itself at risk as Edward III quarrelled with France and the Hundred Years War began. In 1381 came the Peasant's Revolt with the execution of the Archbishop of Canterbury by the mob in London and the last of the rebels executed in Norwich. All this played itself out against two enormous ecclesiastical struggles, firstly the Great Schism of 1377, with Henry Despenser, Bishop of Norwich, leading an army to fight on behalf of the Pope in Rome, a crusade which was defeated, with many from Norwich dying in the process, and second, the struggle against Lollardy. The first English Bible, translated by Wycliffe and others, had appeared in 1390 while a group of English Bishops, led by Henry Despenser, requested the death penalty against the Lollards, which was granted. The Lollards' pit, where they were burned, was not far from Julian's cell.

In and amongst all this death Julian herself desires death:

> *I desired three graces by the gift of God... the second was bodily sickness... And I wished it to be so severe that it might seem mortal... Whilst I myself should believe that I was dying. In this sickness I wanted to have every kind of pain, bodily and spiritual which I should have if I were dying.*
>
> *Then I said to those who were with me: Today is my Doomsday. And I said this because I expected to die..."*[5]

So both women are surrounded and interpenetrated by death. What can we say about this parallel phenomenon? Although separated by so many years and by so much else, these two women exhibit similar responses which focus on the place of the body. Both women, of course, lived through a 'holocaust'. In that holocaust, however different, both women deliberately 'embrace' death. And by death here we mean something more than mere physical death, although that is part of it. They embrace the phenomenon, the theological reality, of death. Moreover, both women identify entirely with the suffering of their people – Etty with the Jewish people, Julian with her 'even christen', and both women exhibit this 'death' in their bodies – Etty by her weakness, Julian by her near death.

Let us pause for a moment over this question of the centrality of the body. We have to recognise that for both Etty and Julian, the response to the holocaust was not simply an intellectual one. They responded to what was happening in the body of society with a bodily response. This was not just a question of what they said but a question of what happened to them as a whole, 'in the body'. They suffered 'in the body' what the body of society was suffering.

Moreover, both of them were acutely aware of the importance of their bodies. Etty is always deeply conscious of her body. She constantly records details about warmth and cold, pain, exhilaration, physical or sexual contact, other peoples' bodies and so on, all of which are deeply important. This is no less the case for Julian, although for her what happens to her body is intimately linked with Christ's body and vice versa. This parallel is interesting for two reasons. The first is that contemporary research into the texts written by mediaeval women reveals that the period between 1200 and 1500 saw the development of a new attitude towards the body in which physicality came to be seen 'less as a barrier than an opportunity'.

> *The goal of religious women was thus to realise the opportunity of physicality. They strove not to eradicate body but to merge their own humiliating and painful flesh with that flesh whose agony, espoused by choice was salvation. Luxuriating in Christ's physicality, they found there the lifting up and redemption of their own.*[6]

This can be seen in the writings of other women at this time besides Julian, especially, perhaps, Margery Kempe.

The other reason this phenomenon is interesting is because it chimes in with contemporary interest in the body and physicality. We do not have to look very far to see this obsession blazoned across our culture and I think one of the reasons why Etty is so fascinating for contemporary people, women in particular, is because of her way of thinking through her bodily senses. The question which remains unanswered for us is whether this is actually as unhealthy as many have suggested or whether it is really one of the ways in which we must 'think' today and one of the central elements in a wholesome spirituality. Can we really do without our bodies in the approach to God? Julian and her contemporaries deliberately espoused physicality as a way to share in Christ. Etty found, perhaps somewhat surprisingly, that by 'luxuriating in her body' she was brought closer to what she in the end called 'God'. In other words they come to the same place, but one deliberately, the other by introspection. The unanswered question is whether this is only possible at a time of physical suffering.

I now want to look in closer detail at the two different responses of these two women to the 'deaths' which they embraced. First let us look at Etty Hillesum. I have become aware that people do not always know a very great deal about Etty, so perhaps a few facts about her life will be in order.[7] She was born of educated Jewish parents in Middelburg, Holland, in 1914. Her secondary education took place in Deventer where there is now a Study Centre devoted to her life and the study of the Holocaust. She read Law and Slavic Languages at university (Amsterdam) in the late 1930s, which perhaps was not surprising as her mother was Russian. She moved in Jewish left-wing intellectual circles and lived as the housekeeper (and mistress) of a widower, Han Wegerif. In 1941 she met Julius Spier, a psychochirologist, who had been trained by Jung and became part of his circle. He was the love of her life and an enormously beneficial influence on her. Spier introduced her to the Bible and St Augustine and taught her to deal with her own depressive bent. She read Rilke, who was hugely important to her, and between 1941 and 1943 she kept a diary. This filled eleven exercise books. In 1942 she worked for the Jewish Council, but in July 1942 at her request she was transferred to work at the transit camp at Westerbork. She became quite ill but returned. In July 1943 Etty was permanently at Westerbork. She and her family were sent to Auschwitz where she died on 30 November 1943. A postcard was dropped from the train which read 'We left the camp singing'.

A word about the diaries themselves. They cover the years 1941–43 and have now been published in English, notably in the abbreviated form titled *An Interrupted Life*.[8] They are important documentary evidence of the Jewish response to the Holocaust in Holland, but have also become important spiritual reading, especially as they represent a very non-ecclesiastical spirituality. They are also important for those who are interested in how human beings respond to physical and emotional extremes and Etty's life and her response bears comparison with a number of others at this time including Edith Stein and other Christian martyrs of the Holocaust. Etty says that she wishes to chronicle these dark times. "I want to become the chronicler of many things from this period of time."[9]

And she makes it clear that she is the chronicler of the most terrible things.

> *Just now I clambered up on a box in order to count the number of goods wagons, there were 35... The goods wagons were completely closed, here and there a plank had been removed and through the gaps, hands stuck out, waving, just like people drowning. The sky is full of birds and nearby, before our own eyes, mass murder was being perpetrated, it is all so inconceivable.*[10]

But she also recognises that she is engaged upon a particular spiritual exercise and that she wishes the words to be not just an account, a chronicle, but to come from a deeper place, a place which, through her sufferings, she had accessed directly. She says:

> *And suddenly I was sure again: this is how I want to write. Only words which grow organically within a great silence. Just like that one Japanese picture with the flowering twig downstairs in the corner. A few tender strokes of the pencil.... so I would like to pencil in a few words against a wordless background. And it will be more difficult to depict and find the soul of that stillness and silence, than to find the words.*[11]

It actually took Etty a little while to reach that place of stillness and silence and the diaries are a record of her personal development from a very active and sensual woman whose activity disguises an inner turmoil, to somebody who thought of themselves as the thinking and praying heart of a camp devoted to the transportation of thousands of people to their deaths. The diaries begin with an account of her inner turmoil. She says:

> *I am accomplished in bed, just about seasoned enough I should think to be counted among the better lovers, and love does indeed suit me to perfection, and yet it remains a mere trifle, set apart from what is truly essential, and deep inside me something is still locked away… deep down something like a tightly-wound ball of twine binds me relentlessly…*[12]

But it is also clear that she desperately wants to put some sort of order into her life and she knows that she has to do this herself and that this is something which must come from within. She writes:

> *Perhaps it is my task in life, my sole task, to put some order and harmony into that chaos which is myself. I must, no doubt, stop trying to find the answer outside.*[13]

And gradually, as you can see if you read through the diaries slowly, she comes to rest in an inner peace and finds herself praying.

> *Last night, shortly before going to bed, I suddenly went down on my knees in the middle of this large room, between the steel chairs and the matting. Almost automatically. Forced to the ground by something stronger than myself. Some time ago I said to myself, 'I am a kneeler in training.' I was still embarrassed by this act, as intimate as gestures of love that cannot be put into words either, except by a poet…*[14]

She discovers God within her, at the deepest point.

> *God I thank You for having given me so much strength: the inner centre regulating my life is becoming stronger and more pivotal all*

> the time... I think I work well with You God, that we work well together. I have assigned an ever larger dwelling space to You, and am beginning to become faithful to You. I hardly ever have to deny You anymore. Nor, at frivolous and shallow moments, do I have to deny my own inner life any longer out of a sense of shame. The powerful centre spreads its rays to the uttermost boundaries.[15]

And she comes to believe that all of life is beautiful, a phrase which she repeats constantly in her diaries.

> Yes, life is beautiful and I value it anew at the end of every day. And you must be able to bear your sorrow ... you mustn't run away from it, but bear it like an adult. Do not relieve your feelings through hatred. Do not seek to be avenged on all German mothers, for they too sorrow at this very moment for their slain and murdered sons.[16]

And the diaries end:

> I shall simply lie down and try to be a prayer.
> I have broken my body like bread and shared it out among men. And why not, they were hungry and had gone without for so long. We should be willing to act as a balm for all wounds.[17]

There is a great deal more that could be said about Etty's journey of self-discovery in the face of death. Questions have certainly been raised. Some have believed that her writing is hardly genuine, but concocted, something of a literary artifice. Others cannot accept that what she says is real.[18] How can anybody welcome, they say, the enormity of such evil, how can a human being welcome every evil and every suffering as though they were fated to be, as though they were all part of cosmic harmony? Should there not be a greater element of rebellion against such suffering? Of what use is such a mystical approach? Learning from Rilke Etty even comes to the point where she says that God cannot help us but that we must help him. She says:

> You cannot help us, we must help You....

> *There doesn't seem to be much that You Yourself can do about our circumstances... neither do I hold You responsible.*
> *We must safeguard that little piece of You, God, in ourselves. And perhaps in others as well.*[19]

Etty, of course, was no theologian. She was ignorant of the work of resistance theologians such as Bonhoeffer and Barth who were both active while she was writing, and whose collaboration in the Barmen Declaration led to the establishment of a network of churches and pastors known as the Confessing Church, which was in direct opposition to Hitler. Indeed her 'theology', if that is what it was, took a quite different tack. Since the war, of course, the debate between action-based theologies (such as those of Bonhoeffer and Barth) and approaches based upon an idea of presence and the redemptive capacity of presence has sharpened, particularly as Christians become more aware of the need to work for a more just and peaceful world. What Etty does is to assert that we can affirm the presence of God in the midst of great suffering and that we can allow that presence in us to become redemptive. Being there, being 'the praying heart of the barracks', was, to her, not useless. This is, of course, all very redolent of Julian, especially Julian's belief that all is in the hands of God and that all shall be well. But that is to jump to conclusions. Before we make too much of the comparison let us turn now to Julian and look a little more closely at her response to the 'death' which she faced in her day.

As we know, Julian asked for death. She asked for 'the mynd of the passion', for 'bodily sickness' and for 'three wounds'. These wounds were:

> *The wound of true contrition, the wound of loving compassion, and the wound of longing with my will for God...*[20]

Her request for the mind of the passion is, of course, indicative of a shift of interest across Europe in the thirteenth and fourteenth centuries from an understanding of Christ as hero or vindicator (a Christology associated with Anselm), to understanding Christ as the suffering one. What we moderns need to understand is that this request was not a desire for some sort of mystical ecstasy, but rather represented a desire by Julian to enter into the passion of Christ and its costly transformation of her life. Her desire for 'wounds' was a favourite way of talking of a number of the Beguine writers, especially Mechthild of Magdeburg, who says,

> *Whosoever shall be sore wounded by love*
> *Will never become whole*
> *Save he embrace the self-same love*
> *Which wounded him*[21]

In the Long Text Julian develops the imagery of woundedness and relates it to the wounded Christ. Woundedness becomes the means of finding wholeness.

> *When we come up and receive that sweet reward which grace has made for us, there we shall bless and thank our Lord, endlessly rejoicing that we ever suffered woe; and that will be because of a property of the blessed love which we shall know in God, which we might never have known without woe preceding it...*[22]

An embrace of 'woundedness' appears strange to modern ears, just as Etty's movement to embrace the suffering of her days caused Todorov to question her authenticity, but Grace Jantzen points out that:

> *In spite of their strangeness to modern conceptions, solid commonsense pervades these prayers. Julian was not praying for visions for their own sakes, or for strange spiritual or physical occurrences to gratify a religious mania. She was praying rather for greater integration, compassion and generosity; and it seemed to her that these means would enable her to develop them.*[23]

In all sorts of ways the same could be said of Etty Hillesum. Both women recognise that bodily suffering, or 'woundedness' is somehow 'of use'. It is not neutral nor a purely negative experience, which is, sadly, the modern understanding. It is 'of use', particularly when placed within some sort of theological or transcendental reference.

Julian knew this instinctively, Etty slowly came to realise it through her experience.

But Julian does not stop there. She not only asks for death, but also has a vision of the crucified and dying Christ, which is vouchsafed to her. So she records the vision complete with "the red blood running down from under the crown, hot and flowing freely and copiously". But once again this is not simply a gruesome vision; it leads to a further understanding, this time of the Trinity.

> *And in the same revelation, suddenly the Trinity filled my heart full of the greatest joy, and I understood that it will be so in heaven without end to all who will come there.*[24]

This is interesting because for us, perhaps because of the Protestant legacy still within us, in spite of everything, the crucifix is indelibly associated with the atonement, the saving power of Christ's death, but for Julian the vision of the crucifix is the gateway to God, to the immensity of the Trinity. Moreover, the Trinity is described in totally integrating language, inclusive and binding together. "The Trinity is our maker, protector, everlasting lover…" And while the term 'Mother' comes later in the Long Text we can begin to see foundation for that here. 'Mother' develops out of her theology of the Trinity; it is a metaphor for the all-inclusive and enfolding love of God. So the embrace of the crucifix, the embrace of death, is also an embrace which allows us to be bound into God.

Julian's vision of God is, moreover, not simply an integrating one, a God who 'encloses' us, but also a totally sustaining one. God it is, we discover as we read on, especially in the Third Revelation, who never lets anything fall from his hand. This means, and Julian states it clearly, that there can be no such thing as chance, for God does everything.

> *So I understood in this revelation of love, for know well that in our Lord's sight there is not chance; and therefore I was compelled to admit that everything which is done is well done, for our Lord does everything.*[25]

And she continues:

> *See, I am God. See, I am in all things. See, I do all things. See, I never remove my hands from my works, nor ever shall without end. See I guide all things to the end that I ordain them for, before time began, with the same power and wisdom and love with which I made them; how should anything be amiss?*[26]

This again is moving stuff, especially as she was writing in the midst of the most terrible suffering and in the midst of so much conflict. How could she say this? For Julian God is not just the creator, not just the sustainer, but the author of all things in the present. Though it might appear that men or the evil one is in control, in and through appearances God is doing everything and doing it well. 'How should anything be amiss?'

For as we saw with Etty this is a remarkable assertion. But towards the end of her 'Showings' Julian makes another remarkable and related assertion, namely that at the deepest part of the soul Christ the Lord dwells continuously. She says:

> *I saw the soul as wide as it were an endless citadel, and also as it were a blessed kingdom... In the midst of that city sits our Lord Jesus, true God and true man... He sits erect there in the soul, in peace and in rest, and he rules and guards heaven and earth and everything that is.*[27]

This is the source of her statement that nothing can be amiss, because Christ the Lord sits erect in the soul and rules everything that is.

Julian made the same discoveries that Etty made. Like Etty she discovered God at the bottom of her being, which is the place where God says, "I am the ground of your beseeching". Like Etty Julian has an enormously powerful understanding of the participation of the soul in God in which all the ills of the world are redeemed by love. And Julian's vision of the all-embracing Trinity relates well to Etty's statements about 'being in your arms, O God'.

I believe it is remarkable that either Etty or Julian can even begin to think in these ways when faced with the sort of 'deaths' which they did. They both came through to seeing things in the most positive and hopeful ways, partly because the suffering they faced and embraced drove them deep into themselves. They were forced to the depths of their beings and there made remarkable discoveries – that God had not abandoned them or his world, that 'Life was beautiful' and that 'all would be well'. Perhaps this sort of discovery can only be made when we suffer and bear that suffering well?

I think it is interesting that the deeply affirmative vision of things that Julian propounds, which in many ways was not so unusual in the Middle Ages, was cruelly and dishonestly removed from the hearts of Christian people at the Reformation and replaced by a much more cynical and negative view of human nature which still inhabits us. The importance of Etty is that it is vouchsafed to her, a secularised Jewish woman, to rekindle something of that vision for us in the twenty-first century. One of the few positive things abut the Holocaust is that it forced people to think differently about how they saw God. Etty and a number of other writers, like Paul Celan,[28] are among those pioneers who ask how we shall now talk about God. Etty asks us to use a different theological language, a language which is not transfixed by post-Reformation ways of talking, but one in which God is simply 'you' and where we live best by a movement of the soul towards 'you' and towards each other. For her the self is not an isolated 'I' but simply a movement or set of movements towards another, and she suggests that to accept and live by this new way of being 'self', where the 'self' is best defined as 'movement towards the other' or 'welcome to the other', and to do theology by this new way of 'speaking', where theological language is more a 'word out of silence', than a set of fixed theological constructs, this is to live theologically, that is 'before God'. I believe that in rediscovering this way of living before God Etty had found something which Julian knew and practised instinctively, but where even Julian, the Christian solitary, had to delve deep into herself and find herself in serious conflict with the church of her day in order to speak in this way. In this way both Etty and Julian are subversives, subversive of official Christian ways of talking and being and we need them now when we risk falling into the trap of thinking that there must always be some sense in official ways of talking about God.

I want to end this essay with two quotations. They are both about the importance of suffering well, which is really the brunt of both Julian and Etty's messages to us. The first is from the theologian F.C. Bauerschmidt:

> *Christians can have hope in disaster. Julian's words 'all shall be well' are not a counsel of inaction. Rather, the belief that every event is enfolded in the being and action of God can liberate Christians from the tedious need to safeguard their lives, thus opening them to the risk of imitating Christ's compassion.*[29]

The other is from a secular source, from Alain de Botton's reflections on Proust, called *How Proust Can Change Your Life*. He says:

> *In Proust's view, we don't really learn anything properly until there is a problem, until we are in pain, until something fails to go as we had hoped... He tells us that there are two methods by which a person can acquire wisdom, painlessly via a teacher or painfully via life, and he proposes that the painful variety is the far superior... 'Infirmity alone makes us take notice and learn, and enables us to analyse processes which we would otherwise know nothing about...*[30]

. . . .

This essay was originally given as a lecture to The Friends of Julian of Norwich at their Festival in May 2008 and this much revised version is reproduced with the kind consent of the Trustees.

Notes

1. John Chrysostom, *Sermons*, quoted by Poliakov, Leon (1974), *The History of Anti-Semitism*, New York, Vol. 1, p25.
2. Luther, Martin *On the Jews and their Lies*.
3. Etty, Hillesum (2002), *The Letters and Diaries of Etty Hillesum 1941–43*, Eerdmans [from which all diary quotations are taken], p459. In these notes I have given the date of the entry rather than the page numbers of this edition as this will facilitate finding the quotation in the different editions of the diary which are available.
4. Ibid.

5   Julian of Norwich, *Showings*, Long Text Chapter 2 [Quotations from Julian are all from the edition of *The Showings* published in the series Classics of Western Spirituality by The Paulist Press, transl. by Colledge and Walsh (1978) and references are to chapters of The Long Text].
6   Caroline Bynum Walker, cited in Beckwith, Sarah (1996), *Christ's Body: Identity, Culture and Society in Late Mediaeval Writings*, Routledge, p115.
7   An excellent introduction to Etty and her life and writings is Woodhouse, Patrick (2009), *Etty Hillesum: A Life Transformed*, Continuum.
8   Hillesum, E. (1999) *An Interrupted Life*, London: Persephone Books.
9   *Diary* 13 August 1941.
10 Ibid. 8 June 1943.
11 Ibid. 13 August 1942.
12 Ibid. 9 March 1941.
13 Ibid. 12 October 1941.
14 Ibid. 13 December 1941.
15 Ibid. 9 January, 1942.
16 Ibid. 28 March 1942.
17 Ibid. 13 October 1942.
18 See esp. Todorov, Tzvetan (1999), *Facing The Extreme: Moral Life In The Concentration Camps*, London: Weidenfeld and Nicholson.
19 *Diary*, 12 July 1942.
20 *Showings*, Long Text, Chapter 2.
21 Mechthild of Magdeburg, *The Flowing Light of the Godhead*, 2.14.
22 *Showings*, Chapter 48.
23 Jantzen, Grace (2000), *Julian of Norwich: Mystic and Theologian* (2nd Edition), London: SPCK, p61.
24 *Showings*, Chapter 4.
25 *Showings*, Chapter 11.
26 *Showings*, chapter 11.
27 *Showings*, Chapter 68.
28 See Matthews, Melvyn (2006), *Awake to God: Explorations in the Mystical Way*, London, SPCK, chapter 5.
29 Bauerschmidt, F.C. (1999), *Julian of Norwich and the Mystical Body Politic of Christ*, University of Notre Dame Press, p199.
30 de Botton, Alain, (1997), *How Proust Can Change Your Life*, Picador, p72.

Schools of Formation: What kind of theological education is needed for a learning and missionary Church?

Graham Dodds

Introduction

In 2003 the Church of England's General Synod accepted the report, *Formation for Ministry within a Learning Church* (FMLC), which sought to address the issues of, and make provision for, the future leadership training necessary for a missionary Church. In 2004 the same Synod also accepted the report entitled *Mission Shaped Church* (MSC) which outlined experiments and thinking beyond the Decade of Evangelism and into the new millennium. In response to these reports, the Anglican diocese of Bath & Wells decided to reorganise its ministerial educational resources to form a *School of Formation*.

As an adult educator and priest working in the Anglican Diocese of Bath & Wells, I have been intimately involved in the implementation of the proposals of these reports. As a Bishop's advisor in the diocese, responsible for the provision of education and training for ministry, I advise the Bishop on the creation of policies, the implementation of educational planning, and the likely outcomes of such actions for the churches of the diocese. Being regularly in contact with both the senior staff of the diocese and the parochial ministry of nearly 500 parishes, I am able to observe a broad range of concerns and hopes. I therefore discuss this field of enquiry from a confessional practitioner perspective. What this chapter seeks to achieve is to critique the principles behind the creation and establishment of the *School of Formation* and to highlight how this might signify something of the direction of theological education for the future of the Church.

What is the School of Formation?

While *School of Formation* is not a generic term for education in dioceses, areas or districts, many church organisations are beginning to respond to a decrease in available leaders. The movement towards a reinvigorated laity, which has been one of the marks of pre- and post-Vatican II ecclesiologies, is causing church planners and authorities to consider structural changes. These are beginning to emerge through synods, covenants and more informal agreements. The Anglican Diocese of Bath & Wells has put a name to the educational enterprise that supports these changes – *School of Formation*. In so doing, it has recognised something of the responsibilities and accountabilities that are necessary for sustained growth.

The *School* is in one sense virtual as it embraces all the educational activity in the diocese. Every church and Christian agency that is involved in any kind of education is able to be part of it. Ranging from lent and house group study courses to induction training for church officers, to whole church development, the *School* offers advice, direction, materials and support as part of its work. It provides coherence for vocation work, mission work, training and education within ministry, strategic thinking, local teams of clergy and laity working together as well as advice to senior staff and pastoral planners. It is also involved in conversations with many practitioners of education such as Foundation Governors, Headteachers and the like through the work of the Diocesan Board of Education.

In another sense the *School* is visible, in that the employees comprise nine full-time equivalent staff occupying a departmental building at the Diocesan headquarters. They publish programmes for a variety of leadership training, learning programmes for lay people, consultancy to church governing bodies and congregations. The staff is directed by the senior staff of the Diocese as well as being responsive to individual incumbents and congregations through an intensive listening facility (focus groups, questionnaires, longitudinal studies, qualitative research projects etc). The essence of the enterprise is twofold; to work collaboratively in order to form a coherent learning strategy across the diocese and region; and to be proactively responsive, that is, active in conscientising leaders and members of parishes, benefices, local ministry groups and the like to understand the nature of the changes taking place. Clearly the word 'School' is familiar, but the question is often asked 'Why formation?' The formation part of the title is used because the Church is never fully formed and the *School* is endeavouring to shape or sculpt the ecclesiology of the Diocese. It is also used in a biblical sense of being 'formed' as part of the journey within the image of God and the likeness of Christ. Therefore, the *School* seeks relationships with individuals, groups, and official bodies, senior policy makers, those outside of the Church and leaders within. Its vision is the vision of the Diocese. In the event of this changing, it remoulds itself to support it. At present the vision is:

> *To inspire and encourage confidence in Christian communities throughout the diocese and region, to assist them to express a joyful hope in the Christian gospel for the sake of the world in which they serve.*

It may be asked, 'What is the difference between the *School of Formation* and previous or other departments of training and ministry development?' Because of the nature of the change taking place, there are several differences. Rather than managing learning in the Diocese, the *School of Formation* is endeavouring to model it. If ecclesiology involves being a learning Church, then the *School* needs to show how to be a learning community. For this, the framework offered by Nicola Slee when considering a theology of education is adopted. She delimits this by means of three dialectics: individual vs communal; cognitive vs affective; and developmental vs conversion perspectives.[1] Recognising the hermeneutical commitment of each of the members of the learning community, learning is encouraged in all its work. For example, nearly all the staff is involved in some kind of formal as well as informal learning; learning is taken seriously in personal development, team appraisals, overall strategy and evaluation of projects.

Clearly, there is much in the detail, but one particular element that has become distinctive is the format of the regular staff meeting. The meeting begins with a reflection led by a different member of staff each week. These range in style from theological reflection on current issues to practical tasks to Bible study. The second part of the meeting is given over to a visitor – someone that the *School* is engaged with directly or who wants to speak about their work and make it known to the staff of the *School*. The final part is business with a paperless shared agenda set up with wireless facilities to each staff member's laptop. Paper is used minimally and the agendas are hyper-linked. The business tends to be project-based with beginning and completion dates linked to an operational plan. It sets budgets and produces statistics of its work, but it is not like the usual committee with standing members and operates more like a working party or troubleshooting unit.

At the time of its inception, the concept of a *School of Formation* was a departure into the unknown for the Diocese, to cope with immense changes in the leadership of the church (a dramatic decrease in the number of clergy over twenty-five years), as well as a response to the thinking behind the FMLC report. Although there had been a robust and vibrant Department of Training, which later evolved into the Department of Ministry Development, it was felt that the changes that were influencing the Church needed a new configuration using the experience of the past and meeting the needs of the future in a changing Church. Under the banner of *Changing Lives, Changing Churches for Changing Communities*, the new project was inaugurated.

This reflection on the work of the School will first highlight how it is attempting to respond to change, noting the nature of the change. Second, it will examine how it is endeavouring to recover something of the true nature of theological education, which to some extent has been lost. Third, it will highlight the notion of a *School of Formation* in the context of the Anglican Church's recent reports on theological education. Finally, it will reveal the sources of educational theology and ecclesiology which have influenced its creation and establishment.

A Changing Church

After the FMLC and MSC reports were received at General Synod a period of organisational turbulence occurred. This is not entirely surprising. Gilbert Rendle suggests two ways that change can be described, linear and chaos.[2] Linear change occurs when something is wrong, needs attention and a replacement or rebuild can solve the problem. Looking at the 'as is' of a situation and the anticipated vision of the future can suggest aims and an action plan. Rendle describes this as a linear type process of growth through change. Five-year plans or fixing a faulty component on a photocopier are examples of linear changes. However, there is another agenda of change which these types of activities cannot effect. Rendle calls this chaos change and it occurs when life-changes take place, such as marriage or bereavement, or a paradigm shift begins to arise. This type of change requires a different response, one which might be epitomised in the phrase 'looking at the world through different eyes'. What is needed is a change of perspective and attitude – getting used to living in a different way. Linear changes may form part of the new way, but they cannot replace what is requisite to chaos change. It is necessary to see things differently. *Mission Shaped Church* began to hint at this when it suggested *fresh expressions* of church, but the hearts and minds of people in Church will likely take more than a report's findings to persuade them of the need for change. The ecclesiology in practice in churches, parishes, circuits, districts and dioceses is not one which can be changed quickly. Chaos is an apt term for the confusion that resulted from the publication and attempts to implement the reports, but it can also be regarded as an accurate technical term, signifying a higher agenda, which requires a certain style of process to resolve.

Rendle uses the metaphor of wilderness to define chaos change, signifying the biblical journey from Egypt to the Promised Land. It is quite possible that the nature of the change, which is still occurring in the Church, is perceived as linear while in fact it is chaotic. Looking at the problem through a linear lens means attempting to fix the ministerial training provision; adding in lay training to resource the clerical recruitment pool; ordaining many new priests sometimes without adequate training; reversing the decline in leadership and membership numbers through emphasis on mission; measuring the educational provision with academic measurements (degrees, etc). All the signs appear to point toward an approach based on an assumption of linear change. However, considering the turbulence which ensued after the reports were published, 'chaos change' appears to describe the situation better. At the heart of the turbulence were confusions concerning varying ecclesiologies. For example, the Anglican lack of clear and articulated ecclesiology, highlighted by Stephen Sykes[3] from the late 1980s, coupled with a desire to be in covenant with the Methodist Church, resulted in misunderstandings and a lack of clarity. However, what was even more significant was the way in which theological education had been driven in its progress during and since the Enlightenment. This has been narrated in various places with perhaps the seminal work by Farley at the forefront.

Theological education and the lack of habitus

Edward Farley's book, *Theologia*,[4] helpfully outlines the progress of theological education from the early Christian Church through to the present day. However, the subtitle, *The Fragmentation and Unity of Theological Education*, alerts the reader very quickly that the struggle to find integrity and consistency in the approach towards providing theological education is not easy. This will hardly surprise educational theologians, teaching practitioners in theological departments in colleges or universities, and Church teachers in dioceses and districts. They know from practical experience that theology is a subject which involves many sub-disciplines. For example, philosophy, biblical studies, history, ethics and literary criticism are but a few. Likewise, education is constituent of many disciplines, such as psychology, management, learning theory and politics. To put the two together to form a theology of education or educational theology is something of a minefield. Farley does not attempt this here, but he does problematise the issues and highlights something of what might be missing. His thesis maintains that present attempts at the project have lost something of the 'habitus' of the early Church. In his view, theology is, in part, something expressive of the actual and individual cognition of God, and things relating to God. It attends to faith and has a final goal of eternal happiness.[5] He describes this as the habit of faith which he terms the *habitus*. This may not be exactly how others might describe *habitus*, yet what he is describing is in the same general category of engaging in education because of a yearning towards, an intuitive desire – what LeClerq explores in his masterful book *The Love of Learning and the Desire for God*.[6] This loss of *habitus* becomes a lament about the almost uncontrollable bent towards controlling education. Education born out of utilitarian demand and gross national products may be a part of what is necessary for communities to survive, but without a deeper motivation and meaningfulness it loses something of the *esse* of life. In a sense, Farley resonates with Paulo Freire's concept of 'banking education' outlined in *Pedagogy of the Oppressed*.[7] The educational agent attempts to fill the potential learner with knowledge, something to which Freire was totally opposed. What Freire fought for so vehemently was a political revolution for the soul and mind of the learner. His methods of living with a community, becoming aware of significant language used, reflecting it back to the community, gave rise to his famous conscientisation technique. It was, and still is a powerful tool in the armoury of those who seek to learn. To become aware of deeper meanings, histories and trajectories of experience and practice is key to achieving ambitions and goals. Like Freire, Farley's concern is for the individual learner to become reflexive and use self-awareness to grow.

However, when the subject matter of education is theology, and the aim to provide theological education, particularly for a learning and missionary Church, the integration of the disciplines becomes more complex and controversial. For example it can become dualistic as is often seen in modern national curricula – learning about God, learning from God. Even though there is debate, at least among some educationalists, about whether there is in fact any conceptual distinction between learning about and learning from, this phenomenologistic approach is insufficient when it comes to a faith community. In learning about and from God, the learner is introduced to and explores the phenomena of religion. This can be a fascinating experience, as was seen in the popularity of the BBC series *Around the World in 80 Faiths*. The presenter, an Anglican priest, provided a sympathetic and enthusiastic look at many of the world's famous, and not so well known, religions. Talking with people of faith, the presenter enabled the viewer to hear and see religion. This pre-reflective experience can be valuable to form something of an understanding of different religions. However, this would seem insufficient for a leader of a church. No doubt a congregation would feel betrayed if the leader were only introducing them to various religious stances. He or she might be a very good teacher of religion or educator in Christianity, but communities of faith have come to expect leaders of faith. The theological component of theological education, when applied to a local church context, requires more than knowing about or abilities to learn from. It requires the actual and individual cognition of God, and things relating to God. It requires attention to faith and its goals – the *habitus* that Farley laments as somewhat lost in contemporary theological education.

Arguments for a faith stance in Church leaders provoke the question, 'What is the test?' One of the foremost educational theologians of the contemporary world, John Hull, puts it very succinctly and systematically in a short essay. He provides a brief taxonomy of those who he believes can do theology, and those who can theologise.[8] The distinction will become clearer presently. His argument begins by dividing humanity into three basic groups. His first division is between those who are influenced by Christianity and those who are not. Clearly all in the western world are to some extent influenced by the rise of Christianity. From secular laws to seasonal celebrations, to the vast number of ecclesiastical buildings in rural and urban communities, the influence of Christendom is ubiquitous. Secondly, of those who are influenced, there are those who are aware of this and those who are not. Thirdly, of those who are aware of this there are those who confirm these influences, identifying with the religion, and seek to be further moulded by their participation, and those who do not. The group who confirm these influences, which he terms the *community of faith*, take an active decision to consciously pursue faith. As well as delimiting the field of who can do theology, he also argues for a distinction between theologising and studying theology. He states: 'Theologising (which must be distinguished from the study of theology) [...] takes place within the community of faith, and its subject matter is the experience of the faithful, or of those who, knowing they are unfaithful, see even in this self-recognition a summons to faith'.[9] He concludes his argument with this statement: 'In other words, doing theology is characterised by participation in the intentionality of theologising, but studying theology is examination of the phenomenology of that intentionality and is thus characterised by empathy rather than by sympathy'.[10]

It could be argued that in some sense, all of the sub-groups of Hull's taxonomy are part of a Christian culture, to different degrees,[11] and this is where he illustrates or at least provokes the nub of the problem. What is the place of faith in theological education? Conversely, a question arises as to what place theological education has in the faith of the Church.

This is of particular interest to another educational theologian, Jeff Astley, who termed the phrase *Ordinary Theology*. He defines this as:

> *Ordinary theology is my term for the theological beliefs and processes of believing that find expression in the God-talk of those believers who have received no scholarly theological education. Ordinary theology is routinely ignored by academic Christian theology. As John Hull put it at a symposium hosted by the North of England Institute of Christian Education in July 1996, 'If theology is what goes on in people's lives, we know amazingly little about Christian theology'.*[12]

In a thorough treatment of his thesis, Astley makes the case for the study of *Ordinary Theology*, defending it from a variety of potential criticisms.[13] He argues for a *liminal* Church, one where Christians who exist on the threshold of the Church, enable, encourage and sometimes demand its doors to be opened. Ordinary theologians exist in open Churches and often appear as anonymous Christians (Rahner) or in Churches with open doors and great windows (Barth) or even the Church outside of the Church (Solle). He concludes:

> Clearly these discussions raise profound questions for ecclesiology and the theology of Christian identity. In particular, they bring us back to the question of the locus of authority or the beliefs of the Church. Most Churches distinguish different roles and offices within the Church, and locate authority differently ('appropriately') for different roles. But most will now allow the lay baptized some say in the debate about and definition of doctrine, if only by recognizing the importance of the exercise of reason in the pursuit of truth [...] and of the 'primacy' or 'authority' of the conscience of the ordinary believer. A proper recognition of proper authority and hard-won freedom of belief are constituents of the practices that shape all Christian believers.[14]

It is this shift in the place of the lay baptised which is causing most Churches of the west to examine how they approach theological education, both for their leaders and members. To illustrate this, what follows is a brief analysis of an initiative set up by the Anglican and Methodist Church in England in the first decade of the new millennium.

Anglican General Synod reports at the beginning of the new millenium

Formation for Ministry within a Learning Church (FMLC) was accepted by the General Synod of the Church of England in 2003. It offered the opportunity to the Church of England to change training patterns for ministerial education in the forthcoming years, and sought to alter radically the training of ordained ministers and lay disciples. Clearly this was not simply an educational exercise, but one which begged the question: 'What kind of Church is appropriate for the future?' Although it arose from a problem in the cost and location of theological provision for the Anglican Church, inevitably the report was destined to suggest at least an implicit ecclesiology by its suggested proposals for leadership and membership training in the Church. This was not explicit in the interim report, made more explicit in the final one, but rather unsubtle and naïve in its handling of ecumenical matters.

For example, in Chapter 2, an outline of issues that had driven the working party's work demonstrated how wide and far ranging the issues it addressed were. They included:

- A theological approach to Church and ministry
- Formation for ministry
- Expectations of initial and continuing ministerial education
- The relationship of initial training for ordination to adult learning in the Church
- The size of training establishments
- The place of research
- Ecumenical considerations
- Partnerships with other providers of ministerial and theological education and UK higher education
- Issues arising from the framework for learning and the regulations for training
- A norm for the qualification for the clergy
- Financial issues[15]

Clearly there is an implicit reordering of the shape of the Anglican Church latent in these proposals. The contribution the report made to the ministerial training of the Church of England, however, is summarised towards the end of Chapter 2 under twelve headings.[16] Of the twelve points it makes, only number one, 'outlining theological principles that underlie the Church of England's ministry', and number six, 'creating a structure that has the potential to be developed with our ecumenical partners in other Churches'[17] could be said to be explicitly ecclesiological rather than educational.[18] Others, such as 'addressing the smallness of many of our training institutions', 'rethinking the initial ministerial education of the clergy', and 'establishing norms for the theological and ministerial qualification of the clergy',[19] can be seen to be more educational in nature. However, both the specifically ecclesiological, and many of the educational proposals would likely affect the structural organisation of the Church and therefore could be said to instigate ecclesiological changes. Without an adequate statement of intentionality in terms of the ecclesiological impact of the proposals, the report was almost bound to cause more confusion than clarity.

The report also clearly wanted to comment on lay ministry. This is alluded to in various sections and summed up in the proposals for Education for Discipleship.[20]

> *We recommend that:*
> 1. *opportunities for learning, under the general title of Education for Discipleship, are offered on a Church-wide basis for a range of students, which might include lay people seeking to deepen their Christian discipleship, trainee Readers and other lay ministers and potential candidates for ordination.*
> 2. *prospective ordinands are encouraged to engage in such preliminary studies before they enter training.*[21]

Two points that may be noted here are the add-on impression of lay participation in the enterprise, and the strong suggestion that the definition of lay education is exclusively pre-selection training for ordination. The *Issues that have driven our work* section, (Chapter 2 of the report) failed to mention lay education as a discrete area of enquiry at all. In the interim report, the *Education for Discipleship* proposals were absent. They were only added later, which gave the impression that they were not part of the original thinking. This in turn suggested that the report was not in fact about education for discipleship at all, but rather, education for the Church's official ministry.

Education for discipleship should not be confused with education for an office in the Church for fear of creating everyone official. One of the dangers for any ecclesiology is a lack of a specific and distinct laity. The priesthood of the Church can only be justified if it seeks to serve the rest of the Church, the priesthood of all believers. As David Rankin states, 'The Church is not constituted by the existence of a clerical order.'[22] Congar, likewise, sees the Church's task as a partnership between priesthood and laity, at least in terms of mission.[23] As he said in *Lay People in the Church*, 'there is no particular mission differentiating the faithful and the ministerial priesthood.'[24] The report raised some disturbing questions about the place of lay people. The almost obsessive preoccupation it demonstrated with providing training for priests using lay training as staging posts towards ordination, without any central funding for lay education, and without adequate knowledge of what had been provided in dioceses and districts, seemed to demean the viability of lay people. And all this was happening in a time when the *Mission Shaped Church* report was being written to encourage Churches to experiment with new forms of mission. The result is that it is difficult to see anything more than an attempt to form proposals towards clergy training. This suggests that a theology of ordination was assumed. It lacks much of the rest of a satisfactory doctrine of Church. In fairness to its authors, they were not commissioned to write an entire ecclesiology, and should they have attempted the task it would have made their work highly complex. However, without it, the church may lose touch between an espoused theology and a theology in practice, thus also risking credibility and authenticity.

MSC attempted to offer an ecclesiology based on mission; even the title of the report suggests this. For example, there are sections that mention the Lambeth Quadrilateral, the royal assent and the notes of the church. However, these are not any more than a mention. There is no real attempt to allow them to inform the ecclesiology of the report. Again, in fairness to the authors, they were forming an argument to persuade the Church to engage in mission, which, since the Decade of Evangelism, had become a specific part of the Church's larger agenda. However, without the security of purpose and direction that an ecclesiology brings through its vocational nature, the overall effect was that its theological basis was weakened.

What the reports show is that two ecclesiologies were in fact in competition. *FMLC* advocated, in effect, an ecclesiology by beginning with the training needs of the clergy. This is an attempt to shape the church through a top-down model. Not only was this incongruous within the culture of the Church, it was also becoming increasingly impossible as the number of clergy declined. It suggested that the Church needed to amend its practice by advocating a clerical cascade-type educational process. Without paying close attention to what lay people have to say, as in Astley's sense of *Ordinary Theology*, this was almost doomed to fail. *MSC* appeared to adopt another kind of approach as it encouraged Church planting and *fresh expressions* of being Church. However, it did this without an adequate ecclesiological framework to enable people to become Church. In effect a bipolar ecclesiology was created. *FMLC*, by not stating its ecclesiology, ran the risk of creating a Church full of leaders without any laity. *MSC*, by not stating its ecclesiology very fully, ran the risk of creating new Christian communities that bear little resemblance to a Church in any satisfactorily ecclesiological way. Ecclesiologies vying for authenticity like this are likely to create unhelpful tension and confusion.

With these insights beginning to form, the educational enterprise of a *School of Formation* began to emerge and if it were to succeed in any measure then it needed to address the problem of conflicting ecclesiologies. To do this some parental theologians of ecclesiology were employed.

The theological parents of the School of Formation

John Henry Newman's great legacy to the Church included a profound view of the role and place of the laity. His concern that they breathe together (*conspiratio*) with the clergy was prophetic and pragmatic. In his view it is a well-educated laity that is able to witness to the glory of God by knowing what it believes and why. As he wrote:

> I want a laity, not arrogant, not rash in speech, not disputatious, but men who know their religion, who enter into it, who know just where they stand, who know what they hold, and what they do not, who know their creed so well, that they can give an account of it, who know so much of history that they can defend it.[25]

His view was to prove influential throughout the next century and on into this one. It would influence Vatican II in terms of its emphasis on lay people and beyond that, the ecclesiology developed in its wake.

This was, in part, due to the French theologian and champion of a theology of the laity and Newman's thesis, Yves Congar.

Congar's theology of laity

Congar's contribution to a theology of laity is immense. What he constructs, based on Newman's theology and in a Newman-like way, is a Church that understands laity as exercising priestly, kingly and prophetic ministry for the world. In his portrayal of mission the Church exists for the world (laity being secular in the sense of missionary), and the priesthood of the Church exists to support the laity in order to be missioners. This pragmatic emphasis is demonstrated in some of the documents of Vatican II, which contribute greatly to a theology of laity[26] (in some ways, as Carriquiry suggests, it brought it to maturity.)[27] In Vatican II, the laity has a recognised calling. The calling comes directly from union with Christ as head of the Church. As a result, charisms are given. Laity has a distinctive role in the apostolic ministry through circumstances of life, family, job and leisure. In a final section of *Lumen Gentium*,[28] the perfect example of this theology of 'laypersonhood' is exemplified by and through Mary,[29] who personifies a ministry of sacrifice (her heart was pierced) and wisdom (pondering in her heart).

It is relatively easy to detect the hand of Congar in the chapters of *The Apostolate of the Laity* decree,[30] and Vatican II embraces his theology, enhancing the role and ontology of the layperson. In the documents of Vatican II, lay people have a calling that is marked by a distinctly secular and spiritual quality.[31] They are to collaborate with clergy and bishops;[32] act as an organic body;[33] present the Word in liturgy, catechetical activities, the care of souls, and administration;[34] and infuse the Christian spirit in the local, national and international arenas.[35]

He writes, in *Lay People in the Church*, that lay people have for too long been subordinate in the Church, kneeling before the altar and sitting in the pew.[36] They need to become fully part of the Church, even defining the role of clergy:

> May we not be on the eve of a new spring, a vigil of Pentecost? The demands of a laity awakening to consciousness of its place and responsibilities in the Church already give us clergy some inkling of what the welcoming, the cultivation and ripening of such crops will call for from us.[37]

Congar was clearly prophetic in his assessment of the needs of clergy training. Seeing the laity as subjects, the clergy then take their supportive role of enabling mission. Vatican II spells this out further when it directs the whole Church, working together, to construct a temporal order directed to God through Christ.[38] Groups need to unite their efforts by pooling their resources,[39] with hierarchy promoting and supporting the projects,[40] and dioceses specifically set up through councils to assist lay activity.[41] Not withstanding the subsequent failure of Vatican II to live up to its expectations, and despite attempts to spell out the co-responsibility of laity, deacons, priests and bishops,[42] the theology of laity promulgated at the Council was astonishing. *Lumen Gentium* demonstrated a reshaping of ecclesiology in its location of the section concerning the *People of God* immediately after the opening *Mystery of the Church*, particularly before the chapter on hierarchical structure. This confirmed how far the Roman Church had travelled from Vatican I. It is also notable for its famous ending in the rehearsal of Mariology.

Congar's missiology embraces reconciliation of the world to God, demonstrated in his diagrammatic representation of the laity's part in the Church's priestly function.[43] However, Lakeland cites this as one of the main causes for the crisis of identity among the clergy in the post-conciliar period.[44] He suggests that although the theology and event of Vatican II were exciting, the voices were to some extent silenced by Congar's radical views on priesthood, which saw both lay and clerical priests operative in Church and world. Yet the voice of the laity needs to be heard, for as Congar believed, the Church exists 'in the meeting and harmonising of hierarchical communication from above, and a community's (sic) consent'.[45] This consent can only be given if the voice of the community, not just the individual, is heard. Democratisation, that sees the Church making its decisions through one person with one vote, cannot apply here. Laity is the *pleroma* of the hierarchical priesthood[46] and its missionary responsibility is kenotic – to go to the lowest place in order to begin to scale the heights.

Based on Newman and Congar's vision the *School* has become involved in the project of mobilising the laity. A mantra that has been used extensively, attributed to Hans Ruedi Weber, is that:

> *The laity are not helpers of the clergy so that the clergy can do their job, but the clergy are the helpers of the whole people of God so that the laity can be the Church.*

After the creation and establishment of the *School*, which largely began the work of mobilising the laity through providing local courses accessed through electronic media, learning opportunities in small groups or through partnerships and lay leadership training, the second phase has embarked upon bringing clergy and vocational work into the same arena.

Conclusions

The *School of Formation* has been developed largely through a collaborative-intuitive process. As such it can be defended as a two-way approach to ecclesiology. First it honours the 'gut feelings' of all involved and keeps close to the ground in terms of what is needed. However, intuition, when explored collaboratively, is strengthened by those with a desire to embrace universal principles – principles such as a desire that all work in the Church should lead towards the notions of ministering congregations, no one working alone, the core aspirations of the diocese which can be thumb-nailed as calling, reshaping, renewal and transformation. These, and other theological stances offered by parishes, deaneries and senior staff have determined its general undergirding. It is not a blueprint for all other organisations but it is an example of a response to the changing nature of the shape of the Church. It is consistent in its modelling of a learning community for individual leaders, parishes, local ministry teams and groups, diocesan structures and regional partnerships. Because of its responsive nature it is dependant on the 'conscientisation' process which is labour intensive and a slower process than linear change techniques. Some dioceses and districts have adopted a top-down, imposed, managerial approach, 'buying in' leadership courses or trainers. At one level this is a quick process, but it can result in quick fixes that only exasperate the learning that necessarily needs to be addressed in an unhurried way. Some would argue that the Church does not have time to think things through at present – it needs action. Yet when an organisation experiences chaos change, growth depends upon spending time facing up to new situations.

Theological education will be partially responsible for the shape of the church to come. If it notes the explicit and implicit nature of the changes the church is engaged in; if it takes seriously the role of the laity as well as the clergy and enables the breathing together that Newman advocated; if it seeks to join up its thinking about ministry and mission; if it bases its theology of education on some foundational principles; if it takes seriously the need to develop a clear ecclesiology or at least monitor it as it emerges, then the Church might expect that it will serve its mission and fulfil its true purpose.

Notes

1   Slee, N. (1993) in Jarvis, P. and Walters, N. (eds), *Adult Education and Theological Interpretations*, Malabar: Krieger Publishing, pp323–346.
2   Rendle, G.R. (1998), *Leading Change in the Congregation*, Washington, D.C.: The Alban Institute Publishing, pp77–103.
3   Sykes, S. (1992), 'The Genius of Anglicanism' in Rowell, G. (ed), *The English Religious Tradition and the Genius of Anglicanism*, Oxford: IKON.
4   Farley, E. (1994), *Theologia*, Eugene: Wipf and Stock Publishers.
5   Ibid. p31.
6   LeClerq, J. (1961), *The Love of Learning and the Desire for God: A Study of Monastic Culture*, New York: Fordham University Press.
7   Freire, P. (1972), *Pedagogy of the Oppressed* (tr. Myra Bergman Ramos), Harmondsworth: Penguin Books.
8   Hull, J.M. (1990), 'What is theology of education' in Francis, Leslie and Thatcher, Adrian (eds), *Christian Perspectives for Education*, Leominster: Gracewing, p4.
9   Francis and Thatcher (1990), p5. Brackets in original.
10 Ibid. p5.
11 This is reflected in a dichotomy that led two theologians to offer a major critique of mission in today's society in the West. Barrow and Smith's *Christian Mission in Western Society* is set

Schools of Formation

within a dichotomy revealed in its first and last chapters. Smith paints Europe's religious landscape in a bleak fashion. In his view, people seem to have dispensed with Christian tradition, which they feel is no longer true. By contrast Simon Barrow, at the end of the book, while agreeing that Christendom has had its age, sees the Church on the brink of waking up to new models of Church with, 'a new kind of deliberately anti-exclusionary community founded on a rejection of violence, a costly embracing of the outsider, a local embracing of the global and a Christ-like willingness to stake their lives with those crucified "outside the gate" of our brave neo-liberal world.' Barrow, S. and Smith, G. (eds) (2001), *Christian Mission in Western Society*, London: Churches Together in Britain, pp239–240.

12   Astley, J. (2002), *Ordinary Theology*, Aldershot: Ashgate Publishing, p1.
13   Ibid. pp123-145.
14   Ibid. p162. Emphasis in original.
15   *Formation for Ministry within a Learning Church*, G.S. 1496. (2003), London: Church House Publishing, pp15–24.
16   Ibid. p25.
17   Ibid. p25.
18   In contrast, an earlier report such as *A Strategy for the Church's Ministry* (Tiller report) provided a clearer ecclesiological statement – Tiller, J. (1983) *A Strategy for the Church's Ministry*, London: Church Information Office, pp59-132 – while the sister report to *FMLC*, *Mission Shaped Church*, concluded that no new experiment in Church should be attempted unless a clear ecclesiology is provided. It stated: 'The time has come to ensure that any fresh expressions of Church that emerge within the Church of England, or are granted a home within it are undergirded by an adequate ecclesiology (doctrine of the Church).' *Mission Shaped Church GS 1523* (2004), London: Church House Publishing, p84.
19   *Formation for Ministry within a Learning Church*, p25.
20   *Formation for Ministry within a Learning Church* 5.22-5.24, pp61-62. It is interesting to note that in a large document of nearly 200 pages, a major proposal to change formal lay education only commands three paragraphs, and less than two full pages.
21   *Formation for Ministry within a Learning Church*, p133.
22   Rankin, D. (1995), *Tertullian and the Church*, Cambridge: CUP, p130.
23   Congar, Y. (1967), *Priest and Layman*. (tr. P.J. Hepburne-Scott), London: Darton, Longman & Todd, p255.
24   Congar, Y. (1965), *Lay People in the Church*, London: Geoffrey Chapman, p25. NB this was included as an addition made by the author in 1964 and can be found in the revised edition.
25   Newman, J.H. (1851, 1872) Prepos. *Lectures on the Present Position of Catholics in England*, p390.
26   However, note that this was not without frustration and difficulty. For an account of the changes and trajectories of the various views of the laity in Vatican II see Klostermann, F. (1969), in Vorgrimler, Herbert (ed), *Commentary On the Documents of Vatican II* (tr. W. Glendepel and others), London: Burns and Oates, Vol. 3, pp273–404.
27   Carriquiry, G. (1998) in Apostola, N. (ed), *A Letter from Christ to the World*, Geneva: WCC Publications, pp107-113.
28   *Lumen Gentium* <http://www.vatican.va/archive/hist_councils/ii_vatican_council/documents/vat- ii_const_19641121_lumen-gentium_en.html>
29   Abbott, W.M. (ed) (1966), *The Documents of Vatican II*, London: Geoffrey Chapman, p4.
30   *The Apostolate of the Laity* <http://www.vatican.va/archive/hist_councils/ii_vatican_council/documents/vat-ii_decree_19651118_apostolicam-actuositatem_en.html>
31   Ibid. p29.

32 Ibid. p25.
33 Ibid. p20.
34 Ibid. p10.
35 Ibid. p13.
36 Congar (1965), p xxiii.
37 Ibid. p xxxi.
38 Abbott (1966), p7.
39 Ibid. p18.
40 Ibid. p24.
41 Ibid. p26.
42 See Cardinal Suenens's work, Suenens, L.J. (1968), *Co-responsibility in the Church* (tr. Francis Martin), London: Burns & Oates, pp92-135, 152-164 and 187-211.
43 Congar (1965), pp181-183.
44 Lakeland, P. (2002), *The Liberation of the Laity: In Search of an Accountable Church*, London: Continuum.
45 A point made by Lakeland (2002), p56 and from Congar (1965), p250 (NB p263 in the edition from which Lakeland worked [2004]).
46 Congar, (1965), p313.

Are the 'New Atheists' the 'New Fundamentalists'?

John A. Harrod

It is an honour to be part of this Festschrift. I first met John Newton when still at school – attending a 'travelling fellowship' in the Lincolnshire village of Nettleham. He spoke on 'redeeming the time.' Ever since I have honoured John as a scholar minister, a man of signal Christian grace, and a Methodist minister of the calibre that makes one feel privileged to belong to the same order.

. . . .

Recent years have seen vitriolic attacks on religion by the 'New Atheists'. Their passion certainly owes something to alarm at religious extremism and maybe also to a sense of being cheated that religion has failed to do the decent thing and, at the behest of the enlightened, simply die out. The description 'New Atheist' is not my own and it needs to be remembered that not all atheists associate with their stridency.[1] That said, Dawkins's *The God Delusion* is an astonishing publishing phenomenon. Of the same genre are books by Daniel Dennett, Sam Harris, Christopher Hitchens, Anthony Grayling, Michel Onfray and others.

The new atheists are not exactly chuffed to be called 'fundamentalist'. Dawkins[2] seeks explicitly to rebut the charge, and even in his bonsai *Against all Gods* Grayling spares a whole chapter for it. But they both define fundamentalism in a way that allows them to declare themselves acquitted. Thus important questions are circumvented. I have no interest in fashioning an uncomplimentary label to stick on people. The question posed in the title of this paper does not admit of a simple answer, yes or no. Indeed it is probably preferable to speak instead of atheist extremists. What I do wish to argue is that the fundamentalist mindset has certain features of which the new atheists are not entirely innocent. This is a much more modest thesis – but it is significant enough.

The word arose in the USA in the 1900s. Over and against perceived liberal betrayals there was the call to preserve the 'fundamentals' of faith. Words, however, have a history as well as an origin. In contemporary usage the word has no tight definition. Nonetheless, in a general way it describes a mindset which has certain characteristics. Here I concentrate on just two. There are of course others which are implicit, for example an intellectualism which downplays the significance of the social, economic, political and psychological – and not least reactions to marginalisation and injustice.

1. Over-simplification and over-confidence

First, the fundamentalist world view is straightforward and simple, confident and certain. It is about straight lines and neat edges. Ambiguity, puzzlement and mystery are banished. Fundamentalists do not do nuance.

These characteristics of religious fundamentalism are mimicked in the new atheists' simplistic confidence in their treatment of religion. The ambiguities are bleached out in a simple contest between the rational and the irrational, the enlightened and the superstitious, the good and the irredeemably bad. And this is made possible by mammoth misrepresentations of religion.

I begin with a more respectable instance of this over-simplification. Dawkins embraces scientific naturalism, or materialism. The real is confined to the material. It is not simply that science is methodologically empiricist – a claim I would not dispute. Rather the only route to knowledge is through the scientific method – the examination of empirical evidence, the formulation and testing of hypothesis, and so forth. We see Dawkins's scientific naturalism is his assumption that if there is a God then God must be established by an appeal to empirical evidence. Again and again he asks for evidence – failing to acknowledge that few theists would see theism as attested by a straightforward appeal to scientific data – which is not to say theistic belief is without reason, nor that such data is irrelevant. The assumption is that God is a finite being – part of the physical universe – a kind of powerful super agent. There is no other option available for a god.

But most theists would not play the game on that pitch. For a start God is not finite, but the one ultimate in rationality, being and value and upon whom all else depends. There is thus the radical alternative that language about God is not language about another empirical reality. Rather such language is complementary to, not an instance of, empirical analysis. There are, in fact, many everyday instances of the language of complementary description. A page of writing may be described in terms of the chemistry of paper and ink. It may also be described in terms of the argument of the text. A symphony may be described in terms of sound waves, but also in terms of musical appreciation. An action may be described in terms of the mechanics of muscles or in terms of the agent's intention. Reality is complex and multifaceted, admitting complementary descriptions sometimes of mind-blowing complexity. In a not dissimilar way claims about creation and the universe declaring the majesty of God speak of a complementary dimension, different from that which science investigates. Thus, as John Haught has argued, we can still sing Watt's 'I sing the Almighty power of God' despite the radical differences between the science of his day and our own.[3]

I do not deny that such claims are problematical, neither do I deny the difficulty in understanding how these complementary descriptions and modes of cognition fit together. Such is the stuff of debates within philosophical theology. But at least we here locate real questions rather than questions that are beside the point.

Scientific naturalism – as an all embracing metaphysic – is not without its problems. For a start, if we say the real is confined to the material, what exactly is this material? There are the age-old problems of the relationship between appearance and reality – given particular focus by contemporary physics, which suggests the 'real' world is mysteriously different from that of our structured experience. Moreover, it is not necessary to endorse a substance dualist philosophy of mind to acknowledge that even if an 'emergent' characteristic consciousness is so novel a phenomenon that it serves as a signal pointer to the fact that the 'material' remains profoundly elusive. The 'material' after all is not as straightforward as it seems; and it follows that a 'scientific method' is not as straightforward either.

And what confidence does materialism give us that we may trust our processes of rational thought? Rational thought is a strange sort of thing if it is merely reducible to the physical activity of a brain evolved to locate predators and food in the middle distance. What sort of thing is rational judgement if it reduces to brain processes? There is indeed an experiential validation of some of our thought processes – but by no means all. It is interesting that Darwin himself was puzzled by this[4] and interesting that Descartes found in theism a confidence that our honest and painstaking inquiries might be trusted to yield some insight into reality.[5] And a crucial related issue – on what basis does materialism assume reality is ultimately intelligible?

Space does not permit me to ask if materialism can give an adequate account of ethical and aesthetic experience or of concepts such as intention and action. I repeat. Materialism is a respectable philosophical position – but it is no less problematical than its major alternative, theism, and I would argue more so.

Embracing scientific naturalism does not make Dawkins a fundamentalist. There is however a tendency towards fundamentalism in his failure even to acknowledge the difficulties or to defend it against its critics. There is simply the breezy assumption as to its transparent adequacy and that it is the only respectable show in town. He assumes simplicity and certainty when in fact there is ambiguity and perplexity. To that extent he is on the verge of a fundamentalist mindset. For Dawkins 'science' is not only an enterprise for investigating the natural world. It is an overarching ideology, a form of intellectual Blitzkrieg. This is seen in his treatment of the debate about differing magisteria. And those who debate the relationship between scientific and theological discourse are guilty of 'Neville Chamberlain' appeasement.[6]

Other examples of over-simplification and over-confidence are more telling. Repeatedly religion is invariably attacked at its weakest points and with misrepresentation, caricature, cheap sarcasm and the assumption that the most extreme and the most naive represent the norm. The abusive portrait of the Old Testament's understandings of

God in Dawkins betrays a total ignorance of Old Testament scholarship. Likewise Dawkins's ignorance of gospel criticism and Pauline theology is abysmal.[7] Is this the man who (justifiably) gets shirty when people fail to do their homework over Darwin? Generally, the new atheists tend to copy religious fundamentalists in giving a 'plain sense' reading of both Bible and Qur'an, plundering selected passages to reinforce their ideology.

Then again, belief in God is like belief in a teapot orbiting the sun (Dawkins following Russell)[8], belief in the Flying Spaghetti Monster (Dawkins)[9] or parallel even to belief in fairies (Grayling).[10] But a fairy (I assume – who knows?) is a quasi-physical entity, even if its empirical credentials are somewhat smudged. No reflective theist has so thought of God. Incidentally, how many of Grayling's fellow professors of philosophy in the UK believe in fairies? But not a few believe in God. The genre of the notion of God is profoundly different from that of fairies. I do not suggest belief in God is in any way coercive. Atheist philosophers who have taken theism more seriously have given it a tough critique.[11] That I respect. But belief in God deserves a serious critique. Simplistic jibes about teapots, fairies and Flying Spaghetti Monsters invite the charge of fundamentalism.

And then we are told that religious education is 'child abuse', no messing. We are even told that the 'long-term psychological damage' of being brought up a Catholic may arguably be worse than physical abuse by paedophilic priests.[12] This is true, it appears, of *all* religious education – not just that which tries aggressively to proselytise or to silence questions, but also that which seeks to equip the next generation to engage critically and creatively with our religious heritage. The assumption of course is that all religion is a bad thing and that all religious education is about infecting the young with the religious virus. But to play the new atheists at their own game, maybe it is child abuse to fail to equip our children for such a mature and informed engagement, and still more to bias them against it as in *Camp Quest?*[13] Maybe Dawkins is guilty of child abuse in his letter to his daughter which foists upon her an epistemological sparseness in his failure to acknowledge that some beliefs may be *rational* even if not in a straightforward way *evidence-based* way, along with its superficially dismissive engagement with theology.[14]

Anthony Grayling spins western history as a 'struggle' between 'humanism' and 'religious conceptions of the world'. Humanism affirms the dignity and glories of human life in art, intellectual endeavour, science, love, friendship and so forth. And it is signally about liberty and the primacy of reason.

As a Christian I too hold these values – subject of course to seeing the small print, including the assurance that we will not neglect justice for those damaged by the harsh winds of a meritocracy based on individual autonomy. But Grayling sees humanistic values as rooted almost entirely in non-religious thought. By contrast religion is the chief and implacable enemy of humanism – and especially of individual autonomy and reason. Religion is about subordinating reason to superstition. 'Religions of the book' are about heteronymous control and the unthinking acceptance of what has been taught. This thesis is developed in *What is Good?* and in *Towards the Light* where the focus is on the development of liberty.

Grayling regards Christians who champion liberty as being only stalking horses for the theme to be taken up by weightier secular thinkers.[15] Moreover, whilst the church's record has indeed often been shabby, Grayling presents it in the worst possible light. He gives more space to Torquemada than to Aquinas.

Crucially for Grayling, the historical record does not show simply that Christians fail to live up to their ideals. On the contrary, the ideals are wrong. Inherent to Christianity is a mindset of unreason, anti-humanism and authoritarianism. But his portrait of Christian faith, indeed of the Abrahamic faiths as a whole, is almost unqualifiedly monolithic. He does not recognise how pluralistic these faith traditions are or how incessant has been intellectual debate within them. Liberty, along with the humanistic values Grayling espouses, is strongly affirmed in the Abrahamic faiths, and with a rich theological rationale. The human is celebrated in a theology which speaks of creation as being 'very good', of humanity made in the divine image, of incarnation and of love and grace. The Augustinian claims that the 'service of God is perfect freedom' and that we may 'love what is commanded and desire what is promised' are hardly rare Christian idiosyncrasies. Likewise, reason has a strong place in the Christian tradition – especially in mediaeval theology. The latter sections of *Veritatis Splendor* are in many ways the exception that proves the rule – many Catholic theologians protested that John Paul II's insistence upon subservience to the teaching of the papacy reneges on the strong Catholic emphasis upon a reasoned faith and a reasoning accessible to all. Religion has been one of the strongest defenders of freedom and reason, even if it has also many times disastrously failed to live up to its own ideals, including times when a proper perception that freedom needs to be balanced with other values –such as belonging and community – has led to an oppressive paternalism.

We could fill pages with the shrill dictates about religion – at best one-sided but often grotesque caricatures. Here is a sample. 'Monotheism loathes intelligence' declares Onfray. Monotheism is about 'hatred of intelligence and knowledge.' There is 'the requirement to obey rather than think.'[16] For Dawkins the burqa is simply about oppression and egregious male cruelty.[17] Does Dawkins not know it may also be an expression of a self-respectful Muslim identity and a protest against western commodification of the female body?[18] And then God is routinely described as the invisible policeman and similar caricatures.[19] Of course Paul the Apostle is not beyond criticism. But for Onfray the epistles are the 'ravings of a hysteric' one who is 'sick, misogynistic, masochistic', and guilty of 'ideological brutality, intellectual intolerance' and 'hatred of intelligence'. His 'hatred of self turned into a vigorous hatred of the world... life, love, desire, pleasure... joy, freedom.'[20] Incidentally, both Onfray and Hitchens attack the practice of circumcision with high octane outrage, but curiously when Paul attacks it, it is a 'wasteland of rant, nonsense....and bullying.'[21]

It is not surprising that the old myth of a 'warfare' between science and religion is resuscitated into radiant health. This is a persistent theme in Dawkins. Those who sit at the feet of Grayling are told nothing of Christian thinkers who have explored positively the theological implications of Darwinism. Instead Darwin is presented without qualification as fuelling a 'religious crisis.'[22] Onfray treats us to rhetorical flourishes in the tradition of Russell. Monotheism is characterised by a 'hatred of science'.[23] Because of this the 'forward march' of western civilisation fuelled by the scientific enterprise was impeded by the Catholic religion for a millennium 'inflicting incalculable damage.' But again, such fundamentalist simplicities fall when confronted with the tiresome facts of history. These can be subversive of atheist as well as of Christian triumphalism. The truth is more complicated.[24]

The fundamentalist certainties – accompanied by not a little intellectual arrogance – excuse the new atheists from engaging seriously with theological thought. Why should they since it is all dim-witted superstition appealing either to the neurotic or to those who employ religion to deliver power? Grayling defends a refusal to study religious thought. By the same token, why should we study the contrasts between sidereal and tropical astrology?[25] That a professor of philosophy should so regard an awareness of theological thought, once seen as part of a liberal education, is certainly cause for thought. No wonder John Haught complains that their engagement with religion is so shallow that they lack theological challenge.[26]

2. Polarisation

Fundamentalist simplicity and confidence lead to something more sinister – the polarisation between 'them' and 'us', between the children of light and the children of darkness, good and evil, sanity and stupidity, rationality and superstition. The new atheists have little sense of the ambiguity of their position. They are the children of light and religion is painted in the grimmest of terms.

To be more specific, there is first a polarisation between the intelligent, critically thinking and healthy-minded atheist and indoctrinated 'faith heads.'[27] Maybe there is some cogency in Dawkins's defence of the self-description 'Bright', since it is cheerful, whilst 'Atheist' seems stuffy. [28] That said it is a bit disingenuous to insist this is a noun and not an adjective. The clear implication is that religious believers are dim. Speaking of a rise of conversions to Roman Catholicism Grayling observes: 'Amazingly, some were intelligent.'[29] How amazing indeed that some who disagree with Grayling are actually intelligent. Dawkins refers to 'religious but otherwise intelligent scientists.'[30] So, when scientists profess religious faith they are suspending their intelligence. Then again, Grayling contrasts the 'utter certainties of faith' with a whole gamut of intellectual virtues (intellectual courage, open-mindedness, intellectual integrity) which apparently are not expected to be evidenced by people of religious faith.[31] And to crown all we have Onfray's extraordinary statement: 'Monotheism loathes intelligence'.[32]

But by far the most significant polarisation is between atheists who are the good guys and the religious who are the bad guys. Atheists are invariably people of tolerance, goodwill and kindness. By contrast religion is the root of most evil – so much so that having religious faith is morally culpable, since it involves meddling in something so menacingly toxic in human affairs. 'Religion poisons everything.'[33]

For Dawkins atheism is twinned with happiness, a balanced life, morality, intellectual fulfilment, a healthy mind and healthy heart. By contrast: 'Think of a world without any religion. No suicide bombers, no witch hunts, no Crusades, no persecution of Jews, no Northern Island Troubles, no honour killings, no Taliban. No public flogging of female flesh....'[34] Grayling goes as far as to claim: 'Most human suffering, other than that caused by disease or other natural evils, has been the result of religion-inspired conflict and religion-based oppression.'[35]

Can the 'most' be defended? Can it really be claimed that the motivation of 'most' burglars, rapists, child abusers, domestic bullies, embezzlers, murders, mafia bosses, pimps and drugs barons, tyrants and despots is religious? Yes, and also terrorists? And it is not permitted to venture the observation that the regimes of Stalin, Hitler, Mao and Pol Pot were not exactly paradigms of religious piety. This is dismissed as a 'tired old canard'.[36] But why is it a tired old canard whilst the repeated references to the inquisitions and the burning of witches are not?[37] That said, we do need to clarify what is being claimed. The least is that there is no guarantee that things will be well if only we rid ourselves of religion, and even that these regimes illustrate the dangers when the constraints, inspirations and convictions of the Abrahamic faiths are laid aside. Grayling disowns the atheisms of Stalinism and Nazism because they mutated into a religious form by becoming monolithic ideologies. For atheism this is an aberration. For religion it is intrinsic and universal.

Dawkins and Grayling claim religion is the cause of most war.[38] But this is ridiculous fundamentalist dogma. The causes of conflict and violence are manifold and complex.[39] Yes, religion may sometimes be a factor in fuelling conflict. At worst it can encourage a crusade. But it may also urge the constraints of the just war tradition and uphold the values of justice and compassion. Again the reality is more complex than fundamentalist simplicities allow.

We return to sanity with the balanced observation: '*Religion can be very close to madness. It has brought human beings to acts of criminal folly as well as to the highest achievements of goodness, creativity and generosity.*'[40] Christians should acknowledge the first, and indeed invariably do so. Should not atheists acknowledge the latter, as indeed many do, although not the 'new' ones? And then we can have a sensible debate about the resources and dangers of religion in human life – a debate which goes beyond the fundamentalist simplicities of any camp.

But to single out just three strands of this charge – there is first the charge that religion by its inner logic encourages fanaticism and intolerance, judgemental attitudes, harshness or even persecution. And of course terrorism and suicide bombers. The dynamics of this are easily stated. I believe in God who is ultimate and who has revealed his truth and way. Those who differ from God are blasphemous and 'error has no rights'. My privileged access to divine revelation entitles me to absolute certainty and to despise and even persecute those who differ.

Alas this grim picture of the religious 'know all' who is excused human decencies is sometimes a reality. But the critics fail to see that religion has profound counterbalancing forces. The transcendence of God relativises rather than validates what is human, confronting the idolatries of our smug religiosity. As Richard Niebuhr classically argued, 'radical monotheism' critiques the idolatry of anything that is not God – including a theology which is too big for its boots.[41] Moreover, truth is apprehended through persuasion not coercion, and the other person is beloved of God and is so to be respected.

And to what extent does religion itself engender intolerance, and to what extent do intolerant personalities seize upon and mould religion for expression and bogus validation? In our sin we will always use religion – along with other things and other people – for our own ends. Again the reality is complex and nuanced and does not conform to fundamentalist simplicities. Of course those who know they are right can be tempted to intolerance. Christians are indeed sometimes guilty of this. But such intolerance is not absent in the new atheists. But maybe that is OK – after all they are right and their intolerance is justifiable because it is aimed at liberating people from the virus of religion.

There is secondly the charge that religion encourages evil by demanding blind obedience and a faith which has no rationality. We thus fail to honour our intellectual duty. Such 'heteronomy' diminishes our lives. This is to misunderstand faith. The majority will insist there is 'reason for the faith that is in them.' Faith is libellously misrepresented when Dawkins describes it as blind and brooking no argument.[42] Faith is more like an adventurous response of love, trust and loyalty – supported by reason. The Christian tradition has given a high place to rationality, claiming belief in God is eminently reasonable – be it according to canons of rationality more expansive than some atheists allow. The new atheists are fully entitled to argue that on this pitch they win the game. But they have no right to accuse religious believers *en masse* of picking up the ball and refusing to play.[43]

Thirdly, moderate theists are in bad odour because they provide a culture of respectability within which religious extremism can flourish.[44] There may indeed be contexts where this is the case – such are the manifold complexities of human affairs. But again we meet fundamentalist simplicity and over-confidence. Where is the evidence (yes, Professor Dawkins – evidence?) that moderate religion encourages fanaticism? Maybe it is more readily enflamed by the elitist sarcasm of the new atheists? Moreover, in the churches a massive amount of moderating takes place through the cut and thrust of debate. Contrary to atheistic rhetoric, religious traditions are traditions of intense debate. One high-profile example is how the Dutch

Reformed Church changed its position on apartheid because of the careful critique of the world church.

Fanaticism and extremism belong to the human condition. Certainly religion – along with politics and ethics – is more vulnerable to extremism than, say, cultivating cacti. But again that is a fact of the human condition. Extremism will not go away if 'moderate' theists become 'Brights'. And are we to suspect 'moderate' debate about embryo research or the moral status of the unborn because it encourages 'pro-life' extremism and the bombing of abortion clinics? Are we to relinquish a 'moderate' commitment to animal welfare because we encourage the extremist fringe? Both Grayling and Dawkins support medically assisted dying – and I am personally highly sympathetic. Should this 'moderate' position be disallowed because it opens the door (the 'slippery slope') to Nazi involuntary euthanasia? Are we to silence Darwinian biology because some build on this scientific foundation a harsh politics and ethic? And presumably in order to rid our society of sexual abuse we must abolish sex.

Incidentally, Grayling insists all religions in their essential nature and core texts are 'extreme' and that 'moderate' religion is an aberration.[45] But again this is asserted with fundamentalist simplicity and untroubled confidence and would be contested by a huge majority of scholars. Grayling does not engage with the significant debate on this issue in biblical hermeneutics, and in theological inquiry about the nature of Christian identity – and similar debates in Islam and Judaism.

Conclusions

The new atheists make a serious and dangerous error in externalising the source of evil in something 'out there' – namely religion. Religion is the 'root' of most evil. Religion is the cause of suicide bombers and terrorism and most wars. And so on and so forth. But this is fundamentalist ideology masquerading as serious sociological and historical analysis. The source of evil is not to be so externalised and so blamed. The source of evil is more in ourselves – in all of us – and in our social structures. This false analysis is dangerous because it leaves us ill-equipped to deal with evil; and the new atheists reluctant to acknowledge it in themselves. For in contrast to the great religious unwashed, they are squeaky clean. A typical remark in Dawkins concerns acts of vandalism: he '[does] not believe there is an atheist in the world' who would do such a thing.[46] That claim is ridiculous – unless made true by definition. Does Dawkins admit into the class of 'atheists' only those who take lunch with him in Clare College?[47]

The new atheists love to plunder Christian history for the rich pickings of abuse of power, stupidity, narrow-mindedness, bigotry, cruelty, conservatism inhibiting progress, and deep misogyny. These pickings are there – despite often a lack of balanced historical judgement.[48] They seem unaware how frequent and caustic are critiques of bad religion in the Bible itself. But the crucial question is: *What is our interpretive paradigm?* That of the new atheist tends to be that we humans are basically trustworthy, decent, open-minded and generous unless corrupted by religion. A more realistic paradigm is that we humans are flawed; that these are human and not essentially religious traits. Sometimes indeed they are reinforced by distorted religion, and sometimes they engender religious expression. Sometimes in our folly we hijack religion for our own ends. Invariably these distortions arise when religion's appeal for repentance, compassion, justice and humility, together with the offer of grace, are eclipsed. But again such thoughts go beyond fundamentalist simplicities.

Moreover, because religion is the source of most ills, religious people are primarily responsible for the world's ills, and so potentially dangerous members of society. They are to be treated with suspicion as spreading a dangerous virus. This is seriously worrying. History is littered with the scapegoating of certain groups and the consequences are alarming. Tina Beattie even suggests a parallel between the new atheist attitudes and the Nazi scapegoating of the Jews.[49] Are there hints of an action replay of the Jacobin Terror? At times one wonders how secure is a commitment to religious liberty and tolerance.[50] Rationalism, after all, has its own history of intolerance and persecution.

It is a sound principle that there is no inconsistency in tolerance being intolerant of intolerance, and liberty restricting the liberty of those who abuse their liberty to enslave others. Is this really being appealed to as a justification for a blanket quarantining of religion? I agree that the state should be secular in the sense of not privileging any one faith. But the church, free from Erastian privilege and Erastian control, is thus free to contribute to society for the common good. Grayling appears to want to go beyond a separation between church and state. Religion must be about 'private observance only' and allowed 'no quarter in the public realm'. The reason is clear. The extremism of a Taliban is not an aberration but rather an 'unadulterated and unconstrained' expression of theistic faith. 'It is only where religion is on the back foot… with an insecure tenure in society, that it presents itself as essentially peaceful and charitable.'[51] Where religious people have a sunny smile this is a 'perfumed smoke screen' to cover their real selves which is more sinister. With hands on secular power 'religion… shows a very different face – the face presented by the inquisition, the Taliban.'[52] This again is fundamentalist ideology – offered as it is without qualification. There are of course nasty Christians, and there are nice atheists. But there are nice Christians and nasty atheists. Noble as is the espousal of humanistic values by many atheists, the idea that such values are in safe hands when we are atheist but not when we are theist is ridiculous.[53] Such values are embraced with a rich theological rationale and inspiration by the Abrahamic faiths.

Generally religious people are more self-critical, more self-aware, and more ready to acknowledge their own failings and the toxic elements in their tradition than are the new atheists. Dawkins's self-congratulatory elitism as a scientist prevents him from acknowledging properly the ambiguity of how much medicine is beholden to the lucrative rich, of how much scientific brilliance is devoted to weaponry and of how scientists have been in the pay of wealthy interest groups, and have even been servants of despots and tyrants. What about the misappropriation of Darwinian science by Nazism and Lamarckian science by Stalinism? This is not to say that scientists are any worse than the rest of us. It is simply to say that we are all flawed. By the same token there is an astonishing reluctance of the new atheists to face the implications of the fact that the most obnoxious regimes of the twentieth century were anti-religious.

The Christian insistence that we are all sinners but all under grace speaks a profounder and more liberating truth than the new atheist division of humankind between the enlightened and virtuous 'Brights' and the great religious unwashed.

But finally I have accused the new atheists of displaying the mindset of fundamentalism in embracing simplicity and certainty when in fact there is ambiguity and uncertainty. I have accused them of a polarisation between the children of light and the children of darkness. It would be tragic if Christians responded to like with like. The result would be a bleak polarisation between Christian and Atheist. Instead of decent conversations and cooperation for the good of society, they hurl abuse to and fro across an ever-widening chasm. It certainly feels that for the new atheists the religious believer is not part of the same community, but rather an anthropological curiosity – correction, monstrosity – to be objectified and put in a cage and prodded with condescending superiority like the Hottentot Venus.[54]

There is thus the serious danger that Christians are forced into a ghetto of narrow religiosity, not allowed to be part of civil society, not allowed to embrace a rich and generous Christian humanism, and not allowed to be part of the great enterprise of science. And moreover, in over-reaction to the abuse hurled at them they bite the bait and acquiesce.

Many Christians – the majority I guess – know little of the 'utter certainties' of which Grayling speaks. They have a deep sense of the penumbra of mystery which surrounds their lives. The adventure of faith is about exploration and often tentative. Sometimes they occupy the border territory between theism and atheism. 'Faith' does not have a simple 'on or off' switch.[55] Sometimes they speak of enough faith only to doubt their doubts. But there is the sober conviction that life makes more sense when we maintain a vision of God. And however much they fail to realise it in their own lives, they know the vision of a Christ-like God properly nourishes love, joy, peace and a passion for justice. The service of God is perfect freedom. Such a faith gives them open rather than closed minds since God's thoughts are higher than our thoughts. The deliberately parochial rationalism of the new atheists in fact seriously limits the possibilities of thought and washes away so much colour from our lives. Faith occupies broad territory and gives a perspective from which to critique some of the shallowness of modernity. Their living and loving, their joys, their delight in beauty, creativity and intellectual endeavour are given deeper resonance when they see themselves as living a life which is the gift of God's grace. And there are resources in their faith to meet their sin, anguish and pain. Their lives would be impoverished if they relinquished pursuing that vision, and if they ceased to be part of their tradition and community of faith. Moreover, there is the characteristically Christian virtue of patience, which recognises the deep ambiguities and limitations of the human condition – a patience not always evident in the confidences of rationalism, a confidence that can lead to the intolerances of impatience.[56]

But this is the very opposite of confronting one strident fundamentalism with another.

Notes

1   For example, Michael Ruse, Richard Norman and Peter Bowler.
2   In Dawkins, Richard (2006), *The God Delusion*, London: Bantam Books, pp282ff.
3   Haught, John (2006), *Is Nature Enough?*, Cambridge: CUP, p17.
4   Letter to William Graham in July 1881.
5   Descartes, *Meditations* IV.
6   Dawkins (2006), pp54ff, 66ff.
7   Ibid. pp237, 250ff.
8   Ibid. pp51ff.
9   Ibid. p53.
10 Grayling, A.C. (2007), *Against all Gods*, London: Oberon Books, pp28, 34.
11 For example Mackie, J.L., *The Miracle of Theism*, Oxford.
12 Dawkins (2006), p317.
13 www.campquest.uk/activities.
14 Dawkins, Richard, *A Devil's Chaplain*, London: Weidenfeld and Nicolson, pp242ff.
15 Grayling, A.C. (2007), *Towards the Light*, London, Bloomsbury, p79.
16 Onfray, Michael (2007), *In Defence of Atheism*, London: Arcade, p67.
17 Dawkins (2006), p362.

18. See for example Sa'Diyya Shaikh in Omid Safi (ed) (2003) *Progressive Muslims*, Oxford: OneWorld, pp151–154.
19. For example Grayling, A.C., *Against all Gods*, p62. Also Hitchens, Christopher (2007), *The Portable Atheist*, London: Da Capo, p xxii.
20. Onfray (2007), pp132ff..
21. Hitchens, Christopher, *God is Not Great*, p12.
22. Grayling, A.C. (2003) *What is Good?*, London: Weidenfeld and Nicolson, 2003, p147. For a scholarly analysis of the history see Bowler, Peter (2007), *Monkey Trials and Gorilla Sermons*, Harvard University Press.
23. Onfray (2007), p81.
24. See for example Bowler (2007) and Numbers, Ronald J. (ed) (2009), *Galileo Goes to Jail*, Harvard University Press.
25. A.C. Grayling in *London Review of Books*, November 2006.
26. Haught, John (2008), *God and the New Atheism*, Louisville: John Knox Press, 2008, p xi.
27. Dawkins (2006), p5.
28. Dawkins, R. (2003) 'The Future is Bright', *The Guardian*, 21 June.
29. Grayling, *What is Good?* p213.
30. Dawkins (2006), p107.
31. Grayling *Against all Gods* p63.
32. Onfray (2007), p67.
33. Hitchens, p13.
34. Dawkins (2006), pp1–3.
35. Grayling *What is Good?* p x.
36. Grayling *Against all Gods* p45.
37. Grayling, A.C. (2002), *The Meaning of Things*, London: Phoenix, p100. Also *The New Humanist* July-August 2007.
38. Grayling *Against All Gods*, p51; Dawkins (2006), 259ff.
39. See *God and War: An Audit*, University of Bradford, 2004.
40. MacCulloch, Diarmaid (2009), *A History of Christianity: The first Three Thousand Years*, London: Allen Lane, p13.
41. Niebuhr, H. Richard (1943), *Radical Monotheism and Western Culture*, London: Faber, esp. pp31ff.
42. Dawkins *The God Delusion* e.g. p206, 308; also *The Selfish Gene* p198; also Grayling *Against all Gods* pp15–16.
43. I discuss elsewhere the charge that Christian ethics are based on blind obedience to inscrutable commands in my *Weaving the Tapestry of Moral Judgement: Christian Ethics in a plural World*, London: Epworth Press, 2006, especially chapters 1–2 and 4–7.
44. Dawkins (2006), pp303, 306; Also Harris, Sam (2005), *The End of Faith*, London: The Free Press, p45.
45. For example, Grayling *What is Good?* p207.
46. Dawkins (2006), p249.
47. Ibid. p100.
48. See for example the explorations classically represented by Creighton, Mandell (1895) *Persecution and Toleration*, London: Longman Green.
49. Beattie, Tina (2007), *The New Atheists*, London: DLT, p14–15. Also Cornwell, John (2007), *Darwin's Angel*, London: Profile Books, p141.

50 See Dawkins (2006), pp326ff; Grayling A.C. (2007), *The Form of Things*, London: Pheonix, p82; Harris (2005), pp14-15, 109ff.
51 Grayling, *What is Good?* p208.
52 Ibid. pp71–2.
53 Although the optimism of Grayling is more nuanced than that of Dawkins. Compare Dawkins (2006) pp262–272 with Grayling *What is Good?* p167 and *Towards the Light* chapters 7 and 8.
54 I owe this image to Tina Beattie (2007), p64.
55 I owe the phrase to John Cornwell (2007) p95; also p112.
56 Gray, John (2008), *Black Mass*, London: Penguin Books, especially pp50ff.

Notes on the contributors

Dr Wendy Allen first came across John Newton when she was a Methodist local preacher in St Ives in Cornwall and working as part of a Rob Frost Seed Team. She was then privileged to complete the Methodist Studies unit while training for Methodist ministry at Wesley College, to which John contributed the historical sections. After an MA thesis on the Methodist–Roman Catholic dialogues, under the supervision of David Carter and assisted by John's archive, she completed her doctoral research on Newman's ecclesiology at Bristol University. During this time she became a Roman Catholic. She is currently a teacher of Religious Studies and Philosophy at a girls' school in Bath. She is passionate about teaching students to think, and runs a Socrates Society using the Philosophy for Children techniques originated by Socrates and promoted by the SAPERE organisation of which she is a member. She is currently taking part in a Religion and Science in schools research project funded by the Faraday Institute. Alongside this, Wendy also lectures on the Clifton Diocese diaconal training course at Wesley College.

Revd Brian Beck was born into a long-established Methodist family in Tooting, and entered the Methodist Ministry in 1957. He served in theological education firstly in Kenya, and from 1968–1984 as tutor and latterly principal of Wesley House, Cambridge. From 1984 to 1998 he served as Secretary of the Conference, where his clarity of vision and intellect, integrity, commitment to justice and pastoral concern commanded deep respect. He served as President of the Conference in 1993, presiding over the major debate at which the Conference adopted its current 'Derby' resolutions on human sexuality. His longstanding ecumenical commitment culminated in the award of the Lambeth degree of Doctor of Divinity for his service to ecumenism. Since retirement to Cambridge in 1998 he has continued his teaching, writing and preaching ministry. His publications have included *Reading the New Testament Today* (1977), *Christian Character in the Gospel of Luke* (1989), *Way of Jesus: Four Bible studies in Luke's gospel* (1993), *Gospel Insights* (1998) and *Exploring Methodism's Heritage* (2004). He has made contributions to numerous theological journals.

David Carter is a Methodist local preacher, married to a Methodist minister. He is passionately committed to the Ecumenical Movement. From 1967–1996 he was a school teacher, from 1973 at Wilson's School near Croydon. From 1988, he has been an associate lecturer in Religious Studies at the Open University and, from 1996, an associate tutor at Wesley College, Bristol. He is also a visiting scholar at Sarum College. His main current academic interests are in ecclesiology and ecumenism. He is author of a book on Methodist ecclesiology and of about fifty articles in learned periodicals/books. He is a member of the British Roman Catholic–Methodist Committee and secretary of the Churches Together in England Theology and Unity Group. He also enjoys fruitful contacts with the Catholic Church in Belgium. In 2004, he returned to his native Bristol where his key leisure interest is simply enjoying the West Country.

Dr Mervyn Davies is a Roman Catholic layman, Scholar-in-Residence at Sarum College, Salisbury, an Associate Tutor at Wesley College, Bristol and an honorary Senior Lecturer in the Department of Theology and Religious Studies at Bristol University. From 1992 to 1996 he was Theological Education Development Officer at Wesley with a brief to develop adult ecumenical theological courses in the South-West and a tutor on the West of England Ministerial Training Course. He then became Director of Programmes and Research at Wesley College in 1996. Prior to 1992 he was in secondary and post-16 education. His research degrees were on Newman and he organised four national conferences and one international conference on his life and thought, the proceedings of the latter being published in *Newman Studien* 14 (1990). His current research interests continue to be in the educational thought of Newman, and also in the theology and practice of church Leadership, co-authoring a book to be published by Continuum in 2010. He is currently a co-editor of a three-volume work *Religion and the University* which is in preparation for publication in 2011–13 by T. & T. Clark.

Revd Canon Dr Graham Dodds is an Anglican priest, currently Canon Treasurer at Wells Cathedral. He is also Director of Learning Communities in the Diocese of Bath and Wells' School of Formation, which is an educational and ecumenical enterprise providing resources for clergy and laity. Having served as a curate and Director of Lay Ministry in Southwark diocese, he became rector of a city parish in Bath. He has a degree in music, a Masters degree in adult education and theology and a PhD in theology, particularly ecclesiology.

Dr Martin Forward had a varied career before coming to Aurora University, Illinois, USA, in 2001 as Professor of Religion and Executive Director of the Wackerlin Center for Faith and Action. He worked: at the Henry Martyn Institute of Islamic Studies, Hyderabad, India; as a student chaplain in London University, when John Newton was his superintendent minister; as a Methodist pastor in Leicester and Inter-Faith Secretary of the British Methodist Church; and as Academic Dean of Wesley House seminary, Cambridge, England, and a member of Cambridge University's Faculty of Divinity. Within this variety run common themes of recognising and reflecting about human diversity, and a love of mentoring young people to live faithfully and thoughtfully in God's wonderful world.

Revd Dr John Harrod is a Lincolnian. He took his first degree from London University in sociology and then read the Cambridge Theological Tripos whilst preparing for the ministry of the Methodist Church. He was a Senior Scholar at Fitzwilliam College and Chadwick prize-winner in the university. His later doctorate was in philosophical theology from Manchester University. He has served in pastoral ministry in Methodist circuits, has lectured at Wesley College, Bristol and part-time in philosophy of religion at the universities of Manchester and Bristol, later becoming principal of Hartley Victoria College, the Methodist foundation within the Partnership for

Theological Education in Manchester. The author of book reviews and articles, his main publication is *Weaving the Tapestry of Moral Judgement: Christian Ethics in a Plural World* (Epworth, 2007). Married with a grown-up son and daughter he now lives in retirement in Cornwall.

Revd Dr Tim Macquiban is currently the minister of two city-centre churches in Cambridge (Wesley and Sturton Street) which includes chaplaincy to the Methodist students of both Universities (Cambridge and Anglia Ruskin). He is also a senior member and honorary chaplain at Wolfson College. As Co-Chair of the Oxford Institute of Methodist Theological Studies he contributed to its last conference in 2007 on Charles Wesley and a Theology of Vocation which has recently been published in *Our Calling to Fulfill* (Abingdon Press). His writings include articles on Methodist History, Worship and Spirituality as well as many biographical articles in a number of dictionaries. He is also a member of the British Methodist Church's Heritage Committee and contributes to its work on Methodist Heritage and Contemporary Mission. He was formerly Principal of Sarum College, Salisbury, where he continues to contribute as a Visiting Scholar.

Revd Canon Melvyn Matthews is Chancellor Emeritus of Wells Cathedral. Before being appointed Chancellor of Wells in 1997 he had, as well as being a University Chaplain and parish priest, taught theology in the University of Nairobi where he took over a class from John Newton, and been the Director of the Ammerdown Centre, a centre for reconciliation and peace south of Bath. His many books and articles have focussed on the nature of spirituality and mysticism and include two studies *(Both Alike to Thee*, SPCK 2000, and *Awake to God*, SPCK 2005) which relate the Christian mystical tradition to contemporary post-modernism. He is married to June and enjoys dinghy sailing.

Revd Dr Neil Richardson is a Methodist minister who taught New Testament studies at Lincoln Theological College and Wesley College,

Bristol, where he was also Principal. He also served as a Circuit minister and a university chaplain in the Oxford, Manchester Mission and Leeds North East Methodist Circuits. He is married to Rhiannon, and lives in the Marches near Ludlow, where he continues to write, preach and teach, and enjoy marathon-running. He is the author of several New Testament books: *Was Jesus Divine?*, *The Panorama of Luke*, *Paul's Language about God*, *God in the New Testament*, *Paul for Today*, and (forthcoming), *God So Loved the World. The Attractiveness of John's Gospel*. He was elected President of the British Methodist Conference in 2003.

Revd John Munsey Turner was born in Wolverhampton and read History at St Catherine's College, Cambridge (1949–1952) and was awarded the J.N. Figgis Prize. He trained for the Methodist ministry at Didsbury College, Bristol, now Wesley College. He was awarded an MA from the University of Bristol and was stationed at Colchester, Burton on Trent and Sheffield. He also was appointed chaplain at the University and Polytechnic at Leeds. From 1970–1981 he was tutor at the Queen's College, Birmingham and then went on to become Superintendent Minister at Halifax and Bolton until 1994. He then became part-time lecturer at Hartley Victoria College, Manchester, 1994–2005. His publications include *Conflict and Reconciliation* (1985); *Modern Methodism in England 1932–1998* (1998); *John Wesley and the Evangelical Revival* (2002); *Wesleyan Methodism* (2005) and *The Historian as Preacher* (2006). He was awarded a Cambridge BD in 1986.

Dr John Vickers was born in 1927 and educated at King Edward's School, Birmingham and the University of Birmingham. Teacher and head of Religious Education in several schools, 1953–1967. Senior Lecturer, Principal Lecturer and Head of the Department of Religious and Social Studies at the Bognor Regis College of Education and West Sussex Institute of Higher Education, 1967–1981. British Secretary of the World Methodist Historical Society. Indexer of the *Works of the Rev. John Wesley* since 1970 and winner of the Wheatley Medal for indexing, 1977. Publications include: *Thomas Coke, Apostle of Methodism* (1969); *Preaching from Hymns* (2002); *Myths of Methodism* (2008); and histories of Methodism in Canterbury (1961) and Chichester (1977). Books edited include: *A History of the Methodist Church in Great Britain*, vol. 4, part 1 Documents and Source Material (1988); the religious Census in Sussex (1989) and of Hampshire (1993); *The Letters of John Pawson* (with John C. Bowmer, 3 vols., 1994–95); *A Dictionary of Methodism in Britain and Ireland* (2000; online edition, 2008); *The Journal of Dr Thomas Coke* (2005).

Revd Norman Wallwork is a Methodist minister, a Prebendary of Wells Cathedral and an Associate Tutor at Wesley College, Bristol. He is a former County Ecumenical Officer for Cumbria and a former Religious Adviser to Radio Cumbria and Border Television. His Marian interests include being a Moderator of the Ecumenical Society of the Blessed Virgin Mary, being a Trustee of the Ecumenical Marian Pilgrimage Trust centred on Walsingham and of the newly formed *Friends of Our Lady of Tintern*. He was one of the compilers of the *Methodist Worship Book*, 1999. He was a contributor to *John Wesley: Contemporary Perspectives*, 1998; *Mary for All Christians by John Macquarrie*, 1991; *Workaday Preachers*, 1995; *The New SCM Dictionary of Liturgy and Worship*, 2002; *Church and Theology: Essays in honour of William Strawson* 2004; *A Dictionary of Methodism in Britain and Ireland*, 2007 (2nd Edition).

Revd Sandy Williams is a Methodist minister and was the Senior Methodist Tutor at Wesley College, Bristol until 2009 having been a member of the college staff since 2001. She now has a half-time post as minister with pastoral charge for four village churches in South Gloucestershire. She began teaching in Liverpool and has a background in both Special Education, as a teacher of children with reading and behavioural difficulties, and also in mainstream education. Ordained in 1990, Sandy served in north-west London and was a member of the Methodist Faith and Order Committee, the District Candidates' Secretary. Sandy convened the working party for the Methodist Conference Report: *A Lamp to my Feet and a Light to my Path: The Nature and Authority and the Place of the Bible in the Methodist Church*, 1998 and was a contributor to *Vows and Partings: Services for the* *reaffirmation of marriage vows and suggestions of how to pray when relationships change and end*, The Methodist Church, 2001. Other publications: *Touching the Pulse: Worship and Where We Live* (ed.) (London, Stainer and Bell 1996) and *Mining the Meaning: Companion to the Revised Common Lectionary*, Year C (Peterborough, Epworth Press, 2003).

Revd Professor Frances Young taught theology at the University of Birmingham from 1971, becoming the Edward Cadbury Professor and Head of the Department of Theology in 1986. During her time at the University, she also served as Dean of the Faculty of Arts (1995–97) and Pro Vice Chancellor (1997–2002). In 1984, she was ordained as a Methodist minister, and has combined preaching in a local Circuit and pursuing her academic career. In 1998, she was awarded an OBE for services to Theology and in 2004, elected a Fellow of the British Academy. In 2005, she retired from the University. On 15 November 2005, she preached at the opening service of the Eighth General Synod Church of England, the first Methodist and the first woman to preach at the five-yearly inauguration ceremony. She delivered her sermon at the Eucharist service at which the Archbishop of Canterbury, Dr Rowan Williams, presided. Her books include both academic and more popular theological writings, drawing on her work on the New Testament and on Christianity in its formative centuries, but also on her experience as the mother of a son (Arthur) who was born with profound physical and mental disabilities.